HAWKER
HUNTER

Hawker Hunter

Barry Jones

AVIATION CROWOOD **SERIES**

First published in 1998 by
The Crowood Press Ltd
Ramsbury, Marlborough
Wiltshire SN8 2HR

British Library Cataloguing-in-Publication Data
A catalogue record for this book is available from
the British Library.

ISBN 1 86126 083 0

Photograph previous page: Hunter F. Mark 6s of No.
92 (East India) Squadron in a vertical climb.

Typefaces used: Goudy (*text*),
Cheltenham (*headings*).

Typeset and designed by
D & N Publishing
Membury Business Park, Lambourn Woodlands
Hungerford, Berkshire.

Printed and bound by Butler & Tanner, Frome.

Dedication

To my wife Judy, in recognition of her fortitude in the world
of an aeronautical enthusiast.

Contents

Introduction

The dictionary defines the adjective *unique* as 'being the only one of its kind', 'having no like or equal'. They could very well add 'Hawker'. Trawl through the British aircraft companies and Hawker stands out as the only one who, since its foundation on 15 November 1920, has continuously manufactured just one commodity – single-engined aeroplanes. No other company has been so 'single-minded' and even today's products coming off the line under the British Aerospace banner (which in turn had been preceded by the title Hawker Siddeley), are basically Hawker designs. Names of the past that are the very foundation stones of the Royal Air Force – Hart, Fury, Demon, Hind, Hurricane, Typhoon, Tempest, – all carried the parent appellation Hawker.

Today, the Harrier and Hawk preserve their origin's proud traditions but preceding them was the most *commercially* successful post-war British aircraft and one of the most beautiful ever built, the Hunter. It earned a reputation that was equally as illustrious as its forebears and, because of good overseas sales plus a very active refurbishment programme, was still in service long after foreign aircraft of the same era, such as the F–86 and Mystère, had deceased.

This is its story, 'warts and all'. From it emerges an aeroplane that reaped high esteem by those who flew it. It had its faults – the perfect aeroplane has never been built and I doubt it ever will – but by general consensus the Hunter was a true thoroughbred, upholding the finest institutions of the company – and country – that sired it.

In the course of compiling this book, I am most grateful to have received help and information from many, who, like myself, have great regard for its subject. I would like to express my sincere thanks to Dennis Brown, Peter J. Cooper, Peter Elliott of the Royal Air Force Museum, Bill Gunston, 'Jock' Harvey, Del Holyland of Martin-Baker, Mike Hooks, John Kendrick, Ian Mactaggart, George Pennick, Richard Riding and Michael Oakey of *Aeroplane Monthly*, W. H. Sleigh, Glenn Surtees of GEC Marconi and, in particular, to my family who, most likely, will not feel deprived if they never hear the word 'Hunter' again.

CHAPTER ONE

A New Dawn

By 8 May 1945, Britain had survived five years, eight months and five days of war in Europe. In terms of manpower and equipment, she could not match the United States or the Soviet Union who had been her allies for over three years. In aeronautical technology however, especially the fields of radar, the Cavity Magnetron valve and gas-turbine engines, she was leading the way by a very healthy margin.

The Royal Air Force had had nearly a years' operational experience with the only Allied jet-powered aircraft to see service in the conflict, the Gloster Meteor. De Havilland, immortalized by the versatility of the Mosquito, were starting to produce their first jet-propelled fighter, the Vampire, and Supermarine, with all their Spitfire experience, were addressing Specification E.1/44 which, combined with a Rolls-Royce turbojet engine, was considered, bound to come up a winner. The Hawker Tempest MkV had been in squadron service since April 1944 and, as the RAF's fastest piston engined fighter, had a better performance than the initial squadron Meteors. Lancasters had proved capable of carrying everything wheeled under their cavernous bombbays, including the heaviest bomb ever produced, and the Lincoln, purpose built by the same stable for service in the Far East, held promise of maintaining Avro's reputation. Through this rose-tinted vista, complacency insidiously took root in the ministerial corridors and, coupled with the financial constraints that years of all-out war had generated, officialdom carefully placed the British aircraft industry on the gentle, well-greased decline from which it would never completely reclimb.

There are no doubt those who, casting their minds back to the Society of British Aircraft Constructors (SBAC) Shows of the late forties and early fifties when every year new aircraft appeared overnight like

The Shuttleworth Collection's Hind K5414 at Abingdon in 1990. It typifies the output of Hawker's project office in the 1920s and 1930s, when more than a dozen different designs were produced for British and foreign air forces, the Napier Dagger-powered Hector being the company's final bi-plane. Author's collection

The last Hurricane ever built, Mark IIc PZ865, seen at Finningley in September,1979. Following its production, the aircraft was first owned by Hawker Aircraft, registered G-AMAU and carrying the legend 'The Last of the Many! '- the 'many' being well over 14,000. Now a constituent of the Battle of Britain Memorial Flight, it has flown in a variety of colour schemes over the years; in 1979 as JU:Q of No. 111 Squadron, who flew Hurricanes from December 1937 to April 1941. Author's collection

mushrooms, will dispute this statement. I too consider them the heydays of Farnborough but many of the exhibits were 'one-offs' that disappeared – the Armstrong Whitworth Apollo, Aviation Traders Accountant, Bristol Brabazon, Cierva Air Horse, Fairey Gyrodyne, Percival Merganser, Portsmouth Aerocar, Saunders Roe Princess, to name just a few. Again, there were prototypes of aircraft which were produced in relatively small numbers – Attacker (145), Scimitar (76), Swift (172), Wyvern (89). New technology dictated that the unit price was too prohibitive for companies to 'go-it alone' with private ventures or for the Services to order more than small quantities. The exceptions, Meteor (3,570), Hunter (1,975), Vampire (1,158) and Canberra (925) all provided benefit for their manufacturers by overseas orders but the industry as a whole did not and the small names, such

as Cierva and Portsmouth disappeared, to be followed not too much later by the better known Miles, Airspeed and General Aircraft. In terms of revenue earning for its manufacturer and the national exchequer, the Hunter reigned supreme.

The British have a slightly unfortunate trait. Once a job is done, there is a natural inclination to sit back and have a metaphorical – or even real – cup of tea, before contemplating the next task. Furthermore, if they have got the better of someone, they do not seriously consider that someone can teach them much. Maybe this theory does not hold quite so much water now as it used to, as we are all living in a very different world from that of 1945. Then, Britain had won the war. They had bettered the Axis powers. So it was feet up, kettle on.

America and the Soviet Union, on the other hand, were not hampered by such

idealism. Nor were they so partial to tea! Following the D-Day landings on 6 June 1944 and the successful progress that all the Allied forces were making in converging on the Fatherland from east and west, serious consideration was given by both nations to the fact that Germany had obviously made enormous advances in high-speed aerodynamics, rocket experimentation and operation, missile armaments for interceptors – in fact, contemporary aviation in general. It was considered most expedient to obtain as much data and hardware as possible on all these scientific achievements before they disappeared, thereby saving years of research and countless dollars and roubles. Both countries despatched teams of specialists to follow close behind their respective land forces, in order to glean anything and everything considered relevant, once a particular area had been overrun. By the time Germany surrendered on Luneburg Heath, well over 500 experts in all branches of aviation were having their eyes opened as to the theoretically advanced state of the former foe – and maybe contemplating that it was just as well that the war in Europe had ended when it had. (The fact that another three months of war was yet to be endured in the Far East is not ignored, but it has no bearing on the subject of this book.) It is rather ironic that the net results of the USA and USSR missions, the F-86 and MiG-15 respectively would, within five years, be facing each other in combat over the thirty-eighth parallel dividing North and South Korea.

Eventually, official complacency in Britain dissolved just enough for the Allied Technical Intelligence Mission to be formed, with the brief to authenticate just how far the former enemy had progressed in aeronautical development. The use of 'Allied' in the title is a little puzzling as it was a purely British mission. In view of Army and Navy representatives also being present, it most likely refers to Britain's three armed services as opposed to the wartime allies. As events unfolded, the latter use was certainly misplaced. Rumours circulating among American sources sounded rather fanciful, but the close relationship welded between Britain and our partners from the New World started to become more than a little strained when requests were made for Britain to be advised as to what had been discovered. Hard-nosed business had taken over from partnership under arms. It was every man for himself – and the main course had already been consumed. Britain was scratching among the crumbs and it is due to the persistence exercised by such mission delegates as Handley Page's Godfrey Lee, Roy Chaplin from Hawker and Sir Roy Fedden, Managing Director of Roy Fedden Limited the aircraft component manufacturer, that so much material was actually discovered and brought back.

There was more cooperation from German representatives than from the Americans. In his biography of Sir Roy Fedden, *Plane Speaking* (1992), that historian on all things aeronautical, Bill Gunston, quotes:

The mission spent the first three days at the LFA laboratory, also known as the Hermann Göring Institute, at Volkenrode, near Brunswick. This had been discovered by American troops a few weeks before. It was easily the

biggest aeronautical research laboratory in Europe. Fedden had heard before the war such an establishment was being planned, but there followed only conflicting rumours, some prisoners saying it was in East Prussia and others claiming it had been planned but never built. Now it had at last been discovered. Never in the thousands of reconnaissance flights over Germany had its presence been suspected, though photographic interpreters had looked at it in numerous prints. It had no main road, no rail link and no overhead power line. The whole series of services were brought underground from Brunswick. Yet the place was gigantic. It covered about 1,100 acres in a thickly wooded area. It contained dozens of huge buildings, a great array of wind tunnels far surpassing in size, Mach number and power, anything even planned in Britain and large complexes of laboratories for engines, structures, explosives and weapons (including rocket propulsion and various classes of guided missiles). Yet, so good was the camouflage, even former members of the staff were continually getting lost and having to make huge detours. The biggest wind tunnel, for example, operating up to Mach 1.8, was under thousands of tons of earth in which were growing grass, bushes and small trees.

This mighty establishment was just the first of a succession of surprises. Members of the mission walked miles through ruined machine shops and laboratories to study and discuss huge piston engines, jet engines, rocket engines and new research tools. They discovered a range of optical interferometric methods of picturing aerodynamic flow and even got a tunnel working with a swept-wing model in it. The use of sweepback to delay compressibility drag-rise had been known before the war, but subsequently forgotten and ignored in Britain. But in Germany it was being accepted as standard in all the latest jet aircraft. While the airflow round the model was being explored, a team breezed in from Boeing; next morning Fedden was piqued that the swept-wing model was nowhere to be found (guess who had it). A day or two later Fedden had made up two huge truckloads of books for Cranfield from Göttingen. They were about to leave when the loads were commandeered by US troops on the instructions of a rival US team. Fedden could see there would be trouble and sought the advice of the Allied Control Commission. They did not want to know and the rule seemed to be the law of the jungle. Fedden had no inclination to steal things off the Americans and it was galling when he was robbed of the things he had managed to find for Britain. As he had no troops and could get no backing, he had to let the trucks be driven off.

As Sir Roy Fedden said, the use of wing sweep to delay drag-rise generated by shock waves was raised pre-war at the 1936 Yalta Conference. In Britain the whole concept was virtually forgotten. With the impending unrest in Central Europe making war look more of a certainty month by month, designers were much more inclined to depend on the straight-wing configuration they knew, rather than embark down a research road with a totally unknown length or destination. (Of course, there is the hoary old chestnut question; 'What swept-wing aircraft saw RAF service throughout World War Two?' Answer: 'The Tiger Moth'. But that was to avoid unacceptable CG movements caused by the repositioning of the centre section struts, which had been done to give the instructor a more reasonable chance of getting out in an emergency. It had nothing to do with delaying drag-rise.) Improvements in performance were seen as possible by reducing thickness/chord ratios but then came the question of skin thicknesses having to be increased to retain wing bending strength. In effect, going for a thinner wing created the necessity to increase skin gauge which put up airframe weight. Machined skins with integral stiffeners, which were still in their infancy, went part of the way to solving the problem but really thin wings would possibly require leading-edge slats in order to avert separation of airflow at high angles of attack, which, again, had not been given too much thought in relation to higher speed aircraft. The resources of contemporary design teams were being put severely to the test, while the RAF and Luftwaffe locked horns 15,000ft above them in the late 1940 summer sunshine.

Of course, so much of what was discovered in 1945 about swept wings was purely German research data. They were miles ahead of the Allies in wind tunnel testing and the results were only just being channelled into detailed design work for the future. These were much in evidence in the drawing offices of Focke-Wulf, Messerschmitt, Junkers, Heinkel and Blohm und Voss. There is no doubt that, given another twelve months, the majority of these drawing offices would have turned projects into shop-floor drawings but at the time of the ceasefire, they had not had sufficient time to capitalize on their advanced state of the aerodynamic art. The only *operational* aircraft employing wing sweep were both Messerschmitt products.

Messerschmitt Me 163 Komet

The *Deutsche Versuchsanstalt für Luftfahrt* (DVL) placed a contract with Hellmuth Walter *circa* 1935/36, to produce a small 90lb (40.8kg) thrust liquid-fuel rocket, to be fixed on one wing-tip, for research into roll characteristics of forthcoming aircraft. From this stemmed the concept of the rocket motor being used as the prime engine for a high-speed aircraft. Professor A. M. Lippisch, working at the *Deutsche Forschungsanstalt für Segelflug* (DFS), the German Institute for Sailplanes, had developed several aero-dynamically advanced airframes and Dr A. Baeumker of DVL suggested Lippisch should design a rocket-powered, high-speed research aircraft.

In view of the lack of test facilities at DFS, January 1939 saw Professor Lippisch, together with a team of assistants, join the Messerschmitt AG (although the association was far from smooth and rather short-lived), so that further work on the project, numbered DFS 194, came into the orbit of the Luftwaffe's Aircraft Development Department. The DFS 194 project became designated Me 163 and, following flight trials at Peenemünde-Karlshagen, made by Flugkapitan Heini Dittman, development progressed with a Walter HWK R.11, giving 1,650lb (748.5kg) thrust. This led to the eventual production of the Me 163B, powered by a Walter HWK 109-509A-2 bi-fuel rocket motor, giving 3,750lb (1,701kg) thrust. Fuel was a combination of concentrated hydrogen peroxide (T-Stoff) and a solution of hydrazine-hydrate in methanol (C-Stoff), which gave the aircraft a maximum speed capability in excess of 550mph (885.5km/h), at over 30,000ft (9,144m). Service ceiling was 54,000ft (16,459m) and endurance approximately 2.5 minutes after the climb.

Series production was well under way by the beginning of 1944. The first Jagdgruppe, JG 400, was formed from Erprobungskommando 16 at Bad Zwischenahn and later moved to Wittmundhafen. By the end of July, three Staffel had been established, but production of the Me 163B ended in January 1945, 364 aircraft having been built, although less than fifty were in service by May.

SPECIFICATION	Me 163B.
DIMENSIONS	Span 30ft 7in (9.32m)
	Length 18ft 8 in (5.70m)
	Height 9ft 0in (2.74m)
	Wing area 211sq ft (14.60sq m)
ARMAMENT	Two 30mm MK 108 cannon, with 60 rounds for each
POWER PLANT	One Walter HWK 109-509A-2 bi-fuel rocket motor, giving 3,750lb (1,704kg) thrust. Maximum fuel capacity, 226 gallons (1,028 litres) T-Stoff; 110 gallons (500 litres) C-Stoff
WEIGHTS	Empty 4,200lb (1,905kg); loaded 9,500lb (4,308kg)
PERFORMANCE	Maximum speed 595mph (958km/h) at 30,000ft (9,100m); 515mph (829km/h) at sea-level. Initial rate of climb 16,000ft (4,877m) per minute; Time to 30,000ft (9,000m) 2.6 minutes; 40,000ft (12,200m) 3.5 minutes.

The Messerschmitt Me 163B Komet was the only manned, operational, rocket-powered interceptor used by any of the combatants in World War II. This was the culmination of a series of German rocket-propelled, strategic target-defending fighters that stemmed from the Me 163V1 high-speed research aircraft. The aerodynamics were tested in glider form, following which it first flew under power in August 1941. *Aeroplane Monthly*

On 29 July 1944, Captain Arthur Jeffrey of the 479th Fighter Group US Eighth AAF was flying a Lockheed P-38 Lightning from Wattisham, Suffolk, escorting straggling 100th Bombardment Group B-17s en route to Merseburg. At 11.45hrs he entered into the first Allied combat with a new generation German fighter, a Messerschmitt Me 163B making for the bomber formation. Jeffrey engaged the enemy, see-ing several hits from a deflection shot made at about 300 yards. His P-38 was indicating 500mph when he pulled out from a dive in pursuit of the Messerschmitt and 'blacked out'. He was credited with a 'kill' after examination of his camera gun film but subsequent German records do not mention such a loss and it is therefore presumed that the rocket-powered inter-ceptor escaped.

The second Messerschmitt fighter design to feature swept wings was the twin-engined Me 262.

Again it was the Eighth Army Air Force that had the first encounter, exactly one month after Captain Jeffrey's brush with the Me 163.On 29 August 1944, P-47Cs of the 78th Fighter Group based at Duxford spotted a low-flying Me 262 near Brussels. In taking evasive action to escape the

---

Messerschmitt Me 262

This superbly streamlined, aerodynamic shape had a modest 12-degree wing sweep, which in reality was a straight wing set back to the CG enough to require a leading-edge extension, which swept back from the roots. It was the result of the German Air Ministry's request that Messerschmitt AG should design an aircraft, powered by axial-flow engines being developed by Junkers *Flugzeug und Motorenwerke* AG and BMW *Flugmotorenbau* GmbH. The result was designated Me 262 and three prototypes were ordered on 1 March 1940, the BMW 109-003A engine anticipated to be available in the summer. The Junkers Jumo 109-004 turbojet was selected as an alternative, but polit-ical forces within the Luftwaffe caused the whole concept to be given low priority and Messerschmitt kept the project alive as a private venture, by fitting a Jumo 210G pis-ton engine in the nose for a first flight on 4 April 1941.

A pair of 1,000lb (453.6kg) turbojet engines were delivered in November 1941 and a maiden jet-powered flight was made on 25 November. The crash of the third pro-totype on 11 August 1942, in which a senior test pilot was killed, again raised doubts about the aircraft in official circles. Its initial design as a tactical bomber, with a built-in fighter development potential, kept the design viable. The combined enthusiasm of Göring, Milch and Galland advocated that its use as an interceptor should be given priority, but unsatisfactory engine reliability, coupled with Hitler's desire to broaden the bomber-role, meant that it was only when the defeat of Germany was becoming more apparent, that emphasis on the mass production of the Me 262, as an inter-ceptor, was established.

A total of 1,433 aircraft was built, of which 865 were produced in the last four months of the War. Only about 100 Me 262s were used operationally, although by April 1945, the combination of the aircraft and its battery of twenty-four 5cm R4M missiles, started to have a marked effect on massed bomber formations.

SPECIFICATION	Me 262A-1a
DIMENSIONS	Span 40ft 11.5in (12.49m) Length 34ft 9.75in (10.59m) Height 12ft 7in (3.83m) Wing area 234sq ft (21.73sq m)
ARMAMENT	Four 30mm MK 108 cannon
POWER PLANT	Two Junkers Jumo 109-004B-1 turbojets, each giving 1,980lb (898kg) static thrust.
WEIGHTS	Empty 9,741lb (4,417.5kg); loaded 14,101lb (6,395kg)
PERFORMANCE	Maximum speed 538 mph (866km/h) at 29,560ft (9,009m); 500 mph (805km/h) at sea-level; Initial rate of climb 3,940ft (1201m) per minute Service ceiling 37,565ft (11,450m) Range 298m (480km) at sea-level; 652m (1,049km) at 29,560ft (9,009m)

By far the most technically advanced aircraft operating in the summer of 1944, the Messerschmitt Me 262 could possibly have reclaimed Luftwaffe supremacy in the skies over Germany, had the war lasted another year. This example was found intact by the US Ninth Army, at Giebelstadt, in April 1945. *Aeroplane Monthly*

Thunderbolts, the German aircraft crash-landed in a field. The pilot ran away from the wreckage but was killed as his aircraft was strafed and destroyed by the 78th Fighter Group. The Group's leader, Major Joe Myers and his wing-man Lt Manford Croy were jointly credited with the 'kill'.

The first German design employing wingsweep of any real significance, with the direct aim of delaying compressibility drag-rise, was yet another Messerschmitt, with

whole aircraft, complete with Messerschmitt's project designer Dr Waldemar Voigt and his team, was taken over by a Combined Advanced Field Team under the leadership of Robert J. Woods, Chief Designer of the Bell Aircraft Corporation. They all reappeared in the United States at Wright Field, Ohio in 1946 and within five years, in June 1951, 5-01838, the first of two Bell X-5 research aircraft, looking remarkably similar to the P.1101, flew to com-

than examples from which something could be learned. The hardware commanded more attention than the reams of results accumulated over five years of German research. In fact, a certain amount of scorn and ridicule was heaped upon the statistics – probably because they were so much in advance of current thinking in Britain.

One of the most successful and respected figures in the industry was the gentleman who, in 1923, had joined H. G.

The Tempest MkII was the last piston-engined aircraft produced by Hawker for the RAF, who were due to operate it in the Far East when the war came to an abrupt end. LA607, the second prototype, which first flew on 18 September 1943, has been preserved and is shown getting a rare outing at Duxford in 1981. At the time of writing, April 1997, LA607 is in Kermit Weeks' Air Museum at Tamiami, Florida. Author's collection

the project number P.1101. The nearly completed prototype, fitted with a mock-up of the proposed Heinkel/Hirth HeS 11 A-1 axial-flow turbojet engine, was located by United States ground troops at Oberammergau on 29 April 1945. With the wings having a leading-edge sweep in the order of 40 degrees, a manufacturer's estimated maximum sea level speed of Mach 0.73, increasing to 0.88 at 20,000ft, looked perfectly feasible for this single-seater, with the designed initial rate-of-climb rated at 4,350ft per minute. As a prime example of the 'un-allied' situation that prevailed, the

mence a programme of investigation into the properties of variable geometry wings. There is no doubt that Bell Aircraft enjoyed a great saving in time and money with their acquisition at Oberammergau.

Wind tunnel test results, data and drawings that were brought back to Britain in 1945 to be presented to the British aircraft industry and experimental establishments, had all the impact of a feather landing on a blancmange. Examples of contemporary German operational aircraft and equipment were also put on display at Farnborough in the autumn, more as battle trophies

Hawker Engineering and two years later was appointed Chief Designer of Hawker Aircraft Limited, Sydney (in 1953 knighted Sir Sydney) Camm. Well over three dozen different aircraft designs had already emerged from teams under his leadership and gone into production, with his latest piston-engined fighter, the Tempest MkV, matching the jet-powered products from Gloucestershire. Yet the aerodynamic findings of the Allied Technical Intelligence Mission, when shown to him, were dismissed out of hand. Prejudice is certainly no respecter of status or reputation.

No Airscrew Necessary

In the 1930s, on both sides of the English Channel the turbojet as a means of impelling aeroplanes in their natural environment was developed along different technical lines but on similar time scales.

Using the noun *jet* as a generalistic term, things have been 'jet-propelled' for some considerable time. Long before citizen Fawkes' misguided mission on 5 November 1605, cylindrical tubes, filled with a mixture of sulphur, nitre and charcoal, when ignited have been hurled forward by the action of the liberated gases. Moving on 178 years, it has been mooted that the French papermakers, Joseph and Etienne Montgolfier, considered the application of apertures around the base of their balloon to facilitate controllable horizontal movement. Getting nearer to home, the childhood laughter generated by the erratic flight path taken when the inflated party balloon is released before sealing, converting the air intake into a jet orifice, is universal.

Returning to things Gallic. A year before Louis Blériot left Les Baraques (Calais), got blown off his intended course and finished up on the slopes surrounding Dover Castle in 1909, a fellow countryman, M. René Lorin patented the use of a piston engine without a drive shaft in which the resultant amplified exhaust gases could produce motive thrust. From these proposals, gas turbines evolved to generate industrial power but inevitably they increased in size so that, while their application as an aeronautical power source seemed possible in theory, contemporary materials and state-of-the-art engineering became something of a stumbling block. Further French predominance in the theoretic principles concerning the relevance of gas turbines to aircraft propulsion, was shown by additional patents being taken out by the well-known engineer Guillaume. Technical papers published in 1928 also recognized that there would be a limiting speed at which conventional propellors could operate and thrust generated by the gas turbine would be the logical answer.

Germany's Lead

In view of this advanced thinking on the part of French physicists and engineers, it seems surprising that they were not in the vanguard of the principle's pre-war practical applications. This was taken up on the continental mainland by Germany and in Britain by a Coventry-born cadet at the RAF College, Cranwell. The German was a Göttingen University physics student, one Hans Joachim Pabst von Ohain (who some years later, in 1947, would become the Chief Scientist at the United States Air Force Aerospace Laboratories). He recognized the advantages to be gained by the construction of a working model and, although it suffered a failure of the combustion chamber to contain the flame, his tutor Professor Pohl identified the potential displayed by the model. Fortunately for young von Ohain, his tutor was acquainted with Professor Ernst Heinkel, who since 1935 had been experimenting with the use of rocket propulsion relative to the aeroplane, in conjunction with a young engineer working in the German army missile section, Wernher von Braun.

Born in the southern German village of Grunbach, Ernst Heinkel was one of the great Teutonic pioneers who was blessed with an extraordinary ability to see ahead of contemporary aeronautical thinking. As a mechanical engineering student, he completed the building of his first aeroplane in 1911 and, after holding senior design posts with Albatros, Castiglioni and Hansa Brandenburg, he formed the Ernst Heinkel Flugzeugwerke AG at Warnemünde on 1 December 1922. During the mid-thirties, the first fighter in the resurrected German air force was the bi-plane He 51, which would pioneer the use of the aeroplane as a ground attack weapon in the Spanish Civil War. His later He 70 single-engined four-passenger monoplane transport, capable of over 220mph (354.2km/h), was such a clean, advanced aerodynamic shape that Rolls-Royce purchased an He 70G for £13,000, registered G-ADZF, to be used as a flying test-bed for their new Kestrel V in-line engine. This was collected by the founder member of the RR Flight Test Establishment, Captain R. T. Shepherd, from Heinkel's factory at Rostock on 27 March 1936. In the summer of 1937, Heinkel mounted a von Braun designed rocket in the fuselage of his piston-engined He 112 fighter and several successful test flights were made by the hybrid combination.

Such was the pedigree of the man who engaged Pabst von Ohain in 1936 and sponsored his engine development work as a private venture. The initial engine, burning

While this shows the general profile of Heinkel's Type 178, there is an element of doubt as to whether it is the second prototype, which was slightly larger than the original and never flew, or a general mock-up, the latter appearing to be the more likely. Considering the usual German thoroughness, it is surprising that so little photographic recording was made on 27 August 1939, at the time of the world's first flight by an aircraft powered solely by a gas-turbine engine. *Aeroplane Monthly*

oxygen, started running in the autumn of 1937 and two years later, on 27 August 1939, exactly one week before the outbreak of World War II, Heinkel's first aircraft specifically designed around a gas-turbine engine, the He 178, made a maiden take-off that was the world's first flight by a jet-propelled aeroplane. The event, which was a complete success, was attended by such distinguished Luftwaffe pilots as Generalfeldmarschall Erhard Milch and Ernst Udet. An output of 838lb (380kg) thrust from the installed axial-flow HeS 3B engine developed by von Ohain, gave the single-seat He 178, with a 23ft 7in (7.18m) wingspan and length of 24ft 6in (7.46m), a speed of approximately 300mph (483km/h). The later installation of a 1,300lb (590kg) thrust HeS 6 engine increased performance to a maximum 435mph(700km/h). Heinkel had also designed and manufactured another revolutionary aircraft, the He 176, around a von Braun-developed rocket engine. With a 24in (60.96cm) wide fuselage and wing area of only 58 sq.ft (5.38sq m) – the He 178 wing area was 98sq.ft(9.10sq m) – this little aeroplane made its first flight two months before the He 178 at Peenemünde on 20 June 1939 and eventually, after development, attained speeds in excess of 500mph (805km/h). A demonstration of the He 176 was given to the Führer, Adolf Hitler, and the Luftwaffe supremo, Reichsmarshall Hermann Göring on 3 July, 1939, but it was considered no more than an interesting diversion and the whole concept was to be written off.

Officialdom is officialdom the world over and, as the decade was drawing to a close, Germany was no exception. Twin-engined He 111 bombers and He 115 multi-purpose seaplanes were coming off the lines in numbers for the Luftwaffe, to support an army that had already overwhelmed large parts of Central Europe and was poised to strike across the borders of Poland. This was not going to be jeopardized in any way by the development of some newfangled propulsion concept which Professor Ernst Heinkel had been undertaking and financing up near the German Baltic coast. His job was to turn out the bombers and aircraft that were needed, nothing else. Luftwaffe High Command's obstinacy, brewed by Heinkel's natural tenacity of purpose, prevailed so that even when the He 280, the world's first jet fighter design (and, incidently the first twin-jet powered aircraft) was built, not a single prototype was officially ordered and it saw no service. Furthermore, a contract for jet-engine development was also withheld from

Heinkel and given to Junkers, with Willy Messerschmitt getting the order to design an airframe, which was to become the Me 262.

Britain Catches Up

On this side of the English Channel, in 1923, sixteen-year old Frank Whittle enlisted in the Royal Air Force as a boy

apprentice at Halton.

Despite the constraints of war, an example of the W1X engine, evolved from the WU, was cleared for taxiing in an aircraft George Carter, Chief Designer of the Gloster Aircraft Company, had designed around it to meet Specification E.28/39. In terms of aviation history, the W1X was the first British jet engine to become airborne, albeit unintentionally.

The 'Exceptional to Above-Average' Engineer

Throughout history, certain people have, through their efforts and endeavours, become synonymous with particular achievements. Frank Whittle was such a person.

Born on 1 June 1907 and raised with humble beginnings, his aspiration in 1923 was to become one of the small number of apprentices selected each year for officer training at the RAF College, Cranwell, deep in the heart of the forthcoming 'bomber county' of Lincolnshire. Attaining his goal, three years later Flight Cadet Whittle passed out from Halton to place his feet firmly on the bottom rung of the ladder that was to lead to heights even his ambitious nature could not envisage. He did not look too hard beyond the desire to be a good fighter pilot, which he became, with an assessment of 'Exceptional to Above Average'.

In the course of his education at Cranwell, Whittle became acquainted, like the French, with the insurmountable limitations suffered by a piston engine driving a propeller. He also learned about the respiration problems that reciprocating engines encounter as they climb to higher altitudes, due to the decreasing density of the air. His inquisitive mind explored a way round these constraints and in 1928, in his fourth term at the age of twenty-one, he wrote a science thesis entitled 'Future Developments in Aircraft Design'. This essay considered how it might be possible to power an aeroplane by some form of engine that drew in air, heated it and discharged it at high speed through a nozzle. Completely confident of the logic of this principle, Whittle filed a Provisional Specification for his turbojet in January 1930.

Having completed an officers' engineering course at Henlow, Whittle was seconded to Cambridge University. His creative prowess was recognized by the Air Ministry who, despite his being a serving officer, allowed him to form his own company, Power Jets Limited, in collaboration with two former officers and an investment banker. The engine developed by the company was a reverse-flow centrifugal layout unit and placed with the British Thomson-Houston Company (BTH.) for manufacture. The engine, known as WU was fired for the first time by Whittle himself, on 12 April 1937. Power Jets as a company faced a lack of funding but nevertheless produced a variety of projects and, by cannibalizing a previous engine in order to complete the next, managed to construct and test several of them. In retrospect, it seems amazing that not only did this state of affairs persist until January 1944, when the company was nationalized, but the political *coup de grâce* was the decree that, in future, Power Jets Limited would not be allowed to manufacture jet engines!

Honorary Air Commodore Whittle, taken at RAF Cranwell in March 1945, three years before he was knighted. Sir Frank Whittle is accepted as one of the real giants of engineering in this century and for this he was awarded Britain's highest civil honour, the Order of Merit, in 1986. His pertinacity in the face of technical and financial frustrations is an object lesson that would have defeated many a lesser character. He died on 9 August 1996, at the age of 89. *Aeroplane Monthly*

Frank Whittle continued to exercise his mind on a variety of aviation and engineering projects, as well as undertaking a gruelling programme of lecturing, coupled with many consultancy surgeries. Ill health affected his remaining in the RAF and, when he was invalided out in 1948, holding the rank of Honorary Air Commodore, he was knighted. He was the recipient of many civic and professional awards, the Order of Merit, bestowed in 1986, being his country's highest civil honour.

Sir Frank Whittle's eventual retirement to the United States suited his character – and the exchequers of numerous American political and economic establishments. The British Prime Minister in 1986, Margaret Thatcher, not noted for unnecessary eulogy, put on record when the OM was awarded that 'Frank Whittle's life and work are an object lesson, on the creativity and inspiration of British engineering at its best'. This accolade not only held good, up to his death on 9 August 1996, but will remain permanently valid.

(Top) **A photograph of great significance in the annals of British aviation – the first Gloster E28/39 has been taken from the premises of Regent Motors in Cheltenham, where it was assembled in great secrecy. Heat-sensitive paint strips have been fitted on the rear fuselage sides, the W.1.X engine is installed for taxiing and the original short-stroke nose-wheel unit is fitted. This was replaced by a longer unit before the first flight.** *Aeroplane Monthly*

(Above) **Standard camouflage colours dark green and dark earth, plus an all-yellow underside, were applied for the first flight, together with the serial W4041 and Type A.1 roundels. Seen here at Farnborough in April 1944, end-plates have been fitted to cure slight instability, Type C.1 roundels plus prototype markings have been added, as has the 'G' suffix to the serial, which denoted that the aircraft was to be guarded and given strict security, should it land away from its base. A new W.2/500 engine has been fitted, for a ten-hour flying programme to be undertaken at the Establishment.** *Aeroplane Monthly*

During the second day of high-speed taxiing at the company's Hucclecote airfield in Gloucestershire on 8 April 1941, Gloster's Chief Test Pilot P. E. G. Sayer achieved several 'hops' of between 100-200 yd, in the process rising about 6ft above the tarmac.

The following month a flight-cleared W1 engine producing 850lb (385kg) static thrust was fitted and at 7.45pm on Thursday 15 May 1941, 'Gerry' Sayer lifted W4041, the first prototype E.28/39 Pioneer off the runway at the Royal Air Force College, Cranwell. Seventeen minutes

later he landed and the bedrock of future British aviation was laid. Gloster followed the Pioneer with a twin-engined single-seat design to Specification F.9/40, powered by an improved W1 engine, the W2, giving 1,600lb (726kg) static thrust. From the F.9/40 came the RAF's first operational

A reproduction of 'Gerry' Sayer's test report, covering the maiden flight of W4041 made from Cranwell on 15 May 1941. Author's collection

fighter, the Meteor. In October 1941, a set of manufacturer's drawings of the W2B and a Whittle W1X engine, accompanied a group of Power Jets Limited engineers on a flight to the General Electric Company in America. The brief was to assist GEC to initiate production of the engine in the United States. The value of this action can be deduced from the fact that, within twelve months, on 2 October 1942 the first of three prototype Bell XP-59As made its first flight, piloted by the company's Chief Test Pilot Robert Stanley and powered by a pair of GEC-manufactured Whittle-type W2B engines.

Production of the Whittle-type centrifugal flow engines was put in the hands of Rover Motors at Coventry but they rather quickly discovered the difference between the tolerances required for their usual products and those for the aircraft engine industry. Engineering requirements to the necessarily higher standards took much longer than anticipated, so that delays in delivering engines to Glosters lengthened the development of their F.9/40 prototypes. Rolls-Royce had taken an interest in jet propulsion for aircraft since 1938 and had undertaken research work in the field of turbine blades operating at very high temperatures and rpms. Two years later they commenced to manufacture turbine blades and supercharger casings for Whittle's Power Jets company. The following year, a test plant was established by Rolls-Royce at Derby and the company received instructions from the Ministry of Aircraft Production (MAP) to develop and produce complete Whittle-type engines in conjunction with Power Jets Limited and Rover Motors, the latter eventually accepting that the standard of requirements was beyond their ability and retiring from the project early in 1943, with Rolls-Royce taking over the company's facility at Barnoldswick. The rivernames system adopted by Rolls-Royce for their gas-turbine engines, chosen to indicate the idea of flowing associated with jet propulsion, was started with the W2B/23, christened Welland and much of the flight testing was done with an engine mounted in the rear of a Vickers Armstrong Wellington Mk II Z8570, which later was joined by two hybrid Wellingtons, W5389 and W5518. Two of the new engines powered Meteor Mk1 EE210/G which went to Muroc Air Force Base, California the following month to be bedecked in USAAF star-and-bar markings, in exchange for a Bell XP-59 Airocomet that had been uncrated, assembled and flown at Moreton Valence four months earlier, in September 1943.

Parallel with Rolls-Royce's efforts on the Whittle-type engine, at Hatfield in Hertfordshire the de Havilland Engine Company Limited entered the new era. In April, 1941, under the direction of Major F. B. Halford, the company commenced to design their first jet engine, the H-1. This featured a single-sided (compared with R-R's double-sided) impeller combined with sixteen straight-flow combustion chambers (as distinct from the reverse-flow system at Derby). Within a year, the prototype engine was being bench-run, two months later producing its designed 2,300lb (1,043kg) thrust and within another ten months, on 5 March 1943 at Cranfield, production engines powered DG206/G, the first F.9/40 to fly – Rover's late delivery of W2B engines giving DH the distinction on a plate.

Again America was presented with a gift. A de Havilland H-1 was supplied to the US Air Technical Service Command in July, 1943 and they passed it over to the Lockheed Aircraft Corporation, to become the basis of a power unit for their XP-80 Shooting Star single-seat fighter. Back in Hertfordshire, the H-1 (by now named Goblin) became the first British jet engine to pass the official type-test in the new gas turbine category, being awarded Approval Certificate No.1. Across the road at Hatfield, R. E. Bishop, Chief Designer of the de Havilland Aircraft Co. Ltd, had been quick to design the company's 100th aircraft type in order to provide an airframe for Halford's engine. This was LZ548/G, a little twin-boom, single-seat fighter originally named Spider Crab but, by the time Geoffrey de Havilland Jnr lifted it into the air for the first time on 29 September 1943, it had been given the much more realistic appellation, Vampire.

The British and German learning curves in jet-engine development came closest with Metropolitan-Vickers' involvement. At the Royal Aircraft Establishment (RAE) Farnborough, Dr A. A. Griffiths headed a section which, since 1936, had been researching the principle of gas-turbine engines with axial-flow compressors. The following year, the Air Ministry gave the RAE the go-ahead to place an order for the manufacture of an engine based on their designs and this was placed with Metropolitan-Vickers (Metrovick), on the logic that they had been in the business of manufacturing industrial gas turbines for many years. Their first jet-propulsion engine, designated

The Midland Air Museum at Coventry Airport, Baginton, houses the Sir Frank Whittle Jet Heritage Centre, which includes a fine example of the Rover-built, 1,600lb (725kg) thrust W.2 engine. Author's collection

The first flying test-bed used to further the development of Whittle's jet engines was Vickers Wellington MkII Z8570. Merlin Xs were the main power plants, the test engine being installed in a redesigned rear fuselage, with lateral intakes over the elevators. Testing started in July 1942, with the BTH produced W2B/23 Welland, shown here, which later was replaced by a Rover-built Whittle engine. *Aeroplane Monthly*

F.1 and based on RAE design work, unlike Rolls-Royce and de Havilland, employed an axial-flow compressor. Metrovick's new gas-turbine team was lead by Dr D. Smith and together they believed that the smaller overall diameter of an axial-flow engine gave aircraft designers more flexibility in determining the size of their projects. Development of the F.1 led to the F.2, the first of which was bench-run at the end of 1941, producing 1,800lb (816kg) static thrust. The following year, after modifications had been incorporated, the F.2 passed a Special Category Test giving flight clearance and trials commenced on 29 June 1943, with the engine mounted in the rear fuselage of the much modified first Avro Lancaster prototype BT308. In parallel with these flights, F.2 engines were installed in DG204/G, the third F.9/40 prototype, consequently restyled F.9/40M. Problems with high-idling thrust necessitated these engines being

returned to Metrovick for further amendments but, after reinstallation in the aircraft a month later, DG204/G made its maiden flight on 13 November 1943 from the RAE airfield at Farnborough.

Lancaster BT308 eventually ran out of airframe hours and the subsequent air-testing of progressive F.2 engines was conducted from a similar rear-end installation in Lancaster B.II LL735 and later a pair were fitted on Meteor MkIV RA490. The ultimate engine, the F.2/4A, giving an output of 3,250lb (1,474kg) static thrust at sea level, was named the M.V.B.2 Beryl and became the chosen power plant for Britain's only flying-boat fighter, the Saunders-Roe SR.A/1, of which there were three prototypes, TG263, TG267 and TG271. By the time the third aircraft was ready to fly, the Beryl was rated at 3,850lb (1,746kg) static thrust and when the first prototype TG263 had finished flying in 1951, it was present-

ed to the College of Aeronautics at Cranfield where one of its Beryl engines was removed and installed in Donald Campbell's boat *Bluebird*, for an attempt on the World Water-Speed Record.

Metropolitan Vickers discontinued working on aircraft jet propulsion in 1948 and their final design for a promising large axial-flow engine was taken over by Armstrong-Siddeley Motors Limited at Coventry, who amalgamated it with research on which they had been engaged with their own A.S.X. gas-turbine engine, test-flown in a bomb-bay installation on Lancaster B.III ND784. The results would emerge as the Sapphire which, in its ASSa1 version, was taken into the air for the first time on 18 January 1950, a pair of them being mounted in outboard nacelle positions on Avro Lancastrian VM733. The following year, on 31 August 1951, Gloster Meteor F.8 WA820, with Flt Lt R. B. 'Tom' Prickett

(Left) Metropolitan Vickers' axial-flow gas turbine's progress was furthered when the first prototype Lancaster, BT308/G, was modified to be the test-bed for their 1,800lb (816kg) thrust F.2 engine. Again it was a rear fuselage installation for the engine, which was aspirated via a large dorsal intake, and the combination's maiden flight was made from Baginton on 29 June 1943. *Aeroplane Monthly*

(Below) The later Metrovick Beryl was test-flown in a modified Lancaster MkII, LL735, the rear-end F.2/1 installation being shown here when the aircraft was at Bitteswell, in December 1947. In 1949, the ultimate Beryl, the 3,250lb (1,474kg) thrust F.2/4 version, was fitted in the aircraft's bomb-bay for flight testing. *Aeroplane Monthly*

at the controls and powered by a pair of ASSa2 Sapphire engines, captured four time-to-height records, reaching 40,000ft (12,000m) in 3min 7sec. A licensed agreement gave the United States gas-turbine industry yet more acceleration. Curtiss Wright produced their version of the ASSa1, designated the J65, which powered the Republic F-84F and Martin B-57B (itself a licensed product of a British design, the Canberra). The Sapphire was destined to become a part of the Hunter story.

(Above) **VM733** was the last Lancastrian to be used as an engine flying test-bed. Converted by Air Service Training at Hamble to take a pair of Sapphires in outboard nacelles, it took the Armstrong-Siddeley engine into the air for the first time on 18 January 1950. Author's collection

(Below) Seen here at the 1950 SBAC Display, Meteor F.8 WA820 was also used by Armstrong-Siddeley as an engine test-bed, when it was fitted with a pair of 7,600lb (3,447kg) thrust ASSa2 Sapphire engines. This was just about as much power as the Meteor could safely handle, which was 450 per cent more than the thrust for which it was originally designed! *Aeroplane Monthly*

CHAPTER THREE

The Jet-Age Comes to Kingston

If you follow the River Thames upstream from its estuary at Shoeburyness, through London Docklands, the City and Westminster, you eventually reach a tranquil stretch which has traditionally provided out-of-town homes for English monarchs. When the river was a main thoroughfare, the royalty of England planted their gardens and built their palaces on its banks at Richmond, Kew and Hampton Court, en route to Windsor. On this historic aquatic ribbon stands the market town of Kingston-upon-Thames, where large Golden Bream could be caught in the warm water efflux from the power station and a pungent odour from the tannery wafted in the air. A couple of miles beyond the town centre lies Canbury Park Road.

Shortly before the First World War, H. P. Martin and George Handasyde joined forces to create Martinsyde Limited, a Brooklands based company determined to achieve distinction in aircraft design. They produced the G.100 and G.102 Elephant in 1915 and 271 production examples saw service in the Royal Flying Corps (RFC). There followed the F.1 and F.2 in 1917, the F.3 and F.4 Buzzard a year later. Orders for the Buzzard totalled 1,453, but 11 November 1918 brought cancellation after only 338 aircraft had been built. One year later than Sopwith, in 1921, Martinsyde also went into voluntary liquidation, but from these two unfortunate episodes, a common denominator emerged. A junior Martinsyde draughtsman by the name of Sydney Camm, who had started on the shop floor, joined H. G. Hawker Engineering.

The bulging order books necessitated an expansion of production facilities and the buildings, plus flight-testing airfield, for a new assembly-line were constructed in 1936/7 at Langley, which in those days was in the county of Buckinghamshire. This plant would be an integral part of Hawker aircraft production throughout World War II and feature strongly in Hunter history.

Specifications F.43/46 and F.44/46 were issued for single- and two-seater interceptors respectively. An Air Ministry edict in

---

Aviation Icons

On Monday, 15 November 1920, the private company H. G. Hawker Engineering Co. Ltd was formed. The new company listed Harry Hawker and T. O. M. Sopwith (in 1953 knighted Sir Thomas Sopwith CBE, Hon FRAES) among the directors. It was registered as operating from Canbury Park Road, Kingston-upon-Thames, Surrey, with a working capital of £20,000, in £1.00 shares.

Such was the foundation of what became one of the most famous and respected names in the world of aviation. From his 1910 barnstorming-pilot days, with Claude Grahame-White and Alliott Verdon Roe at the Harvard–Boston Meet in America, T. O. M. Sopwith, who held Aviation Certificate No. 31, set up the Sopwith Aviation Company, with an Australian, Harry Hawker, as the company's pilot. The corner sited building in Canbury Park Road housed design office, drawing office and administration, while manufacturing was undertaken on one side of the airfield set within the Brooklands motor racing circuit at Weybridge, over ten miles further into Surrey. The first successful flying boat built in Europe was the Bat Boat designed by Sopwith, who wanted to combine his passion for yachting with the new joys of flying. With Harry Hawker at the controls, it won the Mortimer Singer Prize in July 1913. November of the same year saw the prototype Sopwith Tabloid first fly, again with Hawker at the controls, followed throughout the 1914–18 war by a succession of scouts and fighters – Gun-Bus, Triplane, Pup, Camel – names that etched the Sopwith Aviation Co. into the annals of that conflict.

With the armistice came the inevitable winding down of the services, cancellation of contracts and complete lack of official incentive for an industry that had evolved in a mere five years. Sopwith was not alone but, by turning to car body and motorcycle manu-

facturing, he existed for another two years, whereupon Whitehall, by dint of the Treasury's claim for an Excess War Profits Duty, removed the chocks from under the company and it was forced to place affairs in the hands of an official receiver. Directors and the Company Secretary voluntarily left their posts in order to effect some savings and, to Sopwith's credit, the Treasury's claim and all creditors were paid in full, one source of revenue being Harry Hawker's taking over the mortgage of the Canbury Park Road buildings when forming his engineering company.

The new company continued producing motorcycles, but with the director's pedigree it was destined to re-enter the sphere of aeronautics. War-surplus de Havilland, as well as Sopwith, aircraft were overhauled and renovated but eight months after its formation, the company received a body blow. On 12 July 1921, ten days before he was due to compete in the Aerial Derby, Harry Hawker was executing a high-g turn in a Nieuport Goshawk, near to the ground, when he suffered a haemorrhage as a result of spinal tuberculosis and died before the aircraft hit the ground. However, such was the stature of the man that his name never faded from the company's title and was preserved in the 1933 establishment of Hawker Aircraft Limited. Two years later in 1935, on the instigation of T. O. M. Sopwith, the Hawker Siddeley Group was formed with Sopwith as Chairman, and with it the Hawker name was perpetuated for over forty years, until the amalgamation that produced British Aerospace (BAe) in 1977. Sopwith had been Chairman of the Society of British Aircraft Constructors (SBAC), from 1925 to 1927 and is still a revered name in aviation, eight years after his death on 27 January 1989.

---

the mid-1940s had proclaimed that a high rate of climb, in order to combat the nuclear-armed high-altitude bomber, was one of the prerequisites for the next fighter generation and such a performance necessitated twin engines.

Sydney Camm argued fervently against such a philosophy, explicating that the fastest fighter had always been single engined and proven to be safer – the history of service pilots attempting to land asymmetrically-powered aircraft was littered with tragic consequences. His opinions were greatly assisted by Rolls-Royce's

release of preliminary details of their B.41 engine, which would later be named Nene. It had been first run on 27 October 1944 and thirteen months later type-tested at 5,000lb (2,265kg) static thrust. He considered that this was a reliable power plant and Rolls-Royce forecast it capable of further development. Around the Nene a single-seat, single-engined fighter could be designed.

Hawker Aircraft's Project Office, under the leadership of Robert Lickley, had introduced a new design numbering system in the early 1940s, commencing at

P.1000. (One early design, the P.1005, was a Hawker rarity – a twin-engined aircraft which actually got to a mock-up stage.) Having initially investigated the possibility of re-engining the Sea Fury with a turbojet, the first original design based around the Nene was the P.1035. As this

The Fighter Master

Two years after joining H. G. Hawker Engineering in 1925, Sydney Camm (later Sir Sydney Camm CBE, FRAES) took over as Chief Designer from Wilfred George Carter, who left to join the de Havilland design team (and six years later, enrolled with the Gloster Aircraft Company, to become Chief Designer in 1937). With Camm's background of founding the Windsor Model Aeroplane Club, plus the essential grounding of shop-floor techniques gained at Martinsyde before he joined the design staff, he was well suited to take Carter's post. He had already assisted in the design of the Cygnet, which gained first and second places in the *Daily Mail* competition for two-seat light aircraft in 1926. The first aircraft to be designed entirely under Sydney Camm's leadership was an adaptation of the Woodcock II night interceptor for Denmark, given the predictable name Danecock, which was built under licence and remained in Danish service until 1937.

Through a succession of outstanding designs built in their hundreds – thousands following the outbreak of World War II and proven by equally outstanding test pilots: Fred Raynham, George Bulman, 'Gerry' Sayer, Philip Lucas, Bill Humble, Trevor Wade, Neville Duke, Bill Bedford and Duncan Simpson – Hawker Aircraft Limited became forever associated with British fighter aircraft, although the odd sortie into light bomber design such as the Hart and Henley was also taken. Camm's policy was always to combine the smallest possible airframe and largest possible engine with a realistic military load, such parameters being exemplified by the inter-war biplanes, through to his monoplane fighters. The new turbojet power source saw no deviation from this principle, with the subject of this book and the Harrier standing as prime examples. Some were aesthetically more pleasing than others. The Fury and Demon looked purposeful, typifying the military aeroplane of the day, while anyone seeing a Typhoon knew it was not built for pleasure flights!

While many will agree that Sydney Camm was not the easiest of men to work with, none will disagree that he was a master designer of fighter aircraft. His roll-call of achievements is as follows: appointed Director of Hawker Aircraft Limited in 1935; awarded the 1949 British Gold Medal for Aeronautics; Chairman of the SBAC Technical Board from 1951 to 1953; knighted for services to aviation in 1953; President of the Royal Aeronautical Society from 1954 to 1955; Chief Engineer of Hawker Aircraft Limited in 1959. These are the accomplishments of a leader in his field, who left aeronautics the poorer with his death on 12 March 1966.

engine had a double-sided centrifugal compressor, it was considered plausible to position the airway inlet close to the power plant, so twin wing-root intakes were incorporated at an early design stage. In order to keep thrust loss down to a minimum which, in view of the Nene 1 producing only 4,500lb (2,041kg) at that time, was a prudent move, Hawker patented a bifurcated outlet located either side of the fuselage behind each wing trailing edge root. Further refinements progressed to the point where project number P.1040 merited detailed design on a private venture basis with a view to submission for Royal Air Force appraisal.

The company authorized the construction of a prototype but before its completion the RAF made known that it did not consider the design offered sufficient improvement over current marks of the Gloster Meteor. The Royal Navy, on the other hand, was of the opinion that the P.1040 was superior to the Supermarine Attacker which was entering service, and consequently Specification N.7/46 was raised to cover the continuation of the design and the construction of three prototypes for naval evaluation.

the wing, was equipped with a Malcolm ejection seat. It was a very graceful looking aeroplane which, following ground running and taxiing trials, was transported by road to the Aircraft and Armament Experimental Establishment (A&AEE) at Boscombe Down in Wiltshire, for its maiden flight. Following reassembly, the prototype P.1040, serialled VP401, was lifted off the vast A&AEE runway by Bill Humble on 2 September 1947. Two further airframes, VP413 and VP422, incorporating wing-folding mechanism more fully met the N.7/46 Specification and a first order for 151 production aircraft given the name Sea Hawk was placed.

Hawker's progress into the realms of transonic flight was gradual. While development trials with the P.1040 continued throughout 1948, the company was attending to a design meeting Specification E.38/46 for an aircraft to investigate the aerodynamics of swept wings. The P.1040 was proving a sound enough design on which to base their contender for the new specification and in the early winter of 1948, the P.1052 emerged. It was basically a P.1040 fuselage and tail unit married to a 35-degree swept wing, with shorter but deeper engine air intakes. The

The P.1040 prototype VP401 is brought close in to the photographer's viewfinder, to illustrate Hawker's patented bifurcated jet-pipe layout from the Rolls-Royce Nene RN.1. Although this was the company's first jet-powered aircraft, the smooth aerodynamic silhouette, for which they would be noted, is already self-evident.
Aeroplane Monthly

In June 1947, Hawker's first jet-powered aircraft was towed from the assembly shops at Langley. The fuselage length was 37ft 7in (11.4m) and a mid-mounted straight wing spanning 36ft 6in (11.12m) had a thickness/chord ratio of 9.5 per cent. An unpressurized cockpit positioned well forward of

new wing at a 31ft 6in (9.63m) span, was 5ft (1.52m) less than its predecessor and 0.5 per cent greater in thickness/cord ratio. Allocated the serial VX272, it followed the path of its stablemate by being transported to Boscombe Down and was first flown on 19 November 1948 with Squadron Leader T. S.

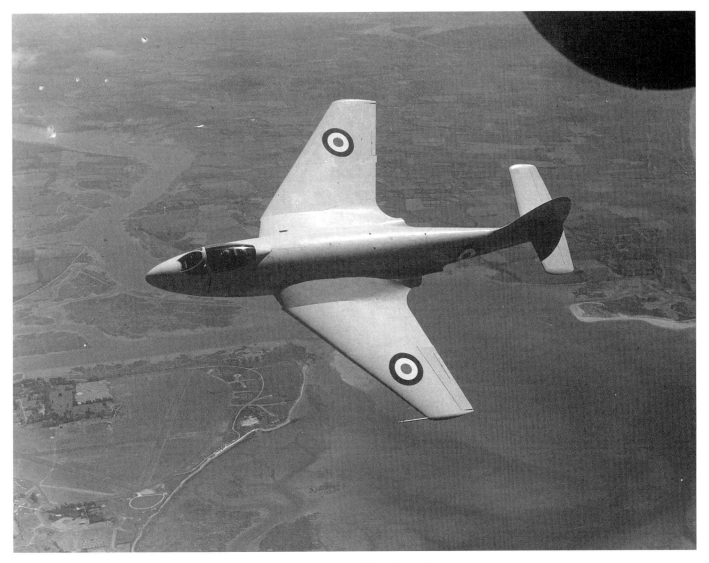

Hawker's first application of wing sweep was on the P.1052. The second prototype VX279, is seen here banking to port over the World War II Fleet Air Arm station HMS Goldcrest, **at Dale in Pembrokeshire. The 35-degree swept wing is married to the basic P.1040-design fuselage and tail unit, with power supplied by a 5,000lb (2,265kg) thrust Nene RN.2.** *Aeroplane Monthly*

'Wimpy' Wade at the controls. Six months later on 13 April 1949, the second P.1052 VX279 had its maiden flight, with the same pilot and from the same location.

Although the tail unit was unswept and the Nene R.N.2 only produced 5,000lb (2,265kg), the P.1052's performance figures were very encouraging, with 640mph (1,037km/h) being exceeded at sea level and Mach 0.85 attained at 40,000ft. An adaptation of the P.1052 to accept an Armstrong Siddeley Snarler rocket motor, at the behest of the Ministry of Supply (MoS), was projected as the P.1078 but this application was met by modifications made to the first P.1040 VP401, under the designation P.1072.

Rolls-Royce were proposing a development of the Nene, employing an increased use of magnesium alloys in order to reduce weight which, fitted with afterburning was forecast as providing a 25 per cent increase in power. A P.1052, fitted with the new engine titled the Tay RTa.1, interested the Australian government as a replacement for their Meteor F.8s, so in April 1950, the second P.1052 VX279 returned to the company's Kingston plant for modification to meet the Australian requirements. The aircraft's bifurcated jet exhaust layout ruled out the installation of an afterburner in that configuration, and necessitated the design of an entirely new rear fuselage and tail unit. So strong was the interest from

Australia, this work was taken on as a private venture and VX279 received a new designation, P.1081. Progress on the Tay became rather prolonged, therefore in order to have the aircraft flying as soon as possible, the Nene R.N.2 was retained but with a straight-through jet-pipe, with plans drawn up for the fitting of an afterburner at a later date.

'Wimpy' Wade took the reconfigured VX279 into the air for the first time on 19 June 1950, the whole conversion having lasted only two months. Delays and the eventual cancellation of the Tay in November 1950, meant that further development of the P.1081 would have to be undertaken based on the Nene – and

Sweep on all flying surfaces finally arrived with the P.1081, together with a straight-through jet pipe. Having started as the second P.1052, as shown previously, VX279 was the only P.1081 produced and it was planned for the Nene to be replaced by a Rolls-Royce Tay, had this engine's development not been so protracted. *Aeroplane Monthly*

Australian interest evaporated. Royal Australian Air Force Meteors were engaged in the Korean conflict and displaying their limitations as interceptors. Consequently a mission went to North American Aviation to investigate the possibility of adapting their Sabre to meet RAAF requirements. A manufacturing licence was acquired and Rolls-Royce retained Australian connections as their first axial-flow engine, the AJ65 produced as the Avon, powered the Commonwealth CA-27 Sabre. VX279 went to the Royal Aircraft Establishment (RAE) at Farnborough early in 1951, to participate in their research programme of high-Mach-number flying but the association was short lived as, four months later on 3 April 1951 the aircraft crashed and the pilot was killed.

His position as Hawker's Chief Test Pilot was inherited by Sqn Ldr Neville Duke, who was destined to be forever associated with the P.1067, which the company had designed and around which Specification F.3/48 had been written. Construction of the first prototype was only two months away from completion.

The Price of Progress

Trevor Wade was born on 27 January 1920 and educated at Tonbridge School, from where he joined the Royal Air Force at the age of eighteen. He learned to fly at Gatwick, took an instructor's course at the start of World War Two and joined Spitfire-equipped No. 92 Squadron, where, having destroyed seven enemy aircraft in the Battle of Britain, he was awarded the DFC, together with the nickname 'Wimpy'. The majority of his subsequent war service saw him as an instructor at the CFS, followed by OC Flying, at the Air Fighting Development Unit (AFDU), Wittering, where he evaluated British and German aircraft, earning the AFC. Similar test work was undertaken on the American continent and, when the war ended, with the rank of Squadron Leader, he joined the editorial staff of *The Aeroplane*.

Aviation via a typewriter was not really fulfilling and when Bill Humble, the Chief Test Pilot (CTP) at Hawker Aircraft, offered him a post of production-aircraft testing on the Sea Fury, it set the seal on the rest of his too-short life. He took over as CTP when Humble became the company's Sales Manager and Hawker's progress into the realms of turbojet-powered aircraft was all administered by 'Wimpy' Wade. His acknowledged abilities as a test pilot were extended to demonstration flying and Hawker's aircraft were always presented to advantage at displays all over Europe.

On 3 April 1951, while test-flying the P.1081 prototype, a situation that has never been 100 per cent resolved required Wade to eject from the aircraft, but at too low an altitude for a successful operation. His body was found still strapped in the seat – which was not a Martin–Baker product – and, ironically, the aircraft, slowed down by the drag of its open cockpit, as well as being lightened by the absence of pilot and seat, crash-landed with a comparatively small amount of damage, which must say something about its constructional strength. This was the company's first loss of a CTP while engaged on a test flight, since Harry Hawker's demise in 1922.

Gestation

The contention of old film scriptwriters was that an aircraft designer had a sudden inspiration, grabbed a serviette at the restaurant where he was lunching and drew out his next fighter or whatever, with a lusty 'eureka'. A fortnight later an intrepid test pilot was throwing it all over the sky! Real life is so very different.

The finished aircraft design evolves and the Hunter was no exception. Specification F.43/46 daytime interceptor requirement was producing a multitude of designs. Many different approaches came out of Hawker's project office but the inherent positioning of engines well forward of the centre of gravity in true piston-engine tradition was generating long fuselages and not all designs adopted swept-back flying surfaces. However, the initial proposals, of either the Nene or Tay centrifugal-flow engines as the power plants, gradually dissolved in favour of the smaller-diametered axial-flow AJ65. Twin side-by-side engine layouts abounded, while at least one project featured engines mounted one above the other to reduce the overall frontal area, although the retention of separate intakes differed from English Electric's later approach to such a configuration.

In the autumn of 1947, the use of a single AJ65 in project number P.1067 was proposed to the MoS during a series of design conferences and early in 1948 Specification F.3/48 was written up for issue to Hawker Aircraft. This was followed by the drafting of Operational Requirement (OR) 228/3 which, through many stages, was to form the basis for future production orders. Although the AJ65 (later named Avon) producing 6,000lb (2,722kg) thrust featured in the P.1067, OR 228/3 stipulated the design should allow for Armstrong Siddeley's axial-flow Sapphire being fitted as an alternative engine, as an insurance against a lack of available Avons. It was written into the original draft that provision should be made in the design for the incorporation of reheat, this being applicable to both engines. Performance requirements were for the aircraft to attain Mach 0.94

(724mph or 1,165km/h at sea level; 620mph or 998km/h at 36,000ft), with a service ceiling of 49,000ft (14,935m). An operational endurance of one hour was required. The specification called for armament to be four of the well established 20mm Hispano cannon or a pair of the newer 30mm Aden guns, which were an Armament Development Establishment version of the German Mauser MG213 revolver-fed cannon with electrically fired ammunition and manufactured at Enfield, thereby creating the acronym.

The installation of an ejector seat was by now considered obligatory in all contemporary designs (at least for the single- and two-seaters, although applications for all members of multi-crew aircraft such as the V-bombers became a rather contentious issue), with the products of Martin–Baker established as the prime choice.

By December 1948, work was concentrating on a mid-wing design with an eliptical fuselage cross-section, nose air intake for a single Avon R.A.2 engine giving 6,000lb (2,722kg) thrust, wings having 42.5 degree backward sweep at the quarter chord and a straight tapered T-tailplane. The armament was four 20mm guns and, with an all-up weight around 12,000lb (5,443kg), a performance in the region of Mach 0.88 was estimated. Two months later, the fuselage design had been amended to have a circular cross-section and an Avon R.A.5 producing 6,500lb (2,948kg) thrust increased the estimated performance to Mach 0.90. The T-tailplane outline became more delta shaped and, with the revised cross-section, two of the guns had to be repositioned in the wing-roots. This stage of development was designated P.1067/1, for which a full-size mock-up was constructed.

Originally designed with a nose air intake, the lateral wing-root intakes had been established by the time this mock-up of the P.1067 had been constructed, in the experimental shop at Kingston. The decision to abandon the T-tail however, had yet to be made. Hawker Aircraft

To Live Another Day

With the increase in operational speeds, slipstream pressures were becoming a serious obstacle when the need for a hurried evacuation from a warplane arose.

Germany had an ejection seat in their Dornier Do 335A *Pfiel* (Arrow), plus Heinkel's He 162A *Salamander* and He 219 *Uhu* (Eagle Owl), all three being actuated by an explosive cartridge. In Sweden, the SAAB-21A pilot's seat was mounted on a powder-driven catapult, which, in theory, threw its occupant clear of the pusher-airscrew arc, once the canopy had been released. Confirmation of any safe ejections from any of these has not been established. In Britain, an idea for a dorsal-mounted swinging-arm, that could be adapted to existing fighters, went as far as a mock-up projected for the Spitfire. But serious proposals arose from a meeting, in the early summer of 1944, between Fighter Command's Wg Cdr John Jewell and James Martin, at the latter's Martin–Baker Aircraft works in Denham, Buckinghamshire.

The Ministry of Aircraft Production (MAP) commissioned Martin to design an ejection seat, and Boulton Paul Defiant DR944 was rescued from towing drogues for the 8th USAAF, to be delivered to Denham, in December 1944, to act as the test vehicle. On 11 May 1945, with its gun turret removed and much modification, the aircraft was flown by Rotol's CTP, Brian Greensted, for the first airborne display of ejecting a dummy in a rocket-propelled seat, before a gathering of high-ranking officers congregated at Wittering.

Gloster Meteor F.III EE416 took over from the Defiant on 6 November 1945 and after seven months of airframe modifications had been made, to convert it to accommodate an additional crew member, a dummy was discharged for the first time on 8 June 1946, the aircraft being jacked up for the test. A completely new canopy was manufactured to cover the front cockpit, with the rear seat position open, to allow unrestricted egress. Two weeks later, on 24 June the first airborne dummy ejection was made, but tangling of the dummy with the seat took another thirteen firings to cure before a successful test was accomplished.

The next step, from dummy to human 'guinea-pig', was greatly assisted by a company fitter, named Bernard 'Benny' Lynch, volunteering to write history by making the first live ejection of a rocket-propelled seat from a turbojet-propelled aeroplane. Ex-Imperial Airways Captain John 'Scotty' Scott piloted the Meteor on 24 July 1946 and 'Benny' Lynch left the aircraft at a height of 8,000ft (2,438m), flying at 320mph (515km/h), with the assistance of a 16g rocket thrust. Eight seconds later, he manually unfastened the straps holding him in the seat, as they both descended on its parachute, to throw himself clear, deploy his own canopy and land on the company airfield at Chalgrove, in Oxfordshire. The whole sequence was a success – but so far removed from today's fully automatic procedure. Lynch went on to make thirty more test ejections and received the British Empire Medal (BEM) for his services.

From that 1946 summer, the principle having been established, manufacturing was put in hand, and the first production seat installed in the Saro SR.A/1 jet-fighter flying boat prototype, TG263. The Mark 8 Meteor was the first RAF squadron service fighter to be fitted with a Martin–Baker seat, while the Supermarine Attacker introduced it to the Royal Navy. Hawker Aircraft jet-powered prototype aircraft were fitted with the Malcolm ejection seat, a product of ML Aviation, but the company discontinued its manufacture in 1951 and by the time the Sea Hawk entered production, Martin–Baker seats were standard equipment, although the P.1067 WB188 was Hawker's first prototype designed to be fitted with this seat. Production single-seat Hunters had the Type 2H or 3H seat, while two-seaters were equipped with the later Type 4H.

Martin–Baker are acknowledged as the leading ejection seat company in the world. Safe ejection can now be made at ground level or operational altitude and speed. The whole sequence can be accomplished with the crewman unconscious and canopies have in-built destructors. Sqn Ldr John Fifield succeeded 'Scotty' as Martin–Baker's CTP and he, together with Sqn Ldr Peter Howard of the Institute of Aviation Medicine, helped to prove the later advanced systems. Some countries install indigenous systems and certain aircraft have tailor-made installations, such as the F-111, for which McDonnell designed an ejectable module. The two-man crew remain within it and the unit descends under a vast Kevlar parachute, fully equipped to touchdown on land or water. However, it is a recorded fact that close on 7,000 aircrew have walked away from disaster, courtesy of the Denham pioneers.

It was at this juncture that the first of several design errors was committed. The preliminary drag and available thrust figures intimated that an internal total fuel capacity in the order of 300 gallons (1,365 litres) would satisfy the specification endurance and performance demands. This was designed as two 130-gallon (591-litre) integral wing tanks, with a 40-gallon (182-litre) collector tank at the rear of the cockpit, and proved to be totally inadequate. Experience with integral wing tanks was limited at this time to a few American transport aircraft and the Airspeed Ambassador in Britain. Structural stresses on these were in no way comparable to those of a fighter and, following several meetings between the company, the MoS and Air Ministry, it was decided that although design work would be delayed, fuel would be carried in bag tanks. With the wing not being very acceptable to the inclusion of bag tanks, fuel was to be carried in tanks situated in every available fuselage space, giving a maximum capacity of 333 gallons (1,515 litres). This achievement was assisted to a small extent by a 2.5in (6.37cm) increase of the fuselage diameter in order to accept either of the engines laid down in F.3/48. The fact that rudder and elevator controls ran through a dorsal spine, completely outside the circular section fuselage structure, helped to make this modification comparatively easy.

Rolls-Royce expressed reservations about the long intake duct from the nose and, in view of Hawker's experience with wing-root intakes from their beginnings in jet-aircraft design, enquired as to the possibility of a similar configuration being applied to the P.1067. It would necessitate deleting the wing-root guns but this was strongly vetoed by the Chief Designer. However, the designed location of the radar gun-ranging scanner in a centre-body within the nose intake was giving cause for doubt as to its accessibility, consequently Camm gave his consent to a redesign of the front fuselage and wing centre section, with two under-nose mounted 30mm Aden guns. The redesign did give Camm some satisfaction, as the cockpit had become increasingly cramped by the gradual inclusion of additional equipment that the Air Ministry was demanding. The modified nose gave some 50 per cent additional volume to the cockpit area.

The matter of a two-gun armament was also a debatable factor. The Sea Hawk had four 20mm guns in a low front fuselage position, with ammunition containers set in the upper fuselage. A similar installation mooted for the P.1067 gave cause for concern, as 30mm shells were a lot heavier and the new aircraft would be much bigger than its predecessor. It was suggested that the answer would be to design a removable pack accommodating both guns and ammunition. Such an idea appealed to Camm and a group in the Experimental Drawing Office perfected an extremely good pack capable of taking four 30mm Aden guns, together with their respective magazines each capable of carrying 150 shells. The fact that the Aden cannon did not require it to be mounted right way up was an advantage. In the designed pack, the inner guns lay on their sides with the lower faces pointed inwards, while the outer pair were mounted upside down. The whole unit could be inserted into, or removed from, a bay positioned behind the cockpit, by three standard bomb winches. For removal the four barrels were unscrewed and remained in the fuselage while the pack was winched down for replacement by a preloaded pack or just the ammunition tanks refilled.

The Aden cannon's rate of fire being 1,200 rounds a minute, the striking power potential of the P.1067 was vastly superior to the F-86A which, being in volume production, was being viewed as something of a benchmark. While the North American aircraft was proving to be very manoeuvrable, as a fighter it was being rather let down by a six 0.5 inch (1.27cm) machine gun armament and was gaining success against MiG-15s over Korea mainly through the greater abilities of USAF pilots. Having said that, it must be admitted that at least they could be fired simultaneously, while a similar action by the P.1067 was going to present airframe problems when gun firing trials commenced.

Wind-tunnel tests intimated that the positioning of a tailplane without sweepback at the top of the fin, could create control problems. Consequently, an elegant new swept tailplane was designed and resited to a position about a third of the way up from the fin/fuselage join, with a reduced area rudder above it. The fin tip was reconfigured with a curve matching the wing and new tailplane tips. Appearance, however, is not everything and another failing at the design stage was the absence of a fully-powered tailplane – commonly called a 'flying tail'. It is very easy to make statements in hindsight but it must be realized that again reference has to be made to the F-86. One of the major features contributing to the F-86E as a fighter (which by December 1950 was in production), was the all-flying tail with linked elevators, which were power boosted and employed artificial feel. Furthermore, Canadian produced versions would be impressed into RAF squadron service at least a year before Hawker's aircraft arrived.

One more original design shortcoming must be mentioned. The P.1067 wing was a lovely and very efficient design, which benefited from the 'better-late-than-never' recognition of wartime German research. The adoption of lateral intakes helped in giving a thick wing-root, which was progressively reduced with the sweep, finishing in tips that gracefully curved back, thereby achieving the greater aerodynamic benefits of a swept wing. Later, when American pilots came to assess the Hunter, with a view to including it in the United States Offshore Procurement Bill – which comes into the Hunter's history later – its superior dive compared to the Sabre was favourably commented upon.

Hawker's experience with swept wings had been gleaned principally through their P.1052 and P.1081 research aircraft. These employed small hydraulically operated dive-brakes fitted in the under surface of the wing centre-section, which really were a carry-over from the original P.1040 design. They were used in conjunction with split wing flaps that were stressed for high-speed operation and which were proved quite adequate on the earlier Hawker designs. They were capable of selection at all speeds up to 540mph (869km/h), whereupon a relief valve in the hydraulic system restricted further increase in flap angle to obviate structure overstressing. The same system was designed into the P.1067 but test flying would show its shortcomings when applied to a transonic fighter.

'Wimpy' Wade banks the P.1081 showing its flap and dive-brake system, which was originally considered adequate for the P.1067. The differing requirements of a research aircraft and an operational interceptor were to be graphically discovered by the Central Fighter Establishment. *Aeroplane Monthly*

Hawker Aircraft's experimental shop, Richmond Road, Kingston-upon-Thames, in the Spring of 1950.
The Rolls-Royce Avon RA.7 is about to be installed in the hand-built first P.1067, WB188 – an event
which obviously gives pleasure to the fitter behind it. With the engine in place, the rear fuselage,
complete with the fin-base, stands on a trestle in position and the port aileron frame looks ready for
skinning. Hawker Aircraft

CHAPTER FIVE

Hunter is Born

For a long time, throughout the British aircraft industry, prototype airframes were constructed on non-production jigs and were colloquially termed 'hand-knitted'. The P.1067s were no exception.

The first aircraft started taking shape in the experimental workshops at Richmond Road, Kingston in December 1949. Serial numbers WB188, WB195 and WB202 had been allocated to the three prototypes ordered in November 1948, the first two being scheduled to receive Rolls-Royce Avon engines and the third Armstrong-Siddeley's Sapphire. Availability of Avons was creating worries at the MoS as not only was Supermarine's venture into swept-wing fighters, the Swift, designed around it, but the new English Electric Canberra bomber had two, while both

Avro and Vickers Armstrong were cutting metal to embark on four engine bomber prototypes employing the same power plant. Therefore the resolution to have the third P.1067 equipped with a Sapphire seemed eminently sensible, and was following the dictates of Specification F.3/48.

By the end of April 1950, components for the first P.1067 fuselage were approaching completion and were being followed by elements of the second. The next month, the MoS generated an air of consternation by stating doubts concerning the 2,000lb (907kg) weight of the Aden gun assembly. While they stated that it could be a disadvantage in terms of the design's all-up weight and advocated using 20mm Hispanos, it is generally believed that they were engaging on a cost-cutting

exercise. Weeks of uncertainty followed, during which Camm, strongly backed by the Board of Directors, brought his strength of character to bear on the ministerial mandarins. The matter was resolved by the end of June – the Aden cannon armament remained.

Prototype assembly continued during the period of uncertainty and throughout the year. Ballast would replace the Aden pack on WB188 and the gun ports in the underside of the nose filled in. During the Spring and early Summer of 1951, manufacturers' tests were completed at Kingston following which the first airframe was dismantled for road transportation to A&AEE Boscombe Down in Wiltshire on 27 June 1951, thereby following in the footsteps of all previous Hawker jet-powered prototypes.

A steady flow of sub-assemblies started arriving at Langley in 1954 and complete aircraft are to be seen in the background. Wings were held in situ **for fuel-flow tests, before they were removed, prior to an aircraft's transportation to Dunsfold.** John Kendrick

The testing of Hawker aircraft had been undertaken at Langley since the late 1930s. By 1950, the growth of London Heathrow Airport, only a few miles away, coupled with the absence of hard runway facilities at Langley, forced the company to look for a new testing establishment. This did not, however, mean the end of Langley's association with Hawker. The assembly shops would continue to be busy for another eight years. In April 1942, an airfield was constructed near the Surrey village of Dunsfold. Wartime operations appear to have mainly involved RAF-purchased American Mustangs and Mitchells.

Camm is on record as telling Bill Gunston, then Technical Editor of *Flight*, 'It's my most beautiful aeroplane'. He did go on to evince, 'But I'll have a fight to keep it that way'. He knew Whitehall – but at least one of the excrescences would be self-inflicted. Another 'family' trait so far as Hawker aircraft are concerned, is the undercarriage. Look through the myriad of designs that the company has produced – they all have strong, wide-tracked undercarriages and, since their first featuring retraction, the Hurricane, they have retracted inwards. Many a service pilot has flown his Hawker aircraft onto the tarmac, grateful that it did

colour, a pale variant of the Fleet Air Arm undersurface of the time which became known by all associated with the P.1067 as 'duck-egg green', was applied over all external surfaces and only broken by national roundels, serial numbers and various small instructional legends.

Going back three months, Hawker's Chief Test Pilot, Trevor 'Wimpy' Wade was closely involved in the P.1067 programme, in preparation for undertaking the first flight. His death in the P.1081 crash on 3 April, put his assistant Neville Duke, who had been a fellow No.92 Squadron Spitfire pilot at Biggin Hill, into the position.

Still a virgin. The prototype P.1067 basks in the sunshine on Boscombe Down's hard-standing prior to its first flight on 20 July 1951. In deference to safety, a spin-recovery parachute housing breaks the outline above the jet orifice. Author's collection

The airfield was declared inactive in August 1946 and the private airline Skyways Limited took up residence, making a great contribution to the Berlin Airlift from the base. In March 1950, Skyways went into liquidation and Hawker Aircraft Limited took over the tenancy, but naturally the move took some considerable time and was not completed by the time the P.1067 was ready to be flown.

Once reassembled and standing on tarmac in the sunshine, the grace of the aircraft could really be appreciated. Sydney

not have the dainty ballerina legs of some designs. The P.1067, with a main wheel track of 14ft 9in (4.48m) was wide, even by Hawker standards.

While in no way meaning to diminish the beauty of the basic design, the appearance of WB188 was enhanced by its simple colour scheme. Another Kingston-upon-Thames company, Cellon Limited, with forty years experience of protective finishes for British aircraft by 1951, recognized the publicity value of donating a new paint for Hawker's first transonic prototype. The

During WB188's reassembly, Hawker took delivery of the first flight-cleared Avon, which was installed in the airframe, and had its maiden run on 1 July. The aircraft/engine combination was given full clearance for flying by the Resident Technical Officer (RTO) and all was set for the prototype to fulfil the promises that had already given the company Contract No. SP/6/5910/CB.7a dated 14 March 1951 from the MoS, for production of the first 113 aircraft designated Hunter F. Mark 1, in a serial block WT555–700. The receipt

A Peer Among Pilots

From the building of scale model aeroplanes at the age of seven and an introduction to flying in the draughty cockpit of an Avro 504K, while still in short trousers, the life of Neville Duke has been entwined with aviation. He joined the Royal Air Force in 1940 as an AC2, which, as he has written in his autobiography, *Test Pilot*, was 'the grandest title I could imagine – AC2, Pilot under Training'. Starting at No.13 Elementary Flying Training School, White Waltham, his first solo flight was made after 8.5 hours, and February 1941 saw him receive his wings. The newly commissioned Pilot Officer Duke was posted to No.58 Operational Training Unit (OTU), Grangemouth, where he was introduced to the Spitfire. He then joined No.92 Squadron at Biggin Hill, his first victory against a Bf 109 being made over Dunkirk. A subsequent posting to No.112 Squadron in the Middle East was scheduled for a six-week duration – it materialized into three years. A mixture of Spitfires, Tomahawks and Kittyhawks yielded Sqn Ldr Duke the acknowledgement as top scoring Allied pilot in the Theatre, with the destruction of twenty-eight enemy aircraft confirmed, three probably destroyed, plus five damaged, which earned him the DSO and DFC with two bars. After the war he passed out as a graduate of the Empire Test Pilot School (ETPS) and, following a posting to the Fighter Test Squadron at Boscombe Down, was invited in August 1948 by Hawker's CTP Bill Humble, to join the company as a civilian pilot at Langley.

He test-flew production Furies and Tempests, as well as the prototype P.1040. He also purchased Hawker Tomtit G-AFTA (now preserved in the Shuttleworth Collection), which he flew at air displays with fellow Hawker test pilot, Doc Morell, flying a Tiger Moth. Duke also joined the Royal Auxiliary Air Force, becoming Commanding Officer of No. 615 County of Surrey Squadron at Biggin Hill, equipped with Spitfire Mark 22s and later, Meteor Mark 4s. Winston Churchill was the squadron's Honorary Air Commodore.

While delivering a Fury to the Royal Pakistan Air Force in May 1949, Neville Duke established two records, from London to Rome in 2hrs 30 min and London to Karachi in 15hrs 18min 36sec. Later in the year, he delivered another Fury to the Royal Egyptian Air Force, again setting a record of 6hrs 32min 10sec between London and Cairo. The year was rounded off by Duke winning the Kemsley Trophy handicap race in the P.1040, at an average speed of 508mph (817.8km/h), one lap being flown at 562.6mph (908.8km/h). Two years later, on 19 January 1951, while flying VP401, which had been the first prototype P.1040 but had now been fitted with an Armstrong Siddeley Snarler rocket motor in the tail and re-designated the P.1072, he encountered an explosion in the motor while attempting to relight it in flight. The tail unit burst into flames and Duke was forced to make an emergency landing back at the motor manufacturer's airfield at Bitteswell, flying on the air-

craft's Nene power alone. Although the aircraft was repaired, official policy regarding rocket motors changed and the P.1072/Snarler combination was never flown again.

Trevor Wade had succeeded Humble, and Neville Duke became his No.2, engaged in test flying all four of the company's jet designs. When he was tragically thrust into the role of CTP, it was typical of his analytical approach to the forthcoming P.1067 flight that he flew a Canberra to become accustomed to handling the Rolls-Royce Avon. He undertook transonic dives in an F-86, flew a Sea Fury with powered elevators, and a Fairey Firefly FR.4 that had been modified to test the powered flying control units for the P.1067. Because of the workload and responsibilities that the new post presented, he resigned his command of No.615 Squadron. All Hawker's flying moved from Langley to Dunsfold and an ex-ETPS instructor, 'Bill' Bedford, became his No.2.

Neville Duke's name flows through the history of the Hunter's early development and, following his retirement from Hawker Aircraft in 1955, he was invited by Sir George Dowty to become his personal pilot. For several years he flew Sir George, in his de Havilland Dove and, later, Beechcraft King Air. He renewed his acquaintance with the SBAC Display in 1980, when he demonstrated the Edgley Optica prototype and remains an active, respected pilot, still maintaining the natural modesty that belies his outstanding career.

---

of this contract, and the assurance of further orders in the future, presented the Hawker Siddeley Group with the problem of making space to fulfil them. It was decided that production of the Sea Hawk would be moved to the fellow Group member company Sir W. G. Armstrong Whitworth Aircraft Limited's facility at Baginton, just outside Coventry.

Taxiing trials commenced a few days after the Avon was first run and Duke began to get the feel of the cockpit and general ground handling. This was his indoctrination into being the first pilot to handle a new type and it was also Hawker's first application of powered controls. Each prototype has its own idiosyncrasies but so far the P.1067 was proving to be comparatively viceless. One problem was encountered on 8 July in the differential wheel braking system, the brakes being burnt out during high-speed taxiing and Dunlop took over a week to cure the trouble. In the afternoon of Friday, 20 July 951, both pilot and aircraft were ready for flying and, with a spin-recovery parachute installed in a housing above the rear jet orifice, WB188 was lifted into the air on its first flight. A point of sartorial interest was

Duke's wearing of an American style 'bone-dome' for possibly the first time in Britain.

He executed a gentle climb to over 20,000ft (6,096m), making verbal recordings of all data readings, throttle and control settings, for the benefit of the ground servicing team. Easy manoeuvres were made both with and without undercarriage and flaps down. The general handling throughout the forty-seven minute flight was fine but Britain had very limited experience with powered flying controls at that time. Consequently, the elevator hydraulic power boost had been disconnected for the first flight although the ailerons remained in use. The result was that elevator forces were far too heavy while ailerons, with power boost working on a ratio of 14:1, were extremely light. Duke rounded the aircraft for a landing, during which the electrically actuated tailplane trimmer's range was found to be unacceptable and the aircraft required great muscular effort on his part to maintain control. Adjustment of the movement range of the trimmer was made and further sorties, each lasting about the same time, were made over the next few days, during which the height and speed

envelopes were increased while a number of check stalls were executed.

Fuel consumption seemed higher than expected during these flights, until a leak was found in the rear fuselage tank. Otherwise, each flight proved successful and on 10 August the whole test programme moved to RAE Farnborough, from where it continued for another four weeks. One particular sortie involved a photocall with photographer Cyril Peckham, who produced some wonderful portraits of the aircraft that confirmed its elegance in its natural habitat. Facilities at Dunsfold were now ready and on 7 September WB188, Duke *et al.* transferred to their new base. In those days the SBAC required ten hours flight testing to have been accumulated before an aircraft could participate in the flying programme at their annual Farnborough-based Show. This having been exceeded, Neville Duke was cleared to display the P.1067 – and have a busy week, as he was also to fly VX272, a naval version of Hawker's P.1052.

Since the early 1930s, fighter development at Hawker Aircraft had been matched by Vickers Supermarine and both companies had tendered designs to the research Specification E.38/46. As already

In preparation for its first appearance at the 1951 SBAC Display, a beautiful set of air-to-air shots was taken of **WB188**, demonstrating it was photogenic from any angle. Hawker were determined that there would be no doubt of its nationality when they applied the upper wing roundels!
Aeroplane Monthly.

mentioned, Hawker designed a swept wing for the P.1040 while Supermarine adapted one of their Attacker fuselages to accept swept wings and tail unit, the design given the designation Type 510. They proceeded through a tortuous four years, via Types 528 and 535, to produce the Type 541 Swift.

ground – when Duke flew it 100ft (30.5m) above the flight line at over 700mph (1,127km/h), it confirmed this impression. It *was* fast and possibly gave the fastest display at an SBAC Show up to then.

Further test flying was conducted after Farnborough and into October, following

Mach 0.97 and progressively increased above Mach 1.0.

Many various modifications were incorporated in an attempt to cure the problem including a reduction of the rudder span, increasing the dorsal fin area, fitting spoilers on the fin and vortex generators, but

The second prototype P.1067, WB195, now named Hunter, fitted with a bullet-shaped fairing at the rear tailplane/fin junction and four-gun armament, was displayed at the 1952 SBAC Show. Seen here, it shares an enclosure with a pair of Supermarine aircraft: WJ965, the second pre-production Type 541 Swift and VX136, the second prototype N.9/47. Author's collection.

While they pre-empted Hawker in having all flying surfaces swept and, in transonic development were ahead of the Kingston company, the Swift was ordered by the Air Ministry principally as an insurance against the P.1067 failing. In the event, the Swift's considerable problems could not be rectified while Hawker's development of the P.1067 went ahead satisfactorily – although later, problems were to arise which were to cause a fair amount of consternation. Both companies' products were at the 1951 Farnborough SBAC Display and while Supermarine's Type 535 was a hefty, purposeful-looking aircraft, the P.1067's sylphlike appearance had an air of looking fast on the

which WB188 was grounded, being stripped down for a complete inspection and some small modifications. Among these were a few local strengthenings to meet minor failures found during a programme of testing on a structural specimen. The main change was the installation of number 244 production Rolls-Royce R.A.7 Avon engine producing 7,500lb (3,402kg) thrust and incorporating variable swirl. This whole inspection lasted six months and WB188 was not airborne again until April 1952, when a programme of high-Mach-number research was commenced, which brought to light high-frequency buffeting in the rear fuselage and rudder vibration which occurred at about

none was really effective. When it was found that the cause was the breakdown of airflow at the bottom of the rudder, a bullet-shaped fairing was fitted at the rear of the tailplane and fin junction. The phenomenon was cured.

The P.1067 had been officially named the Hunter and on 5 May 1952 Neville Duke made the first maiden flight from Dunsfold when he took the second prototype WB195, painted 'duck-egg green' like its companion, into the air. This was the true fighter prototype, being fitted with the four-Aden gun pack, a radar ranging gunsight and a production R.A.7 Avon, together with the tail bullet fairing right from the start. Flying by

WB195 took part in an air-to-air photocall in November 1952, showing the additional fin area fitted, as part of the trials to increase stability, prior to the SBAC Display. A similar fairing was incorporated at one time on the P.1081. Author's collection

both aircraft progressed into the summer, with WB195 being demonstrated to the Central Fighter Establishment (CFE) based at West Raynham in Norfolk, and a deputation of A&AEE test pilots went to Dunsfold to fly WB188, all voicing pleasure at the experience.

Accurate Mach number readings were not attainable on the instruments of the early 1950s, mainly because of unsuitable sitings of static pitot heads and shock waves varying according to the shape of the aircraft involved. It was recognized that the receipt of a sonic boom by observers on the ground would be the only true way to verify a Mach 1+ flight. After several days of flying when up to Mach 1.06 was recorded on his instruments, it was on 24 June that Duke made a shallow

dive from 30,000ft (9,144m) and planted a boom on the ground for all in the vicinity to hear, observing afterwards that he levelled out at about 15,000ft (4,572m) and found the transonic flight quite smooth. The next month, on 10 July he displayed WB188 at the Brussels Air Show and in the first week of September, took WB195 to the 1952 SBAC Display at Farnborough. In a week of varying good-to-atrocious weather, I well remember on the Wednesday seeing a large ball of condensation approaching the Press Tent at very low altitude, with a 'duck-egg green' nose sticking out of its leading edge! His professionalism was further shown to all – including myself – on Saturday, 6 September, by taking off to give a faultless display immediately after witnessing his good

friend and test pilot for de Havilland, John Derry, die, together with navigator Tony Richards, when the prototype DH110 WG236 disintegrated over the airfield. The wreckage ploughed into the crowd, killing thirty people and causing a further sixty-three casualties. That someone can witness such an event and carry out his assigned role aware of similar possibilities, reveals the qualities of a test pilot. The Rt. Hon. Winston Churchill wrote to him, 'My dear Duke, it was characteristic of you and of 615 Squadron to go up yesterday after the shocking accident. Accept my salute. Yours, in grief, Winston S. Churchill'. (*Aeroplane Monthly*, December 1983)It is through them that successful operational aeroplanes such as the Hunter, evolve.

CHAPTER SIX

Problems, Solutions and a Record

The third of the Hunter prototypes, silver-coloured WB202, was first flown from Dunsfold on 30 November 1952, the pilot for the maiden flight once again being Neville Duke. This aircraft differed from the previous two in being powered by an Armstrong Siddeley Sa.6 Sapphire engine rated at 8,000lb (3,628kg) thrust and, in the chronology of the Hunter, was the prototype Mark 2.

A year earlier, in October 1951, a Conservative government had been voted into power in Britain, with the wartime leader Winston (later Sir Winston) Churchill back as Prime Minister. British forces made up part of the United Nations (UN) military effort supporting South Korea's defence against the Communist North Korean invasion, started in 1950. Initially, the UN had complete air superiority but the introduction of the swept-wing MiG-15 by Communist forces completely outclassed the F-80, F-84 and Meteor put up against them, an inequality which lasted until the

F-86 was introduced. For Britain's part, the shortcomings of the country's main interceptor, the Meteor F.8, took a while to be digested. In typical 'Churchillian' manner, shortly after taking office, the state of the armed services was evaluated, in particular the replacement of existing RAF aircraft by more modern types. A 'Super Priority' production programme was initiated, in an effort to accelerate five aircraft projects currently progressing at the rather mundane pace generated by the natural lethargy of bureaucracy, allied to the results of an almost complete lack of funding for research and development since the end of World War II. The aircraft concerned were the English Electric Canberra bomber, Fairey Gannet anti-submarine aircraft, Supermarine's Swift and both Hawker designs, the Sea Hawk and Hunter.

While in reality the programme did not greatly affect the introduction into service of any of the types concerned – although it is interesting to ponder what would have

been the pace of development had the programme not existed – it did put into perspective the fact that three prototypes were certainly not enough airframes for Hawker to convert their Hunter into an acceptable operational interceptor. Duke had been joined on Hunter testing by A. W. 'Bill' Bedford, another wartime RAF pilot and ex-ETPS graduate/tutor, who became a Hawker experimental test pilot in 1951, helping to develop the Sea Hawk.

Hawker set up a team of pilots to undertake the testing of production aircraft, under the leadership of an ex-New Zealand Air Force squadron leader, Frank Murphy. It had become obvious that a number of the first batch of aircraft would be required for the many various trials programmes necessary to evaluate the Hunter before its acceptance by the RAF. The company's newly acquired Squires Gate factory, Hawker Aircraft (Blackpool) Ltd., was prepared to extend production facilities and awarded Contract No.SP/6/

Hawker's association with the Sapphire commenced with WB202, the third prototype Hunter, which was the first prototype Mark 2. It was with this aircraft that gun-firing trials were conducted, giving the false impression that all was well. *Aeroplane Monthly*

8435/CB.7a for twenty-six aircraft, while the resources at Armstrong Whitworth's Baginton factory commenced tooling up to produce forty-five of the Mark 2 variant under the terms of Contract No.SP/6/6315/CB.7a. The facilities at Baginton, in fact, were rather better than those at Kingston, where major sub-sections were fabricated, transported by road to Langley for assembly and then transported again to Dunsfold for testing. Modifications sometimes meant dismantling for another road journey back to Kingston. At Baginton it was all on site, with the engines also being products of Coventry.

With the Hunter now confirmed as the RAF's future interceptor, thoughts were being turned to developing the basic design, in order to meet Air Ministry requests. High on their list was an investigation into ways of increasing both range and endurance, while the ability to be a bona fide supersonic fighter was considered a logical future development. Camm's project group had already drawn up an idea on the same lines under the designation P.1083, which was centred upon the marriage of a Hunter fuselage to a new wing with a 6 per cent thickness/chord ratio (compared to the Hunter's 8.5 per cent) employing 50-degree sweep. Power would be supplied by a Rolls-Royce Avon RA.19 developing 10,500lb (4,762kg) thrust with reheat, and the internal fuel capacity was increased to 600 gallons (2,730 litres). It was estimated that a sea-level speed of

(Above) The 1953 SBAC Show saw WB202 displayed beside WG240, the second prototype de Havilland DH110 progenitor of the Sea Vixen and WT827, the third prototype Gloster GA.5 Javelin. The latter too was Sapphire-powered, as was another aircraft present at the same event, the first prototype Vulcan VX770. Author's collection

(Below) WB188 was modified to act as the test-bed for the P.1083's reheat unit, revised fuel system and rear-end lateral airbrakes. The pointed nose and overall scarlet finish shown, are products of the later record attempt, made after the P.1083 project's cancellation. In this configuration, WB188 became the only Hunter Mark 3. Author's collection

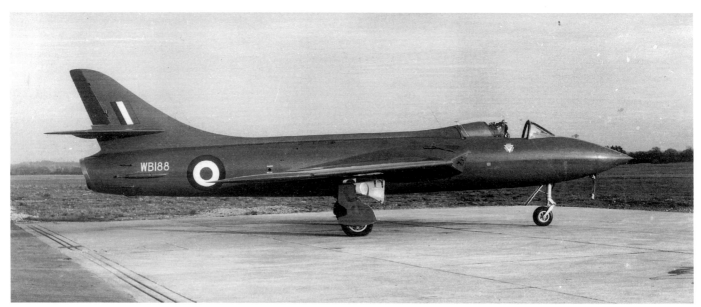

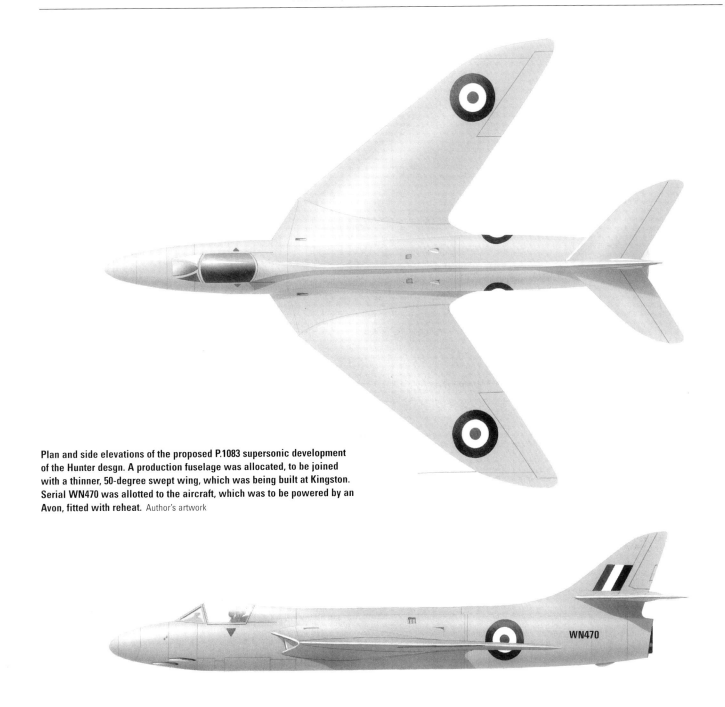

Plan and side elevations of the proposed P.1083 supersonic development of the Hunter desgn. A production fuselage was allocated, to be joined with a thinner, 50-degree swept wing, which was being built at Kingston. Serial WN470 was allotted to the aircraft, which was to be powered by an Avon, fitted with reheat. Author's artwork

Mach 1.2 (912mph or 1,468km/h) would be attainable in level flight. Contract No.6296 was issued to cover the construction of one prototype P.1083 to which serial number WN470 was allocated. The first prototype P.1067 WB188 was withdrawn from the flight test programme in December 1952, for the installation of an Avon with reheat, together with modifications for the wings to accommodate internal fuel tanks and relevant fuel lines preparatory to the P.1083 flying. With the fuselage rear end removed for adaptation

to accept the reheat tail pipe, a pair of hydraulically operated 'clam shell' air-brakes were incorporated, flush to the fuselage skin except for the hinges and hydraulic ram fairings. The need to slow the Hunter down in flight was already being recognized – and the projected P.1083 was going to be a lot faster!

Construction of the P.1083 wings was under way at Kingston and a fuselage allotted for modification to accept them, when the Air Staff had a reappraisal. The considered prodigious thirst of re-heat

engines, coupled with a new Avon 200-series being developed by Rolls-Royce producing the same output 'dry' as the RA.19, led them, on 13 July 1953, to give Hawker Aircraft notification of the P.1083 project's cancellation. It has to be noted that the war in Korea had also ceased by the summer of 1953 and, without wishing to appear too cynical, one cannot discount the historical fact that future aerodynamic research is never high on the British Air Ministry agenda unless conflict is imminent or in progress.

The first production Hunter F.1, WT555 is aligned alongside the second and third prototypes at Dunsfold, prior to making its maiden flight. *Aeroplane Monthly*

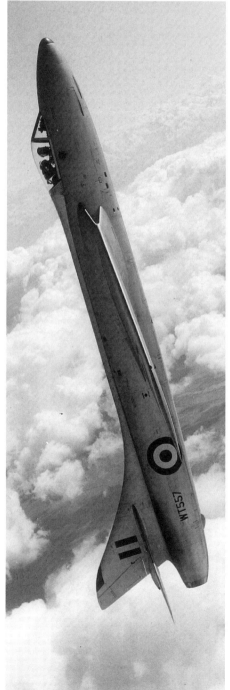

(Below) Aerodynamic grace is exemplified as WT557, the third production Mark 1, climbs above the cumulus during a photographic session held before it embarked on demonstration tours in Denmark and the Low Countries. *Aeroplane Monthly*

Two months before the P.1083's cancellation, Frank Murphy lifted WT555, the first production F.1, off Dunsfold's runway for its maiden flight on 16 May. This was followed exactly one month later by the second, WT556. WT557 first flew on 7 July and WT558 on 24 August, all four immediately being impressed into the trials programme, operating at different times from Dunsfold, A&AEE Boscombe Down, Rolls-Royce at Hucknall and the Radar Research Establishment (RRE) at Defford. On 22 December Neville Duke made his first maiden flight in a production aircraft, this being WT570, number sixteen off the Kingston lines. All of 1953's F.1 production were engaged on various trials, WT558, after utilization on a series of experiments with various wing fences, being the only example to eventually see RAF service, this being for a period with No.54 Squadron. WT556 and 557 respectively, also gave demonstrations in the Low Countries and Denmark, while WT559 was flown by a Belgian evaluation team following canopy jettison trials. WT562 was engaged on trials with various flap arrangements, WT569 would partake in tropical trials at Khartoum the following year and WT570 became the first airframe to be equipped with full-power ailerons.

The F.1 service-handling trials held at Boscombe Down during the summer of 1953 were, in general, quite satisfactory. Nearly all pilots' first reactions to the cockpit layout and controls were favourable, while taxiing was particularly commented upon as being very good, with first rate forward visibility, and the excellent Dunlop wheel brakes with Maxaret anti-skid units proved quite capable of holding the aircraft in position when the Avon RA.7 113 engine, rated at 7,550lb (3,424kg), was opened to full power.

There was no tendency to swing on take-off and the Hunter lifted off the ground quite naturally between 140–150 knots (161–172 mph or 259–277km/h), climbing at 10,000ft (3,048m) per minute to 30,000ft (9,144m). Above this, the rate of climb fell off to 1,150ft (350m) per minute, with 45,000ft (13,716m) being attained in 11.65 minutes – a time which, when the aircraft was in squadron service, was reassessed as being 13.25 minutes.

Mach 1.0 was exceeded in a 35–40 degree dive with very little changes in trim being required, although below a 30 degree angle the aircraft could not be persuaded above Mach 0.97. The average rate of descent was over 6,500ft (1,981m) per minute and as an unpremeditated spin could be produced

Mark 1s start coming off the assembly lines. Eleven new aircraft lined up at No. 5 MU Kemble in the autumn of 1954, ready for operational allocation, WT630 in the foreground going to No. 43 Squadron.
Aeroplane Monthly

when the aircraft was stalled, stalling practices were restricted to above 25,000ft (7,620m). Putting the aircraft into a controlled spin, which gave a rate of descent in the order of 25,000ft (7,620m) per minute, had to be made above 40,000ft (12,192m), with recovery being commenced after the fourth turn. Landing, with 23 degrees of flaps, was recommended between 125–130 knots (143–149 mph or 230–240km/h).

Confidence in the Hunter being a first-rate aircraft induced the decision for it to be entered in an attempt on the World Absolute Speed Record, and WB188, having been taken out of the testing programme to assist in the now defunct P.1083 project, was seen as being the ideal vehicle for such an exercise. The rear fuselage was already modified for a reheat tail pipe with lateral airbrakes installed, and Rolls-Royce had perfected a 'racing' version of the Avon RA.7, designated the

RA.7R, which delivered a 'dry' output of 6,750lb (3,061kg) thrust rising to 9,500lb (4,309kg) with reheat activated. In this configuration the airframe became the sole Hunter Mark 3. Early in August, a highly raked additional windscreen was installed over the standard one and with a pointed nose-cap fitted, WB188 in an overall scarlet colour scheme looked quite capable of taking the record. This stood, at that time, at 715.75 mph (1,152.35km/h), attained by Lieutenant Colonel William F. Barnes of the USAF, flying a North American F-86D Sabre on 16 July 1953. Rather strangely, considering the work that it involved, the lateral airbrakes were removed for the record attempt. The apertures left were skinned over, resprayed scarlet and the WB188 serial numbers repositioned in line with the centre of the fuselage roundel. Two months after the record, in November 1953, the airbrakes

were restored, the actuating jack having a different covering from the original installation and the serials repositioned above them again. One cannot help wondering just how much drag they produced in the closed position and what weight was saved. Also, how much the record speed would have been reduced, had they not been removed, but it is all only academic.

In 1946 Neville Duke had been a member of the RAF High Speed Flight, during which time he became familiar with the Bognor-Littlehampton-Worthing course off the Sussex coast, where the Flight set up a 616 mph (992km/h) record in Gloster Meteor F.4 EE649 piloted by Group Captain E. M. Donaldson on 7 September. The same course was chosen for WB188's attempt and again, the wartime fighter airfield at Tangmere, Sussex would be used as the operating base. On Monday, 31 August, Duke made a practice run over the course in poor weath-

39

(Above) **Squadron Leader Neville Duke, in white overalls, stands behind the nose of WB188 at Tangmere on 7 September 1953, having just succeeded in raising the World Absolute Speed Record to 722.2mph (1,163.22km/h). An additional curved, highly raked windscreen was fitted for the flights.** *Aeroplane Monthly*

After the record flights, WB188 reverted to test flying and the lateral airbrakes were restored. The additional windscreen was removed, its location being evident in the scarlet paintwork when Neville Duke presented the aircraft for this photograph.
Aeroplane Monthly

er but despite the bumpy conditions an average speed of 722.5 mph (1,163.22km/h) was attained. The following day an attempt had to be aborted, due to an undercarriage malfunction which necessitated a two-wheel landing back at Dunsfold. The slight damage sustained required a week for repair – ironically a week of excellent weather!

Sunday 7 September, being the 1953 SBAC Display at Farnborough's Press Day, was perfect weatherwise and publicitywise. Britain regained the record, Duke achieving an average speed of 727.6 mph (1,171.43km/h) in three runs over the Sussex course. As a point of interest, this speed is still the record at low altitude in Britain. Its subsequent raising by Mike Lithgow in Swift WK198 was made over Tripoli harbour, with its higher ambient temperature giving advantageous conditions. When Peter Twiss in Fairey F.D.2

WG774 took the record above 1,000 mph (1,610km/h) for the first time (1,132 mph or 1,122.52km/h being attained on 10 March 1956), it was at 38,000ft (11,582m). This was to all intents and purposes the finish of WB188 in Hunter history. Hawker discontinued developments with reheat engines and it would have been quite uneconomic to restore the aircraft to its original layout. Consequently, the first prototype was sold to the MoS in 1955, who handed it to No.1 School of Technical Training at RAF Halton in Buckinghamshire, for use as a ground

Sapphire-powered aircraft considered the first prototype Mark 2, was allocated for early gun-firing trials and ground firing commenced on 16 February, followed by air-firing trials on 9 March at the A&AEE. The latter were closely monitored, as earlier firing of an Aden gun experimentally mounted in a Bristol Beaufighter indicated that damage to the underside of the aircraft could be sustained from ejected spent cartridge cases and links. However, the trials were conducted with very little problems and gave no indication of what would happen in the future.

RAF West Raynham, whose brief was to combat-evaluate new day fighters prior to acceptance by the Service (a separate squadron performed similar duties for night-fighters). The Commanding Officer (CO) at the end of September 1953 was Wing Commander (later Air Vice-Marshal) Bird-Wilson and he was ordered by Air Commodore Wallace Kyle, Director of Operational Requirements at the Air Ministry, to go to Dunsfold, together with Flight Lieutenant Alan Jenkins, to fly WT555. The pair made four flights to investigate the use of wing flaps as air-

Mark 2 WN888, the first production Hunter to come from Baginton, had its maiden flight on 14 October 1953. It was retained by Armstrong Whitworth for type-handling and performance trials, transferring to Dunsfold the following month. Author's collection

instructional airframe. From there WB188 became a gate guardian at RAF Melksham, Wiltshire for many years, where the combination of the British climate and lack of local care nearly put an end to the aircraft. Thankfully its importance in British aviation history was eventually recognized and, after a lengthy period of refurbishment, it was displayed at the Aerospace Museum, Cosford in Shropshire. Today, it is fittingly back in Sussex. The Tangmere Military Aviation Museum has been set up at the airfield from which it operated for the record runs and WB188 stands there, in recognition of its achievements.

Good as the record-gaining publicity was, there were already stories circulating about certain shortcomings with the Hunter. One of the early problems came to light a lot later purely by mischance. The third prototype airframe WB202, the first

Also early in the Hunter programme, the first serious problem in handling presented itself. That the aircraft was quick, with a terrific rate of roll, could not be disputed but the aerodynamically clean shape made deceleration another matter altogether. The second prototype WB195 started a series of airbrake trials early in its career, beginning with a small flap sited on the wing upper surface and superseded by the use of the landing flaps as airbrakes – a system which worked perfectly on the earlier Hawker jet-powered designs. In the course of these trials, one of many modifications made to the landing flaps was the cutting of a series of vertical slots in their surface but none proved to be a remedy to the problem.

In those days, an Air Fighting Development Squadron (AFDS) existed within the Central Fighter Establishment (CFE) at

brakes but their deployment at high speed and low level caused the nose of the aircraft to pitch down sharply, following which, as the AFDS's CO so euphemistically put it, 'the pilot headed for the canopy'.

Hawker's design office was putting a lot of effort into creating an airbrake that would provide the necessary deceleration without an unacceptable amount of trim change. The rear fuselage application on WB188 was discarded as an operational installation, again because of the resultant pitch change and the options narrowed down to a ventral fuselage-mounted airbrake which, it had to be accepted, would mean its installation being external on the existing outer skin as opposed to the built-in system on WB188. An early fitting on WT566 under the front fuselage did not prove satisfactory and concentration was centred on a rear under-fuselage

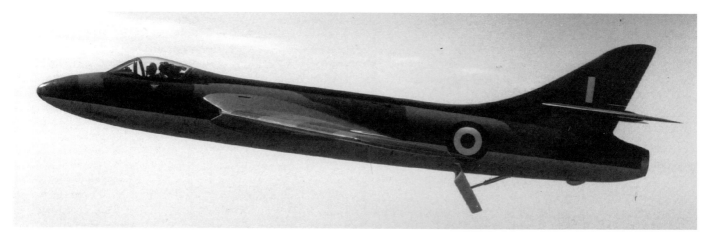

A product of the first batch of Kingston-built Mark 1s, WT594 deploys the finalized airbrake at its full 67-degree deflection angle, followed, after retraction, by a sharp bank to starboard. Author's collection and *Aeroplane Monthly*

installation but ensuring there was not too great a reciprocal action between the air-brake and tailplane.

The Air Ministry had informed Sydney Camm that the airbrake would have to be redesigned before it could be cleared for acceptance by the RAF and it took many months to perfect such an installation, one of the aircraft used on this programme being the F.2 prototype WB202. The ventral position provided so many variables that on 2 and 20 February 1954 Wing Commander Kyle made eight separate flights, each with the airbrake, which was fitted on a pair of rails, set at various positions under the rear fuselage. The final acceptable location was established and now the optimum deflection angle had to be determined. Frank Murphy flew the twelfth production F.1 WT566, with the new airbrake installed, at progressively increased speeds and the deflection angle at different settings up to a maximum of 75 degrees. At this angle, trim change and buffeting became too pronounced and an optimal setting of 60 degrees was agreed as creating enough drag without compromising control. Two months later, further experiments were conducted with WT573, as the contour of the fairing in front of the airbrake itself was found to affect the required trim change. Over the course of trials based at Dunsfold, a fairing shape was designed which enabled the operating airbrake angle to be increased to 67 degrees. By June 1954, the airbrake problem had finally been resolved for Service acceptability, although it never supplied the absolute drag required in all situations and its installed position meant that it could not be deployed during landing as there was insufficient ground clearance.

An increasing number of F.1s coming off the lines at Kingston, Langley and Blackpool, together with F.2s from Baginton, were standing at Dunsfold awaiting the fitting of airbrakes before they could be accepted by the RAF. A concerted effort was put in hand to install the airbrakes and operating jacks, together with the necessary electrical controls and hydraulic actuations, following which Service pilots at the A&AEE had to pass the system for the aircraft to be forwarded to No.5 Mainte-

nance Unit (MU) Kemble, in Gloucestershire, prior to allocation to squadrons. A limited Certificate of Release was issued by the MoS on 1 July, in order that aircraft could be delivered to the CFE, with WT577 and WT578 on 5 July, being the first two of about a dozen F.1s that arrived at West Raynham over the course of a week. During their very concentrated deployment at the CFE, four aircraft took part in Fighter Command's *Exercise Dividend* which started on 18 July and successful interceptions were made on American B-45 and B-47 bombers on detachment to the UK, while at least one participating Canberra crew expressed surprise at being 'jumped' at their operating altitude by Hunters coming from above them.

The fact that this high altitude interception took place within seventy-five miles of

West Raynham was a pointer to further Hunter limitation. The internal fuel capacity of 334 gallons (1,515 litres) was insufficient and neither the F.1 nor F.2 had provision for external tanks. Hawker was fully conscious of this before criticism was received from Boscombe Down and experimental underwing drop-tanks had already been produced, the first having a capacity of 85 gallons (387 litres), while later tanks, holding 100 gallons (450 litres) were made and test-flown on 7 January 1954 under the wings of WB202. Complementary testing was carried out on an F.1 and a satisfactory system based on two underwing pylon-mounted 100-gallon (450-litres) tanks, was cleared for introduction on production F.4s and subsequent marks. This short endurance of the aircraft was to be the contributing factor in the loss of WT590 from

The production airbrake is actuated from the ground handling point, to show the operating jack.
Aeroplane Monthly

(Below) **The Hunter's short endurance received early attention, 100-gallon (450-litre) drop-tanks being the first development. Trials were undertaken by several aircraft, including the fifteenth production Mark 1, WT569, shown here.** *Aeroplane Monthly*

No. 43 Squadron, The Fighting Cocks, was the first to receive the Hunter F.1, in the summer of 1954. In October of the following year, they made goodwill visits to Norway and Sweden, during which their aerobatic team performed at several venues. The team is shown rehearsing a close-formation routine, WN645/'S' nearest the camera, having been built at Blackpool, was the final Mark 1. Author's collection

The Fighting Cocks display team going over the top. The lead pilot in 'N' appears to feel 'g' more than his colleagues. *Aeroplane Monthly*

No.43 Squadron in 1954 and an ETPS aircraft WT628 in 1955. In both instances the pilots were killed, as were two members of the No.54 Squadron aerobatic team for the same reason. The following year, a whole formation of eight F.1s of the Day-light Fighter Leader School (DFLS) flying from West Raynham on 8 February 1956, returned to base after their exercise to find the cloud base had descended below 500ft (152m) and visibility was too poor for them to undertake a landing. A diversion to

RAF Marham, just over ten miles away, enabled the first pair to land, the second aircraft running out of fuel after turning off the runway. The other six all crashed as engines flamed out due to fuel starvation. Four pilots managed to eject safely, as they lost power at a high enough altitude, one made a crash landing at Marham and survived, while the last was killed crashing outside the airfield perimeter. The formation had been airborne approximately 45 minutes.

Paradoxically, the high-altitude ability of the Hunter produced another dilemma. Although the Canberra crew in *Exercise Dividend* were surprised to be intercepted from above, they were quite unaware that the fighter pilots had great visibility problems due to excessive canopy misting and icing during their descent from altitude, a situation which was potentially very dangerous, as they could hardly see each other! The distribution of air-conditioning within the Hunter required urgent attention.

The extent of Langley's involvement in the history of the Hunter is exemplified in these photographs taken in 1955. In the foreground row of front fuselage sub-assemblies is the first batch of Mark 6s, with Swedish Mark 50s and Danish Mark 51s ranged behind. The almost complete airframe in the centre of the lower view is believed to be XE531, in the course of disassembly, for conversion to the only Hunter Mark 12. John Kendrick

The definitive gun-muzzle deflector was exhibited
on Hunter F.6 XE618, at the 1958 SBAC Display.
Two years later, this aircraft, which was one of the
second batch of 100 built at Kingston, was converted
to FGA.9 standard and is believed to have been
transferred to Kuwait in 1967, prior to that country
receiving Douglas A-4KU Skyhawks.
Aeroplane Monthly

(Below) The second Hunter F.1 operational unit
was Odiham-based No. 54 Squadron, who were
also quick to form an aerobatic team. They became
the official aerobatic team of No. 11 Fighter Group
and are seen performing a box formation roll in
rehearsal for the 1955 SBAC Display. The in-line
centre aircraft were built at Blackpool, while
the wing-men are Kingston products.
Aeroplane Monthly

As stated earlier, initial Hunter gun firing was undertaken with WB202, the F.2 prototype, with satisfactory results, and neither Avon-powered prototypes were involved in these trials. No.43 Squadron based at Leuchars in Scotland and commanded by Squadron Leader R. LeLong was chosen to be the first equipped with the Hunter, replacing the Meteor F.4s then F.8s that they had flown since their re-formation in 1949. Four F.1s were delivered in July 1954, the same month that the CFE received their first aircraft and by September, Sqn Ldr LeLong was at full strength.

Almost from day one, No.43 Squadron's Hunter troubles began and the difference between the Avon and Sapphire engines started to become more apparent. Because of the war in Korea at the start of the decade, Hawker was given the green light to prepare for very large Hunter production orders and Rolls-Royce received similar instructions for the Avon. Only forty-five Sapphire-engined F.2s were ordered from Armstrong Whitworth, to be followed later by 105 F.5s, also Sapphire-powered. That was the full extent of Armstrong Siddeley's involvement in the Hunter programme, although at the time of the F.1 and F.2's introduction, the latter was a slightly faster aircraft with a superior rate of climb and the Sapphire proved comparatively viceless compared to the Rolls-Royce engine. Also, rather ironically, it was Sapphire-powered Hunters that first saw action, during the 'Suez Crisis' in July 1956.

Gun firing with the Avon R.A.7 113-powered Hunter caused fierce engine surging due to gun gases being drawn in, and it also had to be accepted that the engine's compressor could sometimes surge for no apparent reason. The gun-gas ingestion phenomenon could occur at any speed, at any height and in any flying attitude, although firing at higher than 25,000ft (7,620m) and faster than 400 mph (644km/h) was guaranteed to present the Avon with difficulties. The gases had been absorbed by the Sapphire without any trouble and no one had given thought to the fact that a different engine may have a different reaction. The Hunter's shape was established and could not be changed. Therefore, the problem was placed firmly back with Rolls-Royce and, although with hindsight it may seem that the aircraft had been prematurely entered into service, the difficulties would have arisen at some time. Maybe the urgency for rectification would not have been accepted so readily

While still rehearsing for Farnborough, three of the aircraft in this No. 54 Squadron formation are different from the previous photograph. The lightning flash on the fin of the leader is yellow, the slot position aircraft's blue on a grey fin. *Aeroplane Monthly*

Representative of No. 54 Squadron aircrew in December 1955 are, *standing (left to right):-* Fg Off J. H. S. Mansfield; Fg Off B. A. Lewis; Fg Off D. G. Carter; Flt Lt D. G. Bleach; Flt Lt D. A. Lamb; Sqn Ldr W. M. Sizer, DFC; Capt R. G. Immig, USAF; Fg Off B. J. Noble; Fg Off P. A. de C. Swaffer; Plt Off T. J. D. Price.
Kneeling:- Fg Off M. A. Crook; Plt Off K. R. Curtis; Fg Off C. Moss; Fg Off B. E. Danton; Fg Off E. T. W.Hill; Fg Off M. J. Hayden; Fg Off K. A. Pye; Fg Off J. Coates; Sgt C. E. Freeman.
   At the time this photograph was taken, Flt Lt Lamb was Acting Commanding Officer, as Sqn Ldr Sizer was awaiting posting. *Aeroplane Monthly*

had they occurred in prototype development and certainly it was the publicity that galvanized all concerned into action. As a short-term measure, Hawker incorporated a fuel-dipping switch in the electric gun-firing circuit, which had the effect of reducing the fuel flow to the Avon when the guns were fired. The fact that a four-Aden broadside produced an enormous recoil just when there was a reduction in engine thrust had to be accepted for the time being. Furthermore, when the guns were fired, they produced a marked nose-down pitch, which certainly did not contribute to the aircraft being an acceptably steady gun platform and this was only

finally eradicated by the installation of downwards directed muzzle deflectors on the gun ports, incorporated on later marks.
   Aircraft were coming off Hawker Siddeley production lines at a steady rate and subcontracting was put in hand for nose sections to be manufactured by the Gloster Aircraft Company, while tailplanes would be produced by Folland Aircraft Limited at Hamble. Final assembly facilities, augmenting those existing at Langley, were set up at Hawker's Dunsfold site and a few months later, in February 1955, the Odiham, Hampshire-based No.54 Squadron became the second to receive the Hunter F.1. Britain was in the embarrassing posi-

tion of having had their first potentially transonic fighter, the Supermarine Swift F.1, introduced into service with No.56 Squadron in February 1954 and proving unacceptable for the role, being followed by the first two Hunter F.1 squadrons, with their aircraft's own litany of problems. The future was to see the Swift F.1 phased out of service within a year, although the later FR.5 did serve with Nos.2 and 79 Squadrons in Germany, while the Hunter would eventually develop into a first-class aeroplane. In the mid 1950s, however, it took a real optimist to think positively – luckily there were quite a few at Kingston-upon-Thames.

CHAPTER SEVEN

More Squadrons and Improvements

The intensification of the Korean conflict early in 1952, coupled with the increasing political hostility between the East and West which Churchill had christened the 'Cold War', accounted for the United States Congress passing the Offshore Procurement Bill. To increase the arsenals of Western powers in as short a time as possible, the US would provide additional finances for selected programmes in Allied countries, which started as paying for services and spares but eventually expanded to incorporate the production of certain aircraft which were deemed vital for Western defence. Such an aircraft to benefit from the Bill was the Hunter and a total of 367 F.4s was ordered for the RAF, with manufacture being spread between Kingston and Blackpool. Further financing for Hunter production in Holland and

Belgium was also agreed, which will be referred to later.

Meanwhile, Hunter F.1s came on the inventory of No 222 Squadron, who shared Leuchars with No.43 Squadron, in December 1954, while Nos.257 and 263 Squadrons, both based at Wattisham in Suffolk, had received F.2s in July and August. The Air Fighting Development Squadron of the CFE took delivery of five F.2s and one, WN919, also went to No.1 Squadron prior to them receiving F.5s, after service with both Nos.257 and 263 Squadrons. The fourth production F.2 was also used for development and went to Canada for winterization trials. Therefore, by the end of 1954 the RAF had five squadrons of Hunters, all restricted by the various limitations placed on the two marks, plus 25 F.1s which went to RAF

Fighter Command, 1950

At the start of the decade, the Royal Air Force had forty-six fighter squadrons on the British mainland, six more in Germany, a further seven in the Middle East and four in the Far East. Of these, fourteen Meteor and nine Vampire squadrons were based in the UK, with three further Vampire squadrons in Germany and four in the Middle East. The remaining thirty-three squadrons still flew piston-engined aircraft, the Hornet equipping four, the Tempest, two and the Mosquito one, which meant that twenty-six squadrons were still operating Spitfires, five years after the end of the war.

The majority of jet-powered aircraft were either the Meteor F.Mark 4 or Vampire FB.Mark 5, with specifications:

	Meteor F.4	Vampire FB.5
POWER PLANT	Two 3,500lb (1,588kg) s.t. Derwent 5	One 3,100lb (1,406kg) s.t. Goblin 2
MAXIMUM SPEED	575 mph (925 km/h)	535 mph (861 km/h)
SERVICE CEILING	44,000 ft (13,563 m)	40,000 ft (12,192 m)
ARMAMENT	Four 20mm Hispano 5 cannon	Four 20mm Hispano 5 cannon + two 1,000lb (454kg) bombs or eight 3in rocket projectiles

Ten years later, in 1960, the Service had been reduced to thirty-five fighter squadrons, but all flew jet-powered aircraft. The Vampire had gone and only one Meteor squadron remained, in the Far East. Fifteen squadrons were now equipped with the Hunter F.Mark 6 and one, in Germany, still flew the Hunter F.Mark 4 – 45.6 per cent of the fighter force had the Hawker interceptor. Fourteen squadrons flew the all-weather Javelin, two reconnaissance squadrons had the Swift, a Venom fighter-bomber squadron operated in the Middle East and one more in the Far East.

Another five years later, the RAF in 1965 was down to twenty fighter squadrons, of which six flew the supersonic Lightning, five had Javelins and nine squadrons operated the Hunter – still 45 per cent of RAF fighters were Camm's design.

The year 1954 was the last that a Mark 1 had a single-aircraft flying slot at an SBAC Show. Here WT631, fresh from Dunsfold and due to go to No. 5 MU in less than two weeks' time, awaits clearance from the Farnborough tower to commence its display. Author's collection

49

Chivenor in Devon, where No.229 Operational Conversion Unit (OCU) had veteran Canadair-built F-86E Sabre instructors. Their experience in operating interceptors at high speed and high altitudes was invaluable in producing qualified Hunter pilots. Although the Sapphire had not suffered the gun-gas ingestion problems of the Avon, restrictions on gun firing under certain conditions covered all the squadrons. Furthermore, the small internal fuel capacity, while meeting the endurance requirements laid down in Specification F.3/48 when experienced test pilots were at the helm, certainly did not give the reserves required for flying by operational squadron pilots.

were also encountered with irregular wheel-cover door retractions due to faults in the sequence circuits. However, pilots were certainly impressed by the overall increase in performance compared to their previous aircraft and were optimistic that the shortcomings would be overcome. Meanwhile, they and their ground crews were becoming accustomed to the Hunter as a new type in squadron service.

Hawker addressed the Hunter's short endurance by incorporating an additional eight small bag tanks in the wing inboard leading edges. Although the rear fuselage tanks had to be removed, the internal fuel capacity was increased to 414 gallons (1,883 litres) and, with the installation of

Sapphire. These marks also fulfilled later issues of OR228 calling for the Hunter to have a ground-attack capability, each inboard wing pylon being able to carry a 1,000lb (454 kg) bomb in place of the external fuel tank. The first contract for eighty-five F.4s to be built at Kingston was covered by the second part of the original 14 March 1951 dated Contract No. SP/6/5910/CB.7a, while a total of 105 F.5s, to be built by Armstrong Whitworth at Baginton, was included in the second part of Contract No. SP/6/6315/CB.7a issued for the production of forty-five F.1s. Frank Murphy's team had grown, with long-time Hawker pilot Frank Bullen, Don Lucey, Hugh Merewether, David Lockspeiser and

On 16 February 1955, No. 257 (Burma) Squadron at Wattisham held a Press Day, to show off its Hunter F.2s. Four F.1s from No. 43 Squadron joined them at the Suffolk base – and took up the foreground in this line-up photograph. Author's collection

As with all new types of aircraft entering into service use, problems were encountered which had not come to light during prototype development. All the first Hunter squadrons had previously been equipped with Meteor F.8s, so the powered flying control units on their new aircraft were somewhat novel and they required time to become accustomed to them, which was not assisted by malfunctions occurring too regularly. Further problems

two inboard wing pylons, each capable of carrying a 100-gallon (455-litre) fuel tank, the total capacity could be increased to 614 gallons (2,793 litres). In this configuration the aircraft was designated the Hunter F.4 when powered by the Avon R.A.7 Rated 113/115 (the first 156 aircraft having the 113, all those succeeding receiving the Avon 115, featuring modifications to reduce engine surge when the cannons were fired) and the F.5 with the

Duncan Simpson joining him in flying production aircraft.

The first Avon-powered airframe to embody these changes was WT701, the 114th production F.1, which in effect became the F.4 prototype and first flew on 20 October 1954, piloted by Frank Murphy. It had been preceded on 19 October by WN954, the forty-sixth Baginton-produced aircraft, itself being the first Sapphire 101-powered F.5, although neither marks

Farnborough's main runway is about to accept Hunter F.2 WN908, on completion of its display at the 1954
SBAC Show, with the Hawker Siddeley Group logo prominent on its nose. Author's collection

Hunter F.1s left the Central Fighter Establishment in September 1955, to undertake a tour of the
Mediterranean area. On their return to West Raynham, WT648/'F' is shown sporting a white modification to
its colour scheme. The aircraft behind it appears to have white paintwork applied to its wing.
Aeroplane Monthly

With rain threatening, No. 257 Squadron F.2 WN949/'M' stands alongside a USAF F-86 Sabre, on the tarmac at Wethersfield, on 21 May 1955. George Pennick

(Below) A picture symbolic of England in the summer of 1955. Small fields, woodlands, villages and a Hunter – in this case, F.1 WT594, before going up to join No. 43 Squadron at Leuchars. Author's collection

trainer for the Fleet Air Arm. The first F.5 was also retained for trials and spent a considerable time at Boscombe Down prior to undertaking a test programme of high speed target towing. Its following Baginton-produced F.5, WN955, was allocated to Armstrong Siddeley Motors for flying trials of their new 10,500lb (4,763kg) thrust-rated Sapphire ASSa7, which was a redesigned version of the F.5's ASSa6 Mk101 and, while never being used as a production engine for the Hunter, would become the power plant for later marks of the Gloster Javelin and the Handley Page Victor B.1.

With the first seven F.4 and five F.5 aircraft all getting impressed into either manufacturer or service trial flying, the first delivery to a Maintenance Unit was F.4 WT708, which went to No.33 MU on 5 February 1955, while F.5s WN959 and WN960 flew to No.5 MU on 26 April. WT708 went on to No.54 Squadron in September where F.4s replaced their original Hunter F.1s,

were prototypes in the usually accepted way, carrying a yellow circled 'P' – in fact, as a point of interest, no Hunter was ever bedecked in this manner. WT701 was retained by Hawker Aircraft for a variety of trials, including the release of external wing tanks in flight, before being engaged on radio trials at A&AEE Boscombe Down and its eventual conversion into a Mark 8

while WN595 joined No.1 Squadron when they relinquished their Meteor F.8s for the Hunter in the same month. From then, a steady allocation of aircraft was continued throughout 1955 and it was decided to re-equip some 2nd Tactical Air Force (TAF) squadrons in Germany with the Hunter. The first was No.98 Squadron based at Jever, near Wilhelmshaven, who got their F.4s in April, followed the next month by No.118 Squadron at the same location. In July, Jever-based No.4 Squadron also replaced its Sabres with Hunter F.4s. Oldenburg, twenty-five miles south of Jever, was host to No.14 Squadron using Venoms and No.26 Squadron flying Sabres, both

units receiving F.4s in June, while the last of the Sabres departed when No.20 Squadron accepted its F.4s at the same location in November.

In the UK, No. 247 Squadron, equipped with the Meteor F.8, shared Odiham with No. 54 Squadron, who had received Hunter F.1s in February 1955. The Meteors started to leave in May, when No. 247 received Hunter F.4s, and the Hampshire base became an all F.4 unit when No. 54 replaced its F.1s with the later mark. At North Weald in Essex, No. 111 Squadron gave up its Meteor F.8s in June and received Hunter F.4s, with which it built up an expertise in spectacular formation flying that, two years

later, equipped with the Hunter F.6, would establish the squadron as the RAF's premier aerobatic team, the *Black Arrows*.

Sapphire-engined F.5s also started service life in 1955, but lack of maintenance facilities in Germany for the Armstrong Siddeley engines meant they served mainly in UK-based units. No. 56 Squadron at Waterbeach in Cambridgeshire gave up the struggle with its Swifts in May and replaced them with Hunter F.5s, while the following month No. 41 Squadron, at the legendary Battle of Britain airfield Biggin Hill, ended over four years of Meteor flying when its F.5s arrived. Another RAF airfield associated with the 1940 air

(Above) **Photographed in winter sunshine at Duxford, on 20 February 1989, Hunter F.2 WN904 had served with No. 257 Squadron and later given Instructional Airframe Number 7544M. The significance of the white '3' on its nose has not been confirmed.** George Pennick

(Below) **A pristine sixth production F.4, WT706, awaits handling trials at Boscombe Down in December 1954. Five years later it was converted to the only T.62 for Peru.** Author's collection

The fifth F.5, WN958 first flew from Baginton early in 1955, and went to the A&AEE for a long series of external stores trials. Here it flies with a 100-gallon (450-litre) plastic drop-tank and twelve 3in (76mm) rocket projectiles, under the port wing – in these sorts of trials there is no guarantee that a similar load is carried on the starboard side. *Hawker Aircraft*

(Below) An example of the mixed loads carried is shown by F.4 WT780, on its way to the 1955 SBAC Display. With the same drop-tank/rocket projectile combination shown on WN958 but under the starboard wing, another 100-gallon (450-litre) drop-tank is on the outboard pylon of the port wing, with a 1,000lb (453kg) free-fall bomb on the inboard one. *Aeroplane Monthly*

battles, Tangmere in Sussex (from where Duke made his world record flight in WB188 two years earlier), hosted No. 1 and No. 34 Squadrons, who were also both Meteor F.8 equipped. In September and October respectively, they began flying the Hunter F.5. The following year, both these squadrons would deploy to Akrotiri in Cyprus, as top cover for Canberras, Valiants and Royal Navy Wyvern strike aircraft engaged on *Operation Musketeer*, the Anglo-French military fiasco to seize, in conjunction with Israel, key points on

the Suez Canal. But the still inadequate endurance meant that their role could not be fully accomplished and the Navy had to provide their own fighter protection with a Hunter predecessor, the Sea Hawk. Also, no doubt by good fortune, Adens were not needed to be fired in anger and the two squadrons returned to Tangmere in time for Christmas. By the end of 1955, there were nine Avon-powered and four Sapphire-powered Hunter squadrons in RAF service, with six of the Avon-equipped mark operating in Germany.

The year 1955 had also seen the sowing of the seeds of change in Hawker Aircraft's position of Chief Test Pilot. On 4 August, Neville Duke experienced turbine-blade failure while flying F.1 WT562 on gun firing trials, not far from his world record flight course. By dint of excellent flying, he landed the aircraft safely on the naval airfield at Ford, for which he would be awarded the Queen's Commendation for Valuable Services in the Air. The Avon was replaced and Duke collected the aircraft two days later. Just after take-off he

(Right) **A production Armstrong Siddeley ASSa6 Type 101 Sapphire, rests on its mobile trestle, prior to installation into a Hunter F.5 airframe, at Armstrong Whitworth Aircraft's Baginton plant.** Hawker Aircraft

When No. 111 Squadron converted to the Hunter F.4 in June 1955, it was quick to build up a reputation for formation aerobatics. Here, Kingston-built WV379/'V', WV264/'A', WT811/'H' and WT720/'Q' come to the top of a loop, with only 'V' and 'H' having cartridge collectors fitted. Aeroplane Monthly

---

An Up-and-Down Test Pilot

Eleven months after Trevor Wade, one Alfred William Bedford was born, on 18 November 1920 and went on to be educated at Loughborough College School. While serving an engineering apprenticeship, World War II broke out and 'Bill' Bedford joined the Royal Air Force, being posted as a sergeant pilot, on gaining his wings, to No. 605 County of Warwick Squadron, which introduced him to the products of Hawker Aircraft. Overseas service with No. 135 Squadron in the Far East – still flying Hurricanes, but later changing to the Republic Thunderbolt – was followed, in 1945, by operations in the North American Mustangs of No. 65 Squadron, until the end of the war.

During the following six years, a Qualified Flying Instructor's post with Training Command was succeeded by graduation at the ETPS and retention there as a tutor. In 1950, he became an MoS test pilot with the Aero Flight at RAE Farnborough.

On retirement from the RAF, as a Flight Lieutenant, Bedford renewed his affiliation with Hawker aircraft by becoming an experimental test pilot for the company, taking over as their Chief Test Pilot in October 1956 and, seven years later, becoming CTP for Hawker Siddeley Aviation, a post he held until 1967. Following development flying with the Sea Hawk and Hunter – his inverted Hunter two-seater spins at Farnborough in 1959 and 1960 are recorded as the sole executions of such a manoeuvre at a public demonstration – Bill Bedford started an association with the world of V/STOL, piloting the P.1127's first tethered totterings on 21 October 1960, with the added encumberance of a leg in plaster following a car crash.

On 14 December 1961, he successfully ejected from the second P.1127 prototype XP837 and two years later,

on 16 June 1963, the first P.1127, XP831, took on board a foreign body in the nozzle-actuation system during the Paris Air Show, the resultant heavy landing by Bedford being made more dramatic by the interference of a substantial chunk of concrete. In February 1963, P.1127 trials were carried out on HMS *Ark Royal* by Bedford and he performed V/STOLs with his No. 2, Hugh Merewether, off Portland. June 1966 saw further carrier operations, on HMS *Bulwark* by the CTP, which were to convince the Admiralty of the advantages of having such an aircraft on their inventory.

Bill Bedford became Sales Manager for Hawker Siddeley Aviation in 1968 and, ten years later was appointed Divisional Marketing Manager for British Aerospace until 1983. His flying life encompassed over 150 different types of aircraft, in which he logged 6,800 hours. Eight international sailplane records were held, including a 1950 altitude record of 21,340ft (6,504m), a height gain of 19,120ft (5,828m), together with the British Gliding Association's de Havilland Trophy, which he won twice, plus the 1950-51 Wakefield Trophy. He was the Chairman and Founder Member of the Royal Aeronautical Society's Test Pilots' Group from 1964 to 1966, a Fellow of the United States Society of Experimental Test Pilots' Society from 1956 to 1967. He was awarded the King's Commendation in 1949, the OBE in 1961, plus other prestigious titles at home and abroad, including a First Class Wings for service to the Republic of Indonesia. With his death on 20 October 1996, the world of aviation became the poorer, but his achievements are recognized every time a Harrier, Sea Harrier, AV-8B or Matador defies the normal rules of flight.

---

encountered a partial power failure (later found to have been caused by a small piece of fluff getting into a fuel-vent valve) at 1,000ft (305m) over Chichester Harbour, which necessitated his flying on idling thrust, to make a forced landing at the No. 2 Air Navigation School base on Thorney Island. With lack of engine control, he touched down at 200mph (322km/h) and commenced a series of uncontrollable bounces, which he felt could be cured by retracting the undercarriage. However,

only one main leg came up and he careered through the airfield perimeter fencing, finally crashing into a ditch. The CTP suffered a fractured spine which, despite a lengthy period of lying on his back while the spine healed, caused him great pain

when executing 'g' force manoeuvres on resuming Hunter test flying. Consequently a year later in October 1956, Neville Duke resigned, the overall responsibility for test flying Hawker aircraft passing to his deputy and friend, 'Bill' Bedford.

(Above) **Hunter F.5 WP188/'V' of No. 56 Squadron lifts off the Waterbeach runway, still without cartridge-link collectors.** Author's collection

(Below) **On 22 September 1956, WP188/'V' was photographed in a similar pose, but with cartridge link collectors installed, accompanied by a similarly equipped F.5 WP104/'A', to commence a sortie in the annual air defence Exercise Stronghold. No. 56 Squadron was not shy, when it came to displaying its colours.** Aeroplane Monthly

Further squadron re-equipping with the Hunter F.4 continued throughout 1956, in both UK Fighter Command and the 2nd TAF, which was in the front line of the North Atlantic Treaty Organisation's (NATO) air defences. Jever became an all-Hunter base when they replaced No. 93 Squadron's Sabre F.4s, while Bruggen, twenty miles west of Düsseldorf, began to lose its Sabres in the same month, as No. 67 Squadron started getting Hunter F.4s. Three months later the Canadian-built fighters had gone and Brüggen too evolved into a Hunter unit, when Nos. 71, 112 and 130 Squadrons all received F.4s in April. Fifteen miles south of Brüggen, the ex-Luftwaffe airfield at Geilenkirchen hosted two more Sabre squadrons but these aircraft also disappeared in May as Nos. 3 and 234 Squadrons accepted Hunter F.4s.

In Scotland, No. 43 Squadron at Leuchars, having been the pioneer Hunter squadron when they received the F.1 in July 1954, upgraded to the F.4 in February 1956, while its neighbouring No. 222

Squadron on the same base replaced their F.1s with F.4s in August. South of the border, the Yorkshire base at Linton-on-Ouse since 1949, housed two long-established fighter squadrons, both of which progressed from the Meteor F.8 to the Sabre F.4. In March 1956, No. 66 Squadron gave up Sabres for Hunter F.4s and the next month No. 92 Squadron followed suit when its F.4s started arriving. The following year, in April 1957, No. 245 Squadron, based at Stradishall in Suffolk, became the last to receive the Hunter F.4, but they only had them for two months before the squadron was disbanded on 30 June.

A total of 365 Hunter Mark 4s was built for the Royal Air Force. As well as the initial Kingston batch of eighty-five, another batch of 100 produced to Contract No. SP/6/6867/CB.7a and a further three to Contract No. SP/6/7144/CB.7a all came from the same factory. Blackpool built their first batch of twenty aircraft to Contract No. SP/6/8435/CB.7a, the second batch of 100 to Contract No. SP/6/9817/CB.7a and

their final fifty-seven Mark 4s to Contract No. SP/6/10344/CB.7a. A further 208 were manufactured on the Continent under licence, ninety-six by Fokker-Aviolanda in Holland and 112 by Avions Fairey in Belgium, for their respective air forces. Export models of the Mark will be detailed in a later chapter.

While endurance of the Hunter Marks 4 and 5 had benefited from the installation of the two inboard 100-gallon (455-litre) drop-tanks, during 1955–56 Hawker was engaged on trials to improve it even more, by providing an additional outboard pylon under each wing. Modification 228 provided the new pylons with their ability to each carry a further 100-gallon (455-litre) drop tank, and to be capable of adaptation for each to accept a battery of twelve 3in (7.8cm) rocket projectiles. WT703, the third production F.4, was the principal aircraft engaged in these trials, which were conducted from both Dunsfold and the A&AEE, the aircraft eventually logging over 244 hours of trials flying before being

The Aden cannon pack, complete with ammunition tank, is removed with the aid of three Type C bomb hoists. In the ground-handling manual, the pack should be lowered onto a castored cradle, ready to be placed on a trolley for being towed away. Maybe the expression on the ground crew in the foreground denotes his wondering where the cradle has got to! *Aeroplane Monthly*

Two pleasant studies of WV325, a Kingston-built Hunter F.4, which first flew on 13 June 1955 and, a month later, went to the Central Flying School. The crest on the port side of the nose has a scroll bearing the legend 'CFS Type Flight'. WV325 was eventually converted into an FGA.73A for Jordan, given the number 846 and delivered in the autumn of 1971. *Aeroplane Monthly*

broken up at Dunsfold in 1964. The fifth Hunter F.5, WN598, was also employed on the rocket projectile side of this programme.

Despite the increasing number of Hunters being accepted by the RAF, guns were still inclined to be their 'Achilles heel'. Behind the Aden cannon ports either side of the retracted nose-wheel, spent ammunition links and shell cases streamed out through separate ejection slots when the guns were fired. The earlier firing trials conducted with a Beaufighter carrying an experimental Aden cannon, indicated the spent elements of the ammunition might cause problems

Between 25 and 27 May 1957, Exercise Vigilant was conducted, No. 74 Squadron being a participant. Hunter F.4 WV269/'H' is shown lifting off the Horsham St Faith operational runway, wearing the whitewash identity panel on its fin applied for the exercise. This aircraft was scrapped at No. 5 MU, Kemble, in June 1961. *Aeroplane Monthly*

From Kingston's second F.4 production batch and first flown by Bill Bedford on 3 June 1955, a very clean WV319 is probably en route to No. 5 MU, Kemble. The aircraft crashed at the base in January 1956, while being flown by a CFS pilot, but was repaired by a Service unit. It returned to Hawker Aircraft in 1958, to be converted to T.8 standard for the Fleet Air Arm and is known to have served with No. 764 NAS at Lossiemouth. *Author's collection*

(Above) **A product of Blackpool's first batch of F.4s, Jever-based No. 98 Squadron's WW658/'O' had yet to be fitted with link collectors in the spring of 1955, when this photograph was taken. The squadron's red and white markings are repeated in miniature, either side of its crest, on the nose.**
Aeroplane Monthly

It is fair to say that a very large proportion of air-to-air photographs of the Hunter, were taken by photographers sitting in the draughty interior of Meteor T.7s. Therefore, while WV325 has appeared earlier, it is interesting to actually see it in formation with the Gloster two-seater.
Aeroplane Monthly

when they were ejected into the slip-stream. However, it had been thought that they would be heavy enough to fall away from the aircraft, but in practice the Beau-fighter predictions came true and Hunters started receiving damaged areas in the fuselage underside and the airbrake.

There was a degree of uncertainty as to whether the cases or the links were the main culprits but a link collector was designed possibly because, as they were not so large as the cases, they would require a smaller unit in which to be contained. The collectors took the form of two large, external, streamlined blisters, mounted under the front fuselage over the link ejec-tor ports, each gathering links from two guns. In keeping with the British sense of humour – so hard to comprehend by some nations – the blisters were colloquially known as 'Sabrinas', in recognition of a television starlet of that name, whose claim to fame rested in being 'well endowed'. The modification worked satis-factorily and nearly all earlier Hunter F.4s and F.5s were subsequently retrofitted with collector blisters.

In squadron service, there was found to be a tendency for gun gases to collect in the nose-cone, which was alleviated by the fit-ting of an air scoop in the underskin of the

gun pack, connected into the electrical fir-ing circuit which opened when the guns were fired, thereby ventilating the inner nose area. Further problems arose as vibra-tions generated by the firing of all four guns in unison created structural cracking in the forward fuselage, which required stainless steel reinforcement sections to be inserted in the affected areas. The consequences of a volley from four closely-grouped 30mm cannon on the carrier aircraft had not been encountered before and Aden operating was restricted to firing in pairs until modi-fications could be introduced on the pro-duction line. As has been stated earlier, malfunctions in the electrical firing mech-anism of the Aden cannon could also cre-ate situations that left much to be desired.

However, not everything was negative and the Hunter was being appreciated by service pilots as being a delightful and rugged aircraft to fly, in the true Hawker tradition. They were firmly optimistic that the niggles would be sorted out and their confidence would prove to be not mis-placed – also, no doubt, their 'grapevine' was active and they knew a good thing was worth waiting for. Rolls-Royce had pro-duced the Avon 200 Series engine and a transformed Hunter, the F.6, was already in production at Kingston.

A Proper Engine

Before the cancellation, on 13 July 1953, of Hawker's proposed genuinely supersonic P.1083 version of their P.1067, a set of wings had been built, a fuselage selected off the Hunter production line and the serial number WN470 allocated for application when the aircraft was finished. As Contract No. 6296 had covered this work, it was decided to use the fuselage for a new Hunter prototype, which would utilize the proposed new Avon that Rolls-Royce had developed.

It has become a bit of a mystery just why the Avon was preferred to the Sapphire at the start of Hunter development. Maybe

The Hunter F.6 prototype, XE833, was built under the company designation P.1099, with the forward and centre fuselage sections of the cancelled P.1083 being used in its construction. Following type flight trials, the aircraft was modified by Miles Aircraft, to undertake testing of a reverse-thrust system being developed by Rolls-Royce. The appalling weather that prevailed at the 1957 SBAC Display had the one virtue of providing a good visual effect during XF833's landing roll, when thrust-reversal was used.
Aeroplane Monthly

Sydney Camm's long and successful association with their engines was the determining factor, but Rolls-Royce are on record as considering the Armstrong Siddeley engine had 'a greatly superior flow/pressure characteristic' to their own engine and it had a slightly greater thrust output than the Avon RA.7. When the surge problems arose with the Rolls-Royce engine installed in the Hunter – the same basic engine powered the Canberra without this phenomenon – coupled with a more-than-occasional reluctance to start and a propensity to break turbine blades, the company realized they had a problem on their hands.

There was a 'gentleman's agreement' between the two engine companies, whereby an interchange of knowledge was entered into, to their mutual benefit. In this climate of understanding, Armstrong Siddeley gave Rolls-Royce data accumulated at the compressor design stage of the Sapphire, which the Derby company recognized as being superior to their original RA.3. The later RA.7 reduced the disparity, but the Sapphire's constant outer diameter proved more beneficial to its operating, compared to the Rolls-Royce engine, which had to have a narrower compressor housing in order to contain the external accessories within the required overall diameter. Another fundamental advantage held by the Armstrong Siddeley engine was the fact that its design ensured the first four compressor stages had considerably less stress loading, irrespective of the angle of attack.

Rolls-Royce designated their first 200-series engine the RA.14 and, while retaining the Sapphire's design in the first four compressor stages, redesigned the following eleven stages, although retaining a straight flow into the combustion chamber. The experience gained with the RA.3's variable swirl was further refined and bench running of the new engine began on 17 November 1951. A 150-hour Type Test programme was undertaken in April 1952, with an output of 10,500lb (4,763 kg) static thrust being assured for the RA.14. Although it had a longer compressor compared to previous Avons, the new engine's application of a true annular combustion chamber, in order to accommodate the increased mass flow, gave it a slightly smaller overall diameter, while the dry weight of 2,860lb (1,297kg) was also less than previous models.

The second production English Electric Canberra B.2, WD930, had been operated by Rolls-Royce's test facility at Hucknall since August 1951. Being capable of undertaking really high-altitude testing, it had assisted in the development of the RA.7 and was now to undertake flight testing of the RA.14. The first flight was made in July 1953 and the aircraft demonstrated the new engine at the Farnborough SBAC Display two months later, in September. WD930 went on to test the later RA.26 and finally the RA.29, before eventually being scrapped, after nine years' trials work, in August 1960.

A further contract, numbered 10032, was issued to cover the new Hunter based on the abandoned P.1083 fuselage WN470 and given another Hawker project number, P.1099. The original P.1083 wings were cast into history and the uprated production wings with four pylon points were fitted, together with an Avon RA.14. The P.1099 prototype, serialed XF833 and designated Hunter F. Mk 6, was completed in record time at Kingston, for Neville Duke to give it a maiden flight from Dunsfold, on 23 January 1954. This was quite a few months before the Hunter F.1, having got through the airbrake saga, was accepted for RAF service, and nine months before the first production F.4 flew. But the earlier marks gave all involved experience in flying and operating the Hunter. Now a new breed of Hunter was airborne.

XF833 went to Boscombe Down on 8 February, for handling trials with MoS pilots, but the new Avon was not trouble-free and, less than a fortnight after its arrival at A&AEE, it suffered a failure, necessitating the aircraft to make a forced landing. It was returned to Dunsfold by road for repairs plus a new Avon, which were completed for flying to restart on 23 April. Five days later, the replacement engine failed and the problem was handed back to Rolls-Royce. Comprehensive ground-running tests revealed the cause to be compressor blade failure due to fatigue, and modified steel stator and rear rotor blades were incorporated to remedy the trouble. These resulted in the basic engine, which had also been fitted with a revised fuel system, being derated from 10,500lb (4,763kg) to 10,000lb (4,536kg) static thrust and now known as the Avon 203, RA.28-rated.

The P.1099 prototype made a second resumption of flight trials on 20 July at Dunsfold and its test programme was completed without further mishap. When its contribution to Hunter F.6 development was finished, XF833 was delivered in the spring of 1956 to Miles Aircraft Limited at Shoreham in Sussex. There, the company was contracted by Rolls-Royce to modify the airframe to accept the installation of a thrust-reversal system that they were developing, with a view to reducing landing roll distances. The modifications included a set of exhaust louvres installed either side of the rear fuselage, about 36in (1.044m) ahead of the jet orifice. While the system operated successfully, the comparative economics of a braking parachute won the day and no further application was employed on the Hunter.

CHAPTER NINE

Construction

With the F. Mark 6 having been produced in greater numbers than any other Mark and forming the foundation of many subsequent conversions, it is used as the basis for this description.

Fuselage

Built in three, circular cross-sectioned, self-contained sub-assemblies for ease of transportation to the site of final assembly, with frames numbered from 1 to 63. While being very strong, the construction is quite conventional, with few large forgings and very little use of steel. Skin panels, rolled to the required curvature, have no integral stiffening – stringers, frames and ribs being built up from light extrusions and formed plate. The front fuselage, from frame 1 to 18A, which has a detachable nose-cone mounted ahead of frame 1, contains the cockpit, all radio equipment, plus the vast detachable armament pack.

The cockpit, being pressurized, is built between frames 6 and 14 with an integral floor. A trunking, on which the Martin-Baker Mk2H or 3H ejector seat is fitted, passes diagonally up through the rear portion of the cabin to carry the flying control runs to the spine. Load bearing for the cockpit coaming plus windscreen, is supplied by the top longerons, which are assisted in carrying canopy-locking loads by frames 10 and 13, the canopy itself being a full-blown plastic element, running on rails and actuated by an electric motor-driven chain gear. The flat bullet-proof windscreen is constructed with two glass plates, between which anti-misting air maintains its dryness through rubber tubing, running from a silica-gel pack to the base of the screen. Both curved quarter-lights are glazed with ¼in (19.5mm) thick Perspex. The fuselage forward of frame 6 houses the retractable nose wheel plus radar-ranging equipment and behind frame 14, the ammunition tank is located, with the radio and electric-control equipment positioned behind it. In this area, skinning varies from 16 swg, via 14 swg where gun-blast has to be contained, to 10 swg at the base of the windscreen framing. The control runs, together with some components of the air-conditioning system, are contained in the unstressed dorsal spine, under a detachable fairing cover commencing aft of the cockpit.

The centre fuselage, from frames 18B to 40A, carries the main body of the engine plus the stub wings. It came from the factory as an entire, equipped unit, ready to accept the front fuselage, wings, engine and rear fuselage at their respective attachment points. It is made up by closely spaced frames, stringers being formed with plate and extrusions, skinning being in 14 and 16 swg sheet. The air intakes are constructed as a part of the centre fuselage, together with boundary-layer bleed ducts and sprung doors to give additional intake area for low-speed flying. No structural loads are absorbed by the intake trunk and the engine intake face is fitted against a rubber seal at frame 31. Principal wing loads are contained through frame 25, which has extended booms and plate webs round two spar members. Frame 34 is reinforced to take the forward engine mounting, with the lower part of nearly all the frames behind being divided, in order to

Seen at Coltishall's 1969 Battle of Britain air display, Baginton-built Hunter F.6 XF512/'34' from No. 229 OCU at Chivenor, carries an SNEB-Matra rocket battery on the starboard outboard pylon. Two years later, the aircraft was converted to an FGA.71, with the number '725', for the Chilean Air Force.
George Pennick

take access panels for the engine and accessories. Frames 37 to 39 are complete and reinforced to transfer some of the load from the fuselage join into the continuous top section, along which the dorsal control line-carrying spine runs. Although the fuselage sections are individual components, separation of the forward one from the centre section is only proposed for transportation or major maintenance, but it obviously became a major factor in the refurbishment programmes.

The rear fuselage is a simpler structure, built with closely-spaced frames from the main join at frame 40B, to frame 57, where the tailcone locates. The rear fuel tank bays extend between frames 41 to 45, stainless steel providing protection to the alloy-lined bays from jet-pipe heat. In the lower section, airbrake jack loads are taken by an 18 swg section from frames 47 to 50, the hinges being contained in channels fitted between frames 45 and 46. On top of the assembly, from frame 46, the dorsal spine changes section to meet the fin contour, the ribs of which attach to the fuselage decking. A reinforced mounting platform for the tail assembly is located on frames 52 to 55, the latter being a stainless-steel forging, sharing the tailpipe support bracket with frame 56. Aft of this, the tail-cone is attached and further use of stainless steel is made in the jet-pipe nozzle, above which the drag-chute housing is situated. The lower fin structure is a constituent of the rear fuselage, with the fin and tailplane unit being mounted on two posts integrally formed with frames 52 and 55.

Wings

With a sweep-back angle of 40 degrees on the quarter-chord line, giving a leading-edge sweep of 44 degrees, the outer wing structure is formed by front and rear spars, with an undercarriage girder running diagonally between them. Rib stations are annotated with numbers 1 to 3 ahead of the main spar root rib and letters A to R from the same point to the detachable wing-tip location rib. An undercarriage pivot bracket runs across the space between the main spar and undercarriage girder. Large, heavy-gauge skin panels, rolled to curvature, cover the whole wing structure, which houses the wing fuel tanks in compartments ahead of the main spar between ribs A and G, stores pylons, flaps and ailerons. The single-spar flaps are

hinged at four points and skinned in light alloy on the underside only, while each aileron is hinged at three points. Wing leading-edge extensions, each comprising a single heavy-gauge sheet wrapped round short plate ribs, are riveted onto the wing skin, between rib J and the wing-tip joint rib R. Langley or Dunsfold took delivery of the wings as complete units, with all fittings, including the main undercarriage legs, installed and tested.

A late Baginton-produced F.6, XF383, is seen as '14' with No. 229 OCU. The outboard pylons and rocket-tier rails are devoid of occupants, the sunlight picking out the ventral blade and post aerials. Sooty deposits indicate that at least the inboard Adens have recently been fired. Author's collection

Tail unit

The Hunter's tail unit assembly consists of the fin, rudder, tailplane and elevators, together with the anti-buffet bullet-fairing – which was the first excrescence to appear on Sydney Camm's beautiful design. Fin sweep-back at the quarter-chord line is 47.5 degrees, while tailplane sweep at its quarter-chord is 42 degrees. Each of the main elements comprises closely-spaced ribs, attached to front and rear spars, with additional formed spars carrying the moving surfaces. The cantilever tailplane is built as one piece and all components of the tail unit are light-alloy skinned.

Controls

Hawker stated that its conventional practice of using flat-sided control surfaces, with fine trailing-edge angles, is followed with the Hunter. Elevator control is full-power operated by Fairey Hydrobooster hydraulic jacks linked to the electrically-

operated, variable incidence tailplane, which is also used for trimming. A three-step plain spring system supplies artificial feel and, in the event of hydraulic failure, elevator control reverts to manual, after a short period in power while the hydraulic accumulators are exhausting. Ailerons are also fully power-operated by Hydrobooster jacks and provided with plain spring feel. Two-speed gearing is incorporated to alleviate loads imposed when flying under stand-by manual control. Rudder control is manual, with an electrically actuated trim tab connected to a Newmark autostabilizer. Operation of the ventral airbrake is hydraulically controlled, the unit only capable of being deployed fully extended or retracted.

Undercarriage

The tricycle undercarriage incorporates a fully castoring nose wheel, which self-centres as it travels through its forward retraction arc. Main wheels, equipped with Dunlop Maxaret units on the disc brakes, retract inwards, and all undercarriage movements are supplied by an electrically actuated hydraulic system. An emergency pneumatic system comes into operation for lowering the undercarriage and operating the flaps, should there be a hydraulic failure, while operation of the Maxaret brake units is maintained by oil pressure supplied by two accumulators situated in the nose-wheel bay.

CHAPTER TEN

A Revitalized Hunter

The lessons learned back in 1951, about undertaking development with too few pre-production aircraft, had been taken on board by all concerned. Contract No. SP/6/7144/CB.7a dated 19 July 1951, had covered three production F.4s to be built at Kingston, the balance of the batch being transferred to Blackpool as Contract No. SP/6/8435/CB.7a. Now, a small second batch of seven airframes under the original contract, was assigned to be employed as provisional Mark 6s, with the new Avons but pre-Mod 228 wings. These aircraft were serialed WW592–598 and Bill Bedford gave the first its maiden flight from Dunsfold, on 23 May 1955, the aircraft partaking in the SBAC Display four months later – the year that sixty-four Hunters, of various Marks, flew at the Display *en masse*. The wisdom of building the interim aircraft from an existing production line was substantiated when Frank Bullen lifted WW598 off Dunsfold's runway on the last

(Above) WW593, the second production Hunter F.6, was one of the seven classified as provisional aircraft and not fitted with Mod 228 wings. First flown on 19 August 1955 by Frank Bullen, it was used for five years on numerous installation trials, at Dunsfold and Boscombe Down, before being converted, in 1961, to FR. 10 standard. The underside silver-grey not continuing aft of the wing seems to indicate that the rear fuselage came from a different airframe.
Aeroplane Monthly

XF374, the second Baginton-built F.6 was used for early 230-gallon (1,046.5-litre) external tank trials and is shown *(right)* with these units on all four pylons, in 1957. However, it was never flown in this configuration, but on 2 October 1958, the aircraft became a long-distance record-breaker and is seen *(below)* taxiing out with the 230-gallon tanks on the inboard pylons only, the outboard tanks being 100-gallon (475-litre) capacity. Hawker Aircraft and Author's collection

day of the year. So 1956 started with six aircraft available for Mark 6 development – the seventh, WW597, first flown on 10 October, had gone almost straightaway to No. 19 MU at RAF St Athan in South Wales, to give service technicians experience of the new aircraft's engine and systems. With the production of all Mark 4s and 5s completed, both Kingston and Baginton (the latter not having built a Rolls-Royce-powered Hunter before) tooled up for Mark 6 production, while Blackpool concentrated on manufacturing export Marks, in conjunction with Dunsfold. This will be covered in later chapters.

utes was still 1.4 minutes slower than the Sapphire-powered F.5!)

On the engine side, the Avon's earlier cartridge starters had often proved unreliable and a new Plessey liquid-fuel system of isopropyl nitrate was perfected for the 200 Series. The positioning of accessories on the new engine was entirely different from the RA.7 and this entailed the removal of the small centre fuselage tanks, which were replaced by a pair of 25-gallon (114-litre) flexible rubber bag tanks, positioned either side of the engine jet pipe. A front fuselage bag-type tank of 200-gallon (910-litre) capacity and four further rubber tanks posi-

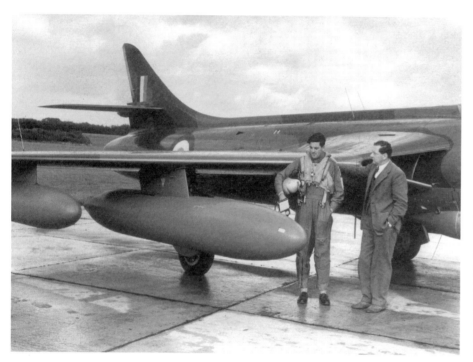

The pilot for the Dunsfold to El Adem flight was Hugh Merewether, who is seen in flying kit, no doubt sharing the observation, with Hawker's Chief Test Pilot Bill Bedford, that the inboard 230-gallon (1,046.5-litre) drop-tanks certainly look big! *Aeroplane Monthly*

Baginton-built F.6 XF449/'S', photographed in 1955 carrying the markings of Church Fenton-based No. 19 Squadron, shows how underwing serials had to be modified when drop-tanks came into general use. *Aeroplane Monthly*

It had been accepted that the Hunter, with its 0.085 thickness/chord ratio wing, would never be a true supersonic fighter and the RAF was to wait until June 1960 before their first, the English Electric Lightning F.1, would be accepted by No. 74 Squadron at Coltishall. Nevertheless, the Hunter F. Mk6, with its time to 45,000ft (13,716m) of just over 7 minutes (compared to the 12.5 minutes for the F.4), was originally accepted into the Service as an interceptor. (As a point of interest, the time to 45,000ft, or 13,716m of 7.1 min-

tioned ahead of the main spar in each wing, collectively holding 140 gallons (637 litres), gave the Mark 6 an internal fuel capacity of 390 gallons (1,774.5 litres). The Mod 228 wing flown on Hunter F.4s, with inboard pylons carrying two 100-gallon (455-litre) capacity plastic drop-tanks, was further modified for the Mark 6, by positioning two additional outboard pylons with the same carrying ability. Furthermore, Hawker had now developed metal drop tanks with a capacity of 230 gallons (1,046.5 litres), which could be carried on the inboard pylons, while the

100 gallon (455 litre) tanks remained on the outboard position. Therefore, the fuel load could be expanded to a maximum of 1,050 gallons (4,777.5 litres), although in practice such an amount would be principally for long-range ferrying, as it constituted a wing loading of approximately 70lb/sq ft (32kg/sq m). In the course of the tank flight-test programme, on 2 October 1958, XF374 was flown the 1,588 miles (2,556km) from Dunsfold to El Adem in Libya by Hugh Merewether, in 3hrs 19min, an average speed of 476mph (767km/h).

During the trials, a mild but unpleasant trait was discovered when high 'g' forces were applied at speed and high altitude. The aircraft entered a pitch-up attitude, for which the A&AEE was entrusted to find a solution. Wing fences did not prove effective but, by extending the leading edge of the outer wing panels forward with a downwards camber, which locally reduced the thickness/chord ratio and moved the aerodynamic pressure centre forward, the problem was cured. This 9 sq ft (0.836 sq m) sawtooth extension was adopted for all Mark 6s, except the first few production aircraft that had already come off the lines, although these were retrospectively modified eventually, as were quite a number of F.4s.

Aden cannon firing still produced a nose-down pitching moment at altitude. The decision to completely eradicate this entailed a programme of firing that Hawker considered had never been equalled by any other gun-firing aircraft, irrespective of the ammunition gauge. Over 20,000

(Above) An anonymous Mark 6 displays the leading-edge extensions installed to cure the pitch-up attitude encountered during high altitude manoeuvres. Author's collection

Hunter F.6 XG290, following delivery to No. 19 MU, spent a large portion of its flying hours on miscellaneous trials for both the RAE and A&AEE. RAE Bedford

(Left) The pilot brings XG290 in close, to present the definitive gun-blast deflectors installed to prevent nose pitching, when an Aden salvo was fired. RAE Bedford

rounds were fired at high speed, with the complete ammunition load being discharged in one burst each time, the aircraft then returning to Dunsfold for rearming, following which it immediately took off for another sortie. On completion of firing 20,000 rounds, the whole gun pack was inspected and, after some very small modifications, reinstalled in the aircraft, XE543, for a second 20,000-round firing spell. To stop the nose pitching, a variety of gun-blast deflectors were tried, the most effective being a welded-steel box mounted in the mouth of each cannon port. A cascade of four vanes in each box channelled the blast away at 90 degrees to the fuselage, providing over 150lb (68kg) of upward thrust from each gun. As the blast deflectors stood proud of the nose contour by over an inch (26mm), they created a small drag factor, which just had to be accepted.

Early F.6s followed all previous Hunters in being fitted with a variable-incidence tailplane, activated by a button on the control column. During the Mark's production, a 'flying-tail' was introduced, which featured the standard power-operated elevator, combined with an electrically actuated follow-up. This altered tailplane incidence in conjunction with elevator movement, and was found to greatly improve longitudinal control at higher speeds.

The continuation of Contract No. SP/6/7144/CB.7a was to produce a second batch of 100 F.6s at Kingston and later a third, of 110 aircraft, from the same plant (although nineteen of this batch were to be transferred to Baginton). The first two true production F.6s, XE526 and XE527, were delivered to No. 5 and No. 19 MUs respectively, on 11 January 1956. Unfortunately, the Maintenance Units were flooded with Hunter F.4s and were unable to handle the new deliveries for some time. Consequently, it was October 1956 before No. 19 Squadron at Church Fenton in Yorkshire started to give up flying the Meteor F.8 and accepted XE561 to become the first squadron operating the Hunter F.6. Later in October, No. 66 Squadron at Linton-on-Ouse, which had been flying the Hunter F.4 for seven months, became the second F.6 squadron. The following month, No. 43 Squadron at Leuchars, No. 65 Squadron at Duxford (the Hunter F.6 being its last aircraft, as the squadron disbanded in March 1961, later to be reformed with Bloodhound ground-to-air missiles) and No. 111 Squadron at North

In 1956, No. 111 Squadron, based at North Weald, replaced their Hunter F.4s with the F.6 and, having been informed that they would form the official RAF aerobatic team the following year, chose a distinctive, overall glossy black finish for their display aircraft, in keeping with their Black Arrows title. A formation is seen here in the original version of the all-black finish, the aircraft nearest to the camera, Baginton-built XF416, later being converted to a Hunter FGA.9. The next aircraft in echelon, XG171, went to the Jordanian Air Force, and its partner, XG194, also became a FGA. 9. The banking-away formation is presumed to be the same aircraft. *Aeroplane Monthly*

Weald, all started receiving the new Mark. One other squadron to follow suit, in November 1956, was Waterbeach-based No. 63 Squadron, which two years later, in October 1958, became part of No. 229 Operational Conversion Unit (OCU) at

Chivenor in Devon. This OCU had been the main Sabre pilot training unit in 1954, before starting to receive Hunters the following year. For the next twenty years, it would be the largest and longest serving RAF operator of the Hawker aircraft. Dur-

ing No. 111 Squadron's time as the RAF's aerobatic team from 1957 to 1961, its aircraft were painted an overall glossy black, in keeping with their official title, the *Black Arrows*. The team went into aviation history and the record books at the

Led by Sqn Ldr Roger Topp in 1957 and Sqn Ldr Peter Latham in 1958, the Black Arrows' **markings were amended to have white outlines to the roundels and a small squadron crest replacing the Union flag on each aircraft's nose.**

Aeroplane Monthly

(Below and bottom) **Another Hunter F.6 that came off the Baginton production line, XF432 had a chequered career. It is seen here, with four 100-gallon (450-litre) drop-tanks , as 'E', with a squadron whose markings can just be seen either side of the fuselage roundel and is believed to be No. 208. Later it was returned to the manufacturer and converted to FR.10 standard, subsequently to be repurchased by Hawker Siddeley for resale to the Singapore Air Defence Command, as one of twenty-two Hunter FR.74Bs the country ordered. Before its delivery in November 1972, it was registered G-BABM to fly at the 1972 SBAC Display, where it carried the national flags of the eighteen countries that had purchased Hunters, over its Singaporean desert camouflage/blue underside paint finish.** *Aeroplane Monthly*

Farnborough bound. Two Kingston-built Hunter F.6s en route to the 1956 SBAC Display, XG128 with eight tiers of 3in (76mm) rocket projectiles on the outboard pylons and 100-gallon (450-litre) drop-tanks inboard. XG129 carries a quartet of asbestos phenolic 100-gallon tanks, both aircraft giving the impression of having had a fair spell of preparation for a CO's inspection! Some years later, XG128 was converted to FGA.9 standard, while XG129's refurbishment transformed it into a Hunter Mark 56A for the Indian Air Force, with the number A936.

Aeroplane Monthly

1958 Farnborough SBAC Display, when their sixteen aircraft formated with six other F.6s from different squadrons, to perform a twenty-two aircraft formation loop – not once, but twice. A world record that still stands and a sight not easily forgotten by those of us who saw it.

The following year, nine more squadrons re-equipped with the F.6. In the UK, No. 54 Squadron replaced its F.4s with the new Mark in January 1957, as did fellow Odiham occupier, No. 247 Squadron, in March. The same month saw No. 92 Squadron at Middleton St George in County Durham go through a similar operation, while No. 263 Squadron at Horsham St Faith in Norfolk, started operating the F.6 in place of their earlier Hunters in November. The *Black Arrows* had been disbanded in 1960 and, in 1961, No. 92 was selected as the Service's official display squadron. A sixteen-aircraft team was formed, titled the *Blue Diamonds* and they displayed for the next two years, until the squadron converted onto the Lightning. In Germany, the 2nd TAF replaced the Hunter F.4s of No. 4 Squadron in February 1957 and No. 93 Squadron in March with the new Mark, both squadrons being based at Jever. Oldenburg's No. 14 Squadron re-equipped with

(Above) No. 92 (East India) Squadron's first Hunter F.6s were not fitted with leading-edge extensions. The Squadron Commander, Sqn Ldr R. W. G. Freer, in XG229/'F', leads Flt Lts D. Arnold, DFC, A. Wright, Flt Lt M. Foster, in XG233/'J', in echelon formation. Flt Lt Wright's XG232/'G' was later converted to a Chilean Hunter FGA.71. *Aeroplane Monthly*

By July 1960, No. 92 Squadron had moved from Linton-on-Ouse to Middleton-St-George and, commanded by Sqn Ldr R. Dixon, formed the reserve aerobatic team for RAF Fighter Command, with the title the Falcons. The following year, the squadron became the official display team, as the Blue Diamonds. In this photograph, the top aircraft is Flt Lt Arnott's old aircraft, XG228, now fitted with leading-edge extensions and gun-gas deflectors, with the squadron's red/yellow checks being repeated across the base of the fins. From the formation, both XF520 and XG137 were later refurbished to FGA.73s for Jordan.
Aeroplane Monthly

1958 was the last year that the Hawker Siddeley Group entered a Hunter F.6 for individual display flying at Farnborough. XF389 was the seventeenth of Baginton's 100 aircraft production batch and is seen complete with 100-gallon (450-litre) drop-tanks , eight tiers of triple 3in (76mm) rocket projectiles, wing leading-edge extensions and gun-blast deflectors. At the same venue, XE618, a much earlier Kingston-built Mark 6 brought up to latest standard, was statically presented, with a forest of Dexion holding variations of armaments and stores the Hunter could deploy. XF389 was later converted to an FGA.73A for Jordan, while XE618, following refurbishment to FGA.9 standard and operating with No. 208 Squadron, is believed to have been transferred to the Kuwaiti Air Force.
Aeroplane Monthly

the F.6 in April, followed by No. 20 Squadron a month later. A year later, in June 1958, No. 26 Squadron was reformed at Ahlhorn with the Hunter F.6, while in the Mediterranean, Nicosia, on the island of Cyprus, hosted No. 208 Squadron who, in March had given up the Meteor FR.9 to commence operations with the new Hunter. In November the same year No. 263 Squadron, re-formed at Stradishall in July from the disbanded No. 1 Squadron and No. 56 Squadron, at Wattisham, both received the F.6. In squadron service, the Hunter F.6's automatic fuel system gave better flexibility of throttle control which, combined with a much improved rate of climb over the earlier F.1s and F.4s, made it a well-liked aircraft.

As an official decision had been made to develop the Hunter as a ground-attack aircraft, which involved a prolonged series of flight trials with an extensive range of external stores, the Hunter F.6 was to be the last pure interceptor Mark. A fourth batch of forty-five aircraft was built at Kingston, as was a fifth, this originally being for 153 aircraft, but 100 were cancelled in the notorious Duncan Sandys White Paper delivered on 4 April 1957. (For the uninitiated, the British Government's Minister of Defence stood up in the House of Commons on that day and announced that fighter development for the RAF was to stop!) This action would have repercussions later in the Hunter's history. Of the fifty-three built in the fifth batch, only twenty-one entered RAF service. The single order given to Armstrong Whitworth at Baginton covered 100 F.6s to Contract No. SP/6/9818/CB.7a and the last aircraft, XF515, took off for delivery to No. 5 MU on 4 December 1956 – although why it was delivered nearly two months later than XF527, the final Baginton F.6 built, has not been explained. A further order for fifty aircraft to be made at Blackpool against Contract No. SP/6/ 13132/CB.7a, was also cancelled, an action that resulted in the closure of the plant.

The ground-attack version was to be designated Hunter FGA.9. However, before this is detailed, the next aircraft in chronological order were the Marks 7 and 8 – the first two-seaters and the introduction of the Hunter to the White Ensign.

No. 208 Squadron was the first unit of the Middle East Air Force to be equipped with the Hunter F.6. Conversion to the new Mark was made at Tangmere and the squadron left for Nicosia on 20 March 1958. Before their departure, a photographic session produced these excellent portraits, all the aircraft depicted later becoming FR.10s. Much later, Baginton-built XF432/'E', XF441/'P' and XF428/'S' were refurbished to FR.74Bs for Singapore, while XF436/'H', and XF438/'R' became Mark 58s for Switzerland. Kingston-produced XE580/'F' became an FR.71 for Chile and, also from Kingston, XJ694/'D' was converted to a T.66E for India. Just why 'D's' XJ694 serial is in black, has not been confirmed.
Aeroplane Monthly and Author's collection

A trio of Hunter F.6s from No. 4 FTS, Valley. Baginton-built XF384/'72' *(top)* was photographed at an Upper Heyford Open Day, on 14 June 1969. It was lost in a collision at the Anglesea base, on 10 August 1972. XG274/'71' *(middle)*, from Kingston's third F.6 production batch, carried the unit's crest on its fin, when it appeared at Coltishall's Battle of Britain display in 1970. From the same production batch, XG185/'74' *(bottom)* was photographed at Bentwaters in 1973, sporting the School's new red, white and Light Aircraft Grey high-visibilty colour scheme, the crest again positioned on the fin. This aircraft is believed to have crashed three years later, while operating from the Naval Air Station at Brawdy.
George Pennick and Philip Birtles

Hunters Made for Two

In 1953, Hawker Aircraft recognized there would soon be a requirement for a two-seat trainer to replace the existing tandem-seating Meteor T.7 and side-by-side seated Vampire T.11. With orders for large numbers of Hunters well in hand, there was no shortage of finance within the company and consequently project number P.1101 was initiated to develop a trainer as a Private Venture (PV) based on the Hunter, up to the construction of a mock-up.

(Top) **The first prototype P.1101, two-seat Hunter, powered by a Rolls-Royce Avon RA21 engine, is seen with the early canopy that gave great airflow problems and started a prolonged schedule of hood-fairing trials. It was fitted with a pair of cannon, as originally proposed for the Hunter trainer, when this photograph was taken early in August 1955.** *(Below)* **A month later, resplendent in a coat of Cellon's 'duck-egg green', XJ615's participation in the flying programme at the 1955 SBAC Display belied the hood troubles. The aircraft was still referred to as the two-seat Hunter at this time.** *Aeroplane Monthly*

The aerodynamic shape of the Hunter lent itself to development in a tandem-seating configuration and it is on record that Sydney Camm preferred this, but prolonged discussions with instructors at the Central Fighter Establishment (CFE) and Central Flying School (CFS) left Hawker's project team in no doubt that a side-by-side seating arrangement was favoured by the Royal Air Force. By March 1955, the mock-up was nearly finished, with a canopy shaped as a double-bubble, schematically following the contours of the crew. Wind-tunnel testing revealed potential airflow problems for such a shape and the canopy was redesigned to a smoother, one-piece cover.

The front fuselage was designed with flowing lines that commenced at the standard Hunter nose-cone and expanded laterally to accommodate the instructor/student crew, both in Martin-Baker ejector seats, to a reduced width that married to the standard fuselage at the front transport joint adjacent to the wing-root air intakes. The four Aden armament was reduced to two guns, but this was something of a moot point between the manufacturer and the Service. While the length increased from the single seater's 45ft 10in (13.9m) to 48ft 10in (14.9m), the wingspan remained the same, at 33ft 8in (10.3m).

Air Ministry approval of the two-seat Hunter design having been given, Specification T157D was written around it, with a contract for the manufacture of two prototypes issued in July 1954. One main proviso of the specification was that trainer airframes could be made by converting fighters, if necessary, without too much trouble – accepting that this would have to be undertaken by the manufacturer. The question of canopy shape took an unexpectedly long time, so construction of the first prototype XJ615, was not completed until the end of June 1955. It was considered something of an interim aircraft and the smaller Avon RA.14 was installed, rather than the 200 Series engine. Following systems tests, XJ615 first flew from Dunsfold, on 8 July, piloted by Neville Duke. This would be the last time he undertook a prototype maiden flight for the company.

During the first few flights, an unpleasant buffeting was experienced that not only produced a high noise factor within the cockpit, increasing in severity with the aircraft's speed, but induced directional pitching and shaking. The enlarged canopy and fuselage cross-section was creating a greatly disturbed airflow, which would have to be rectified before any further development of the aircraft as a trainer could be considered. 'Bill' Bedford has said that when he was fly-

The original canopy design for two-seat Hunters, with a double-bubble contour, was constructed in wooden mock-up form, as shown here, but the configuration did not progress beyond this stage.
Hawker Aircraft

(Opposite) By the time aircraft started assembling for the 1956 SBAC Display, the hood-fairing shape had been finalized and the title Hunter T.7 applied to the aircraft. Seen here on the annual Arrivals Day air-to-air photographic session – for which a Fairchild C119, with the rear-loading doors removed, used to be employed by press photographers, although this may not be correct for 1956 – XJ615 is still fitted with a two-gun armament. Aeroplane Monthly

Taxiing at Yeovilton on 28 June 1971, Hunter T.7 XF321 was a Blackpool-built F.4 when it was first delivered to No. 33 MU, in February 1956. Conversion to two-seat configuration was made in 1958 and, when operated as '728' by the HMS Heron Station Flight, known as Heron Flight, the unit's emblem was carried on its nose.
George Pennick

XL571, the ninth production Hunter T.7, looking immaculate prior to being taken on charge by No. 229 OCU at Chivenor, in July 1958. Author's collection

ing XJ615, he could hear 'a noise like an express train racing through a tunnel'. The shock waves moved backwards as speed built up and were so dense that they were visible from within, as a halo around the rear segment of the canopy. Numerous positioning and grouping of vortex generators were tried, to stimulate the airflow over the canopy, but they were ineffectual, so it had to be accepted that a redesign of the whole canopy, with its hood fairing, was necessary. Nevertheless, XJ615 was flown at the 1955 SBAC Display in the company's 'duck-egg green' livery and titled the Hunter Two-seater.

(Above) **On 15 September 1973, No. 4 FTS, Valley, sent Hunter T.7 XL621/'81' to Coltishall's Battle of Britain display, with a white over-spray on the upper decking, spine, fin and rear fuselage. The reason for this white paintwork has not been confirmed, but it was often associated with air exercises.**

(Left) **A year later, all Valley's Hunters received a new red, white and Light Aircraft Grey colour scheme, as depicted here on XL609/'80', with the outer pylon ejector-gun fairings being absorbed into the wing roundel.** George Pennick and Author's collection

Modifications of various forms were tried, concentrated on the increased fairing cross-section behind the canopy and, in order to keep costs down, metal panels of varying shapes were used for the nearly two dozen different changes made, rather than having new moulds formed for different Perspex contours each time. Cliff Bore, a project engineer at Kingston – who later became the head of research at the plant – was handed the task of curing the trouble and by the spring of 1956 had produced a large, area-ruled canopy and

did have two 20mm Hispano 404 cannons but the Meteor T.7 had no armament at all. A good old British compromise was struck and the right-hand Aden was removed. In May 1956, gun-firing trials at high altitude were conducted with XJ615 and, as was to be expected in view of the aircraft being powered by an Avon RA.14, the old spectre of engine surging raised its ugly head. Now that the phenomenon was understood and it was considered that production aircraft would be powered by at least the Avon 121 or 122, which were not

XJ615 shortly after the finalized hood shape had been fitted, but aerodynamics decreed that it would be preferable to make provision for the parachute within the fuselage rear end. A trial shape hooding over the top of the jet orifice was tested on Hunter F.4 WT780 and a similar fairing was tried on XJ615. After some subtle refinement, the definitive shape was established and a 10ft 6in (3.2m) diameter GQ braking parachute was installed in the first prototype, deploying through two small upwards-opening doors in the

Kingston produced WV318 as a Hunter F.4 in 1955 and, at that time, it was one of only three of the Mark to be fitted with leading-edge extensions. In 1960, it was one of six converted to T.7 standard and later still, was one of four updated to a T.7A, with the servo-operated instruments coming into service on the Buccaneer. Here the aircraft lifts off, carrying the markings of No. 15 Squadron, who operated the Buccaneer S.2 at Laarbruch in 1971. *Aeroplane Monthly*

fairing shape, which completely eliminated all buffeting. The new shape was higher than the original and extended aft beyond the front transport joint. The attempt to keep the two-seat cockpit ahead of this point was a prime cause of the airflow breakdown, so it was a *fait accompli* that had to be accepted.

XJ615 had first flown with a pair of Aden cannons, but there was an element of doubt in the RAF as to whether the two guns were necessary – the Vampire T.11

prone to surge, the gun firing was adjudged successful. Pitch-down of the nose during firing did occur but again this had been mastered and a gun muzzle blast-deflector was fitted later, this being tailored to the two-seater nose configuration, rather than using the design used on the F.6.

Later in 1956, the decision having been made that the trainer would be equipped with a braking parachute, various shapes of housing were tried. A bullet-shaped housing was positioned above the jet outlet on

fairing. It showed off its new deceleration prowess at that year's SBAC Display at Farnborough, in a vivid orange and white colour scheme.

Approval for a second prototype P.1101, based on the Hunter F.6, was given on 31 May 1956 and XJ627, powered by a 200-Series Avon, flew for the first time on 17 November. With Hunter F.6s coming off the Hawker production lines, the Service anticipated that a trainer would be founded on XJ617 to replace the current Vampire

Kingston-built WV372's first flight took place on 15 July 1955 as an F.4. The following year it was damaged by an in-flight fire and, three years later, converted to Hunter T.7 configuration. Photographed here as 'R' of No. 2 Squadron in the late 1960s, it was loaned to the RAE for a period of continuation training and instrument trials, after which it flew with No. 4 FTS at Valley. Peter J.Cooper

Blackpool-built Hunter F.4 XF967 flew for seven years, before returning to Hawker Siddeley for conversion to T.8B standard for the Admiralty. It served with the Royal Naval Air Maintenance Unit (RNAMU) at Changi, but with the rundown of the Navy's Hunter squadrons, several aircraft were passed over to the RAF, XF967 being among them. It was photographed at Greenham Common, on 31 July, 1976, carrying the markings of No. 237 OCU. George Pennick

Taken at Chivenor in August 1974, XX467 had a varied career. Built at Kingston as a Hunter T.7, it first flew
on 14 October 1958, with the serial XL605, to serve with Nos. 66 and 92 Squadrons. In 1966, it was converted
into a T70 for Saudi Arabia, with their number 70/617, and they, in turn, loaned it to Jordan after the 1967
Six-Day War. The aircraft returned to the UK in 1972, was given the new serial XX467 and, after serving
with No. 229 OCU as '92', went on charge to the TWU at Brawdy. P. J. Cooper

Also photographed at No. 229 OCU, Chivenor, on 2 August 1974, Hunter T.7 XL592/'84', with instructor and
student pilot, takes off ahead of F.6 XF439/'26', to begin an early air-interception radar exercise. P. J. Cooper

T.11. But the MoS, aware F.4s currently in service would shortly become available as the Hunter F.6 started reaching squadrons, decided a Hunter trainer would be produced more cheaply by converting earlier Marks. Economy was also supposed to be the consideration with the unsophisticated Folland Gnat T.1 being ordered to supersede the Vampire, but, as it was unrepresentative of any operational aircraft in service with the RAF, this premiss was completely disproved and a lack of official reasoning displayed yet again.

seat trainer, but before construction had started the contract was amended and ten aircraft were transferred to the Admiralty for a Royal Navy requirement, these to be known as Hunter T. Mark 8. The re-location of production did not greatly affect the schedule and Frank Bullen took the first production T.7, XL563, for its maiden flight on 11 October 1957. This aircraft was delivered to the A&AEE at Boscombe Down on 19 December, who retained it for test purposes over a period of four years. After being loaned to Bristol

The first T.7s to reach the RAF went to No. 229 OCU at that lovely airfield location of Chivenor, on the mouth of the River Taw, in Devonshire. XL567 was delivered at the end of May 1958 followed, the next month, by XL570, which became the first T.7 to be lost when it crashed into Barnstaple Bay shortly after take-off on 29 August. Over a dozen T.7s were operating from Chivenor by the end of 1958 and single aircraft were issued to several squadrons that operated Hunter fighters, for instrument and general training flights.

WW664 was built at Blackpool as a Hunter F.4 and, following a forced landing at Ahlhorn in May 1956, was returned to Hawker Aircraft for repair. It was, in fact, rebuilt as the prototype T.8B, as photographed here and served with No. 764 Squadron at Lossiemouth, before again returning to Hawker's, who converted it to a T.75, serialled 514, for Singapore. Author's collection

Contract No. SP/6/12626/CB.9c was issued to Hawker Aircraft Limited for the production of fifty-five new-build aircraft for the RAF and the company scheduled the work to be undertaken at their Blackpool plant. However, the cancellation of fifty F.6s, which had resulted in its closure, forced them to make space at Kingston for the new work. The service designation Hunter T. Mark 7 was applied to the two-

Aircraft in 1961, to act as the chase aircraft during their trials with the disappointing Type 188, XL563 went first to RAE Farnborough and finally to the Institute of Medicine at the same location, before being struck off charge in 1984. Tropical trials for the trainer were conducted at Bahrain in July 1958 by XL566, which was modified to include cockpit refrigeration equipment.

Nos. 1, 54, 56, 65, 66 and 92 (Fighter) Squadrons were respectively the recipients of XL601, XL596, XL609, XL600, XL597 and XL605 during the year.

Further squadrons received individual aircraft during 1959. XL610 joined the *Black Arrows* of No. 111 (Fighter) Squadron on 23 January, while several specialist units, such as the Instrument Rating Squadron and the Day Fighter Leader

No. 764 NAS is represented by two Kingston-built, originally Hunter F.4s, which were both converted to T.8 standard as shown. With the squadron's green and white checks either side of stylized white scales on a black disc, WV322/'687' was present at Bentwaters on 25 May 1968, while WV363/'701' carries a four-tier rocket battery, together with a quartet of 25lb (11.3kg) practice bombs. George Pennick and *Aeroplane Monthly*

No. 899 NAS at Yeovilton had three Hunter T.8Ms, XL580, XL602 and XL603, on charge for airborne instruction on the Blue Fox radar fitted on the Sea Harrier FRS.1. They were specially modified at Holme-on-Spalding Moor, XL603 being the first and shown on RAE trials prior to going to Yeovilton. XL580/'719', resplendent in squadron markings in the static park at Mildenhall's Air Fete '86, appears to be minus a nose-wheel door but it is actually retracted. Author's collection and George Pennick

School of the CFE, both stationed at West Raynham, were allocated some two-seaters. Several fighter Squadron Flights, both in the UK and Germany, received T.7s, as did a unit in Aden and the Hong Kong-based No. 28 (Fighter) Squadron at Kai Tak.

During the year, students at Chivenor were involved in two separate incidents with their T.7s getting into inverted spins. This cast a shadow over the Mark as being prone to spinning vices, but a concerted series of trials were conducted by A Squadron at the A&AEE, in conjunction with the Empire Test Pilots School (ETPS) and Hawker. A Mark 6, as well as the Mark 7, was used for the trials and the Establishment cleared the aircraft as producing no real problems, although they concluded that it would not recover if other than the precise spin recovery action was used. They added that the Hunter had a disorientating spin which could become inverted if the controls, particularly the ailerons, were mishandled. If the pilot was unaware of the fact that he was inverted, recovery could prove impossible. It was concluded that the two original incidents would have to be attributed to pilot error, probably caused by the increased environment of the two-seat cockpit. Later in 1959 and again in 1960, 'Bill' Bedford demonstrated the spinning ability of a Hawker owned, civil registered two-seat Hunter, G-APUX, at Farnborough SBAC Displays. In the second year, he came down from 18,000ft (5,486m) in thirteen spins, with the smoke corkscrews hanging in the air for all to count. Despite this, a ban was put on intentional spinning by RAF squadron pilots which, I believe, has never been rescinded.

(Above) Possibly the only UK civil-registered aircraft with a pair of 30mm cannon, G-APUX, Hawker's Two-Seater demonstration aircraft, displayed not only flying and spinning abilities, but also the Hunter's basic design adaptability. The front fuselage was left over from the Indian Air Force order and was finished for display purposes, at the 1959 Paris Air Show. Following this, components from crashed Belgian-built F.6s IF-19 and IF-67, together with the engine from an RAF F.6, were all married together to produce the orange/white-finished, one-off Hunter Mark 66A. Shown here when engaged on trials of the longer, thinner version of the 230-gallon (1,046.5-litre) drop-tanks plus UHF radio, the aircraft had three years leasing to Middle East countries, before final conversion to a T.72, numbered J-718, for the Chilean Air Force. *Aeroplane Monthly*

One of the aircraft used by the ETPS in the spinning trials was Hunter T.7 XL574. It is shown in one of the modification stages, where a variety of anti-spin devices were installed. The amount of work involved can be gauged by the fact that the rear fuselage is stripped back to the metal, with a temporary serial number stencilled, while a camouflaged production fin has been fitted, with what has the appearance of a camera housing, placed on the dielectric tip. Hawker Aircraft

WV383 came off the Kingston/Langley lines in July 1955, as a Hunter F.4, which was damaged during a wheels-up landing the following year. On return to Hawker Aircraft, it was converted to T.7 standard, seeing squadron service in Germany and the Far East, before returning to the UK. In 1972, it was on the strength of the RAE, for continuation and instrument flying, finished in grey overall, with the Establishment crest on its nose. Two years later, still at Farnborough, but now with a blue nose-flash and tail-unit, the aircraft prepares to touch down. Peter J.Cooper and Author's collection

A pair of two-seat Hunters that never saw squadron service. The green and white XE531 *(top)* started
as an F.6 but, after being engaged on tropical trials, was converted to FGA.6 standard until, while still
at Dunsfold, the MoS ordered an aircraft for test-flying the forthcoming TSR.2's electronics. XE531 was
refurbished to two-seat configuration and, in 1963, became the unique Hunter Mark 12, which, apart from
prototype WB188, was the only airframe to never have any armament. Cancellation of the TSR2 saw the
aircraft retained by the RAE as a trials vehicle, until its demise in 1983. Author's collection

The first production T.7, XL563 *(bottom)*, first flew on 11 October 1957, its first year being spent on testing
programmes for first Hawker, then at the A&AEE. After being loaned to Bristol Aircraft, it was delivered
to the Institute of Aviation Medicine at Farnborough and was photographed at that location in 1971.
Peter J.Cooper

Hawker received an order in 1965 to install the TACAN navigation system in seven T.7s and a T.8, the selected aircraft returning to Kingston the following year for the conversions to be undertaken. The finished aircraft would be designated Hunter T. Mark 7As. Halfway through the work the contract was cancelled, with only four aircraft, XF289 (the former T.8), XL568, XL611 and XL616, having been converted.

One other two-seat airframe, which does not fit into the chronological order of

Royal Aircraft Establishment to conduct trials with a variety of avionics destined for the TSR.2; Hawker chose XE531 for conversion to two-seat configuration, without armament and fitted with an Avon 203. The aircraft was delivered to Farnborough on 8 February 1963 with a large vertical camera installed in its nose and a Specto Avionics head-up display (HUD), housed in a bulge above the nose in front of the windscreen, in readiness for trials associated with the TSR2's proposed terrain-following radar system. In his Budget speech

crashed on take-off at Farnborough on 17 March 1983.

New-build Hunter T. Mark 8 aircraft for the Fleet Air Arm (FAA) were taken randomly from the T.7 production line, their first, XL580, being the eighteenth airframe. It differed from production RAF aircraft by being fitted with an airfield arrestor hook (the T.8 was not stressed for carrier operations and was never considered for such use). The airfield arrestor hook had previously been developed on WT780, a Hawker-retained Mark 4 which

Photographed at Dunsfold before its first flight on 24 April 1959, following conversion to Hunter T.7 standard, originally Blackpool-built XF310 had spent more than two years as a F.4, on charge to Fairey Aviation Limited. The company used it as a flight-test aircraft for their Blue Sky air-to-air missile, which was named Fireflash when put into production. Hawker Aircraft

Hunters, was the single Mark 12, XE531. XE531, the thirteenth production F.6, first flew on 9 January 1956, undertook tropical trials that year and was then operated by Hawker Aircraft. Throughout the first half of the 1960s, one of the major projects occupying the designers at the British Aircraft Corporation (BAC) was the Mach 2+ strike aircraft being produced to General Operational Requirement (GOR) 339, the TSR.2. The MoS ordered an aircraft for the

of 6 April 1965, Chancellor James Callaghan announced the scrapping of the TSR.2 and XE531's *raison d'être* had gone. If production of the TSR.2 had gone ahead, further Mark 12s would have been produced for conversion training. The RAE at both Farnborough and Bedford operated XE531, finished in a pleasant glossy green and white colour scheme, for several years, during which time it operated with an early 'fly-by-wire' system installation, until it

had been engaged on a variety of test trials and featured in the forgettable film *High Flight*. Later, an RAF No. 26 (Fighter) Squadron F.4, WW664, which had crashed at Ahlhorn on 28 July 1956 and returned to Dunsfold for repair, was converted with a two-seat front fuselage, arrestor hook and Mod 228 wings, to act as the prototype Hunter T.8, first flying in this configuration on 3 March 1958. The trials programme, based at Boscombe

(Top left) When RNAS Yeovilton (HMS Heron) sent T.8C WV396/'748' to attend Coltishall's Battle of Britain air show in 1971, it looked far from the usual smartness associated with the Fleet Air Arm. The nose emblem of a blue stylized heron on a small white cloud was applied to Yeovilton Station Flight aircraft in that era. George Pennick

(Bottom left) Later, on 27 June 1992, a much smarter, overall dark sea grey T.8C, XF942/'869', flew from HMS Heron to an Open Day at RAF Honington. Author's collection

(Above) When it comes to being 'ship-shape and Bristol fashion', the first production Hunter T.8, XL580, was flown as an 'Admiral's Barge' for the Flag Officer (Flying Training) when photographed in 1976. Later, the aircraft was converted at BAe Brough into the third T.8M. *Aeroplane Monthly*

Prior to conversion to Hunter T.8M standard, as shown earlier in this chapter, XL603 originated as a T.8 that first flew on 6 December 1958. It served with the naval equivalent of an RAF OCU, No. 764 Squadron at Lossiemouth and then transferred to the Instrument Flight at RNAS Yeovilton, before the Blue Fox conversion. The aircraft, shown here as '738' on charge to Lossiemouth, was photographed in the early 1960s, carrying a bold 'NO STEP' legend on the drag-chute cover doors. Author's collection

Down, was very short compared with usual prototype testing, and delivery of the first production T.8 was made to the FAA at Royal Naval Air Station (RNAS) Lossiemouth, early in the summer. RNAS Yeovilton also received T.8s and construction of the ten new-build aircraft covered by the contract was completed when XL604 flew on 12 December 1958.

The balance of the forty-one Hunter T.8s that saw service with the FAA, was obtained by converting ex-RAF F.4s, the work being undertaken in three batches, the first of which covered seventeen airframes, followed by four additional aircraft converted to T.8Bs. These differed from previous naval aircraft by having the Aden cannon, plus the gun-laying radar, removed and being fitted with the current operational Tactical Air Navigation

(TACAN) system. The final conversion batch of eleven aircraft was designated T.Mark 8C, in which a partial TACAN system was installed. XL604, the last of the new-build T.8 airframes, was used as the test aircraft for this partial system and was considered the T.8C prototype. Later in their lives, many of the FAA trainers, of all three sub-marks, were modified to carry a Harley light for visual tracking, fitted in the extreme nose. Some also had further modification, to carry Bullpup missiles and 2in (52mm) rocket batteries.

Fleet Air Arm use of the Hunter T.8 was very intensive and the aircraft proved most popular. An average of over 2,000 flying hours was achieved by the majority of aircraft, with a small number seeing service as Station Flights on FAA shore-based stations abroad. A further three, XL580 and

XL584 from the new-build contract, plus a conversion airframe, XE665, were specially prepared by Hawker Aircraft for No. 764 Squadron Flag Officer Flying Training (FOFT), HMS *Heron*, at Yeovilton in Somerset. Fitted with two 100-gallon (455-litre) drop tanks, these aircraft were prepared in a special glossy blue/grey and white colour scheme, with the Admiral's flag painted on the nose. For obvious reasons, within the Service they were colloquially known as 'Admiral's barges'.

Utilization of the two-seat Hunter by the Navy continued in 1980 when at least three, XL580, XL602 and XL603, again from the new-build contract, were converted to provide airborne instruction on the Blue Fox radar system, fitted in yet another naval aeroplane with its roots in Kingston, the Sea Harrier FRS.1.

CHAPTER TWELVE

Ground Attack Par Excellence

(Top left) **A pair of Hunter F.6s, of Church Fenton-based No. 19 Squadron, are brought close in. The aircraft nearest to the photographer's Meteor T.7, is flown by Major Richard G. Newell of the USAF, who was Commanding Officer at that time.** Author's collection

(Bottom left) **Back to the nest. The tenth of the 100 Hunter F.6s built at Baginton was progressively upgraded to FGA.9 standard, but not designated as such. It is currently displayed at the Midland Air Museum, situated on the north side of the Baginton airfield, which is now Coventry Airport. The aircraft's last operational use was as '15' with No. 1 TWU, where it carried the markings of No. 79 'shadow' Squadron.** Author's collection

When the Armistice was signed on 11 November 1918, fighting ceased in the majority of the world. However, the British Empire – upon which 'the sun never sets and which is red on the map' – included Mesopotamia (later called Iraq), where the rebellious Arab chiefs in the Northern Territory of Kurdistan, kept eight squadrons of the RAF occupied, including No. 8 (Fighter) Squadron.

In 1945, World War II ended with another signing ceremony, but in the Middle East things were not very different from 1918, except that the claims for territory under British control were being made at full national level and over a broader area. The timetable for a formal withdrawal from the Persian Gulf and Aden Protectorate was drawn up, but it did not satisfy dissident tribesmen and localized operations in many areas involved the RAF, again including No. 8 Squadron, which reformed in September 1946 at Khormaksar in Aden. They progressed over the next fourteen years through half-a-dozen different bases in the Middle East, with the Mosquito FB.6, Tempest F.6, Brigand B.1, Vampire FB.9 and two Marks of Venoms.

The de Havilland Venom was fast becoming the victim of fatigue, and in

If you are going to have a backdrop to a photograph, make it a good one. The Middle East Command's aerobatic team, of four Hunter FGA.9s from No. 208 Squadron, based at RAF Khormakson, put in some formation rehearsal time, against the snowcap of Mount Kilimanjaro, in Tanzania. Author's collection

1958 it was decided to re-equip the RAF in the Middle East with newer ground attack aircraft. The two types being officially considered, on the grounds of cost, were adaptations of existing trainers, the Hunting–Percival Jet Provost and the Folland Gnat. Both types were prepared for trials in Aden, with pilots from the Air Fighting Development Squadron (AFDS) assessing their comparative abilities with the armaments required to fulfil the role. The Hunter was thought uneconomical for the conditions, but Hawker Aircraft did some

modified by a combined RAF and Hawker team at Horsham St Faith, to carry two 230-gallon (1,046-litre) drop-tanks on the inboard pylons. The post-war closure of many overseas bases created longer distances between those remaining active and the UK, thus making the carrying of the larger tanks a necessity. Cockpit ventilation was increased to cater for the prevailing higher temperatures and, due to the small size of so many Middle East airfields, the tail parachute unit developed on the two-seat trainers was fitted, but the

for a new operational application – and not a single new aircraft would be built. The whole schedule was to be undertaken by a masterpiece of refurbishment by Hawker Aircraft and service Maintenance Units.

During the development of the FGA.9's external stores carrying ability, a great variety and permutation of weapons was flown on adapted F.6s. The Mod 228 wing, with its four pylons, meant the Hunter could be fitted with 100-gallon (455-litre) or 230-gallon (1,046-litre) fuel tanks, or 100-gallon (455-litre) tanks used as napalm

XE615 operated as a Hunter F.6 for three years, until being modified, by the RAF and a Hawker Working Party, at Horsham St Faith in 1959, to FGA.9 standard. It is seen here, while serving with No. 1 Squadron at West Raynham, with the tail-code 'G'. In 1970, it was one of the twelve aircraft converted to Hunter FGA.74s for Singapore and given the RSAF number '508'. George Pennick

high-level lobbying and two F.6s, XK150 and XK151 were drawn from No. 5 MU and flown out to Aden to participate in the comparative trials.

While both the officially proposed aircraft performed reasonably well, they were not in the same league as the Hunter and the not-unexpected outcome resulted in the Hawker aircraft winning hands down. It was confirmed as the Hunter FGA.9, for issue to the Service and thirty-six F.6s were

diameter was increased to 13ft 6in (4.1m). These aircraft, which retained the Avon 203 engine, were referred to as Mark 6/Interim Mark 9s but none actually reached overseas bases. Later, most of these aircraft were re-engined with the Avon 207 and modified into production standard FGA.9s.

There followed a unique episode in the history of the RAF. A new Mark of an existing aircraft was to be put into service,

bombs, on any of them. With the FGA.9's strengthened wings, each inboard pylon could be fitted with a 1,000lb (454kg) or 500lb (227kg) bombs, a cluster of six 3in (78mm) rocket projectiles, a honeycomb battery containing twenty-four or thirty-seven 2in (52mm) folding-fin rockets, or a carrier holding a pair of 25lb (11.34kg) practice bombs. Outboard pylons could be removed and individual positions could be adapted to carry four Mk12 rocket rails,

One of nine Hunter F.6s converted to FGA.9 standard by the RAF at No. 5 MU Kemble, in 1965, XG194/'A' taxis at Coltishall on 18 September 1971, in the markings of No. 79 Squadron, when it was a component of No. 229 OCU. George Pennick

No. 54 Squadron took their Hunter FGA.9s to Waterbeach in November 1961 and stayed there for two years, before transferring to West Raynham. While at Waterbeach, they performed a tactical support role with No. 38 Group, Transport Command and, during this time, Baginton-built XF523/'N' was photographed firing a salvo of 3in rockets from the old-style rails used, prior to Matra-type pods becoming standard.

Aeroplane Monthly

each fitted with three 3in (78mm) rocket projectiles; or four 3in (78mm) rocket projectiles with 60lb (27.22kg) heads, interchangeable with rocket launchers produced by Oerlikon, Bofors or Hispano. The standard Hunter four 30mm cannon armament was fully operational irrespective of any external store carried.

The fitting of the larger 230-gallon (1,046-litre) tanks necessitated the cutting away of a portion of the landing flaps, the outboard corner on each being sculptured in an arc. These tanks, originally considered for ferry flights only, were now no longer jettisonable, as a small bracing strut had been fitted between each one and the underside of the wing, in order to clear the installation for combat. A fully tropicalized refrigeration/ventilation system and an increased oxygen supply were developed for the operational aircraft, the first of which, XG135, originally built at

Kingston in the third batch of F.6s, took to the air as an FGA.9 on 3 July 1959, powered by a surge-free Avon 207.

The increasing tension in the Middle East, prompted the re-equipping of No. 8 Squadron at Khormaksar with the Hunter FGA.9 in January 1960, as a deterrent to Iraq's believed hostile intentions against Kuwait. A number of pilots had converted on the Hunter T.7 in the UK during 1959, the squadron currently flying the Venom FB.1 plus a Meteor FR.9 Flight. They returned to Khormaksar to convert the rest of the squadron, whose Venoms had been replaced by FGA.9s by the spring.

In the UK, No. 1 Squadron at Stradishall received its first Hunter FGA.9 in January 1960, followed in March by its neighbour, No. 54 Squadron, and by No. 208 Squadron, who had re-formed at Nairobi from No. 142 Squadron, operating the Venom FB.4, before moving to

Stradishall for conversion to the Hunter FGA.9. By June, No. 208 Squadron, with its complement of Hawker ground-attack aircraft, returned to Nairobi, sending detachments to Khormaksar's ranges prior to another move to Bahrain the following month. The Iraq/Kuwait conflict did not materialize and No. 208 Squadron returned to Kenya, pending that country's independence, when they again took up postings in the Middle East – in time for the next troubles. These involved the State of Yemen, with its new Imam, and the anti-British President Nasser of Egypt.

No. 43 Squadron at Leuchars had replaced its Hunter F.6 with the FGA.9 and, in June, transferred from Scotland to the Mediterranean island of Cyprus. With the increasing pressures in the Yemen, the squadron deployed to Khormaksar to join Nos. 8 and 208 Squadrons, so that when British troops eventually became drawn

On 21 June 1961, No. 43 Squadron, with its Hunter FGA.9s, deployed to RAF Nicosia and a pair of them are seen displaying the Fighting Cocks black/white checks relocation from the rear fuselage, to the aircraft's nose. Both aircraft were later converted to FGA.74s for Singapore, XJ684/'D' becoming '513' and XJ680/'F', '511'. *Aeroplane Monthly*

No. 45 Squadron, which disbanded as a Canberra squadron in February 1970, was re-formed at West Raynham with Hunter FGA.9s for a tactical training role, on 1 August 1972. The squadron moved to Wittering on 29 September and operated for nearly four years. In these two photographs, some of the external differences from earlier Marks are evident, the braced-for-combat 230-gallon tanks on the wing inboard pylons, the outer pylon ejector-gun fairings, the nose IFF aerial and lengthened cartridge case ejector chutes being among them. After these photographs, taken in March 1973, the individual aircraft identification letter system was replaced by numbers. *Aeroplane Monthly*

Tengah, Singapore-based No. 20 Squadron, commanded by Sqn Ldr C. M. Bacon, was heavily involved in the defence of Malaysia, against Indonesian incursions, in the mid-1960s. XJ683/F, armed with 3in rocket projectiles, flies past Pulan Tioman, a jungle-covered mountainous island off the east coast of Malaya.
MoD (RAF)

into the conflict in December 1963, three squadrons of Hunter FGA.9s were available for support. Nos 43 and 208 Squadrons made raids against insurgent positions at Fort Harib, together with numerous frontier guard posts, on many occasions and, by the following May, the main ground fighting was over, leaving the two squadrons to engage in sporadic raids on individual dissident bands in the Radfan, north of Aden, before they too dispersed. An analysis of the operations showed that in the 527 missions collectively flown by the two squadrons, over 176,000 rounds of 30mm ammunition had been fired, as well as 2,500 rocket projectiles. While the older 3in (78mm) rocket

was not the most accurate of missiles, its 60lb (27kg) warhead made it a very useful weapon against the sandstone rock fortifications encountered during the campaign.

From the operations in the Middle East and its first deployment in combat, the Hunter FGA.9 came out very well, with nearly all problems being either climatic or environmental in origin. Lack of sufficient hangar space forced all servicing, except major component replacements, to be done in the sea-salt and dust-laden outdoor atmosphere, where daytime temperatures were seldom much below 40°C. Wear on the Aden cannons due to dust ingress caused frequent gun-pack changes

but their operating ability was only occasionally impaired. Flying in low-level visibility of less than 400 yards (366m), due to wind-borne sand and high humidity haze, presented new operational hazzards, so the fact that there was only one pilot fatality during the whole campaign speaks well of the standard of flying – and the resilience of aircrew who entered cockpits with temperatures approaching 45°C.

The Hunter first saw service in the Far East (euphemistically referred to as 'East of Suez') when No. 20 Squadron, having been disbanded at Gütersloh on 30 December 1960, was re-formed at Tengah, Singapore on 1 September 1961 with the

What a difference ten years can make. At the 1948 SBAC Display, de Havilland Vampire FB. Mark 5, VV218, was displayed with examples of its hardware – 'display' being a rather euphemistic term! In 1958, a Hunter FGA.9 was presented at a Dunsfold photocall, to show that it had a certain margin over the Vampire, although the Fireflash and Firestreaks at the extremities of the exhibits, did not get into operational service with the aircraft. Author's collection and Hawker Aircraft

FAG.9. Five months later, the Kai Tak, Hong Kong-based No. 28 Squadron ended an eleven year association with de Havilland, having flown Vampires then Venoms, when it too started to receive FGA.9s in May 1962, this being the squadron's first Hawker aircraft since its Burma operations with Hurricane IVs in 1945.

Further colonial unrest arose the following year, when the formation of Malaysia was opposed by Indonesia. Uprisings started in the Sultanate of Brunei and Sarawak, where British troops, with elements of the Gurkha Regiment, received air support from No. 20 Squadron, who were directed by a flight of Prestwick Pioneer CC.1s that the squadron operated as Forward Air Control aircraft. Sporadic engagements with guerrilla bands continued through 1963 but when the state of Malaysia was formed in September, an undeclared war saw the Indonesian Air Force operating B-25 and F-51 aircraft, together with more modern acquisitions from the USSR. Il-28 and Tu-16 bombers, together with MiG-17, -19 and -21 fighters, augmented the World War II types in raids during the five-year conflict. The RAF, for their part, employed detachments of No. 45 Squadron Canberras with No. 64 Squadron Javelin FAW.9s, both operating from Tengah, Singapore, who later were joined at the same base by the Victors of Nos. 15 and 57 Squadrons.

Besides many attacks on ground fortifications, the Hunter FGA.9s of No. 20 Squadron acted as fighter escorts to RAF transports undertaking supply drops to British troops in the jungle. The Argosys, Valettas, Hastings and Beverleys that were all used at various times, presented a new discipline to the Hunter pilots, who were much more accustomed to the individual low-level rocket and cannon attacks for which they had been trained. During the Middle East operations, the climate presented conditions for which allowances had to be made when planning sorties. The same applied in the Far East. Tropical storms could break out without any advance notice and No. 20 Squadron pilots learned to keep a good eye on the fuel gauge, in case a diversion from home base should be required at the end of a mission. Despite the large number of sorties flown by both sides during the conflict, there was no actual air-to-air combat, although there are reports of a Hunter/MiG-17 engagement, where aerobatics seem to have taken precedence and no firing button was pressed.

The Hunter FGA.9s of No. 20 Squadron were on active service throughout the dispute and spent various times operating from the airfields of other South East Asia Treaty Organisation (SEATO) members, which included a six-month deployment in Thailand. After the signing of a peace treaty on 11 August 1966, the squadron remained to cover the withdrawal of land units. A detachment of Royal Australian Air Force F-86 Sabres joined them until the New Year, but it was to be 18 February 1970 before the squadron was disbanded at Tengah and returned to Germany where, on 1 December it was re-formed as a Harrier GR.1 squadron, operating out of Wildenrath. Although it took no active part in the Indonesian operations, No. 28 Squadron remained at Kai Tak until it was disbanded on 2 January 1967.

A total of 128 Hunter F. 6s were converted to FGA. 9s – including the Mark 6/Interim Mark 9s – the work being placed in six separate contracts. Number two covered the thirty-six interim aircraft at Horsham St Faith and number six was for nine aircraft converted by No. 5 Maintenance Unit at Kemble in Gloucestershire. The remaining four contracts were placed with Hawker (which, since the end of the 1960s, was known as Hawker Siddeley Aviation Limited), in aircraft batches of forty, thirty-one and two of six. The type operated as the RAF's main strike aircraft, with ten front-line squadrons, among them being Nos. 1 and 54 Squadrons at West Raynham, which made headlines in the national papers when they tried to sink the stricken oil tanker *Torrey Canyon* in 1967. In the mid-1970s, many Hunter FGA.9s were transferred to the Tactical Weapons Unit (TWU) at Brawdy, high on the south-east headland of Pembrokeshire in Wales, where they joined the Unit's F.6s.

With all the earlier problems overcome, the Hunter was now a first-class aeroplane and very much liked by pilots everywhere. The refurbishments that produced the FGA.9 were indicative of its robustness and the re-cycling programme was to be continued still further, for overseas customers, who were encouraged by the operational records in the Middle and Far East. The British services were not finished with the Hunter either.

CHAPTER THIRTEEN

Cameras and Solo Matelots

The small saving grace for the Supermarine Division of Vickers-Armstrongs Ltd, in their unhappy Swift saga, was the FR. 5, which served with No. 2 (Fighter Reconnaissance) Squadron at Geilenkirchen and Jever, plus No. 79 Squadron at Gütersloh. It proved to be a useful and fast reconnaissance aircraft, in the four to five years that it lasted, although long before the last one was 'demobbed' in March 1961, the Ministry of Supply was issuing a contract for the Hunter to be prepared as a replacement.

Hawker had recognized the possibility of a reconnaissance requirement much earlier, seeing the Meteor FR.9 as the type to be replaced. The Mark 4 WT780 that they retained from the production line as a trials aircraft has already been mentioned with the testing of the arrestor-hook installation for the Fleet Air Arm's T.Mk.8. Test flights of WT780, complete with a forward-facing oblique camera in

the nose, proved the feasibility of the photo-reconnaissance concept and the company held the results of the trials in readiness for what they were sure would be an RAF requirement.

They were not wrong and Air Ministry Specification FR.164D showed Service interest in an eventual Swift, as well as Meteor, successor. This prompted Hawker to utilize another production-line-retained aircraft, XF429. This was one of the single production batch of 100 Mark 6 aircraft that Armstrong Whitworth constructed at Baginton, and the trial installation of three oblique cameras, one forward facing and one facing either side of a new nose-cone, was given its first flight by Hugh Merewether on 7 November 1959. The camera bay did necessitate the removal of the standard gun-ranging radar but this was not considered too problematic. XF429 was established as the Hunter FR. 10 prototype, with the standard

FGA.9 external tank-carrying ability and braking parachute. Besides the three cameras, the FR.10 would have a UHF radio replacing the standard VHF and an additional radio compass installed.

The MoS issued a contract in 1959 for thirty-two aircraft, to be manufactured by another refurbishment programme undertaken by Hawker Siddeley. Work started soon after receipt of the contract and five aircraft were completed by November 1960. XE585 is believed to have been the first aircraft delivered, when it went to No. 19 MU on 28 November , before being allocated, the following month, to No. 4 Squadron at Gütersloh. Deliveries to the squadrons continued through 1961, No. 2 Squadron at Jever also replacing its Swifts in March with the FR.10. The squadron joined No. 4 Squadron at Gütersloh in September and this airfield, in the Nordrhein area of Germany, became the principal North Atlantic Treaty Organization (NATO) tactical

Baginton-built XF429 came off the line as a F.6 which, in 1959, was modified to become the prototype Hunter FR.10 seen here, with three oblique cameras in a new front fuselage nose-piece and ' Mod 228' wings. Following five years' RAF service, the aircraft was bought back by Hawker Siddeley for conversion to one of fifty-two Mark 58As supplied to Switzerland, between 1971 and 1975, with the Swiss AF number J-4131. Hawker Siddeley

(Above) Kingston's second batch of Hunter F.6s produced XE585, in April 1956 and it was returned to Hawker Aircraft, for conversion to FR.10 standard, three years later. In this mode, it served with No. 4 Squadron at Gütersloh and was photographed as 'A' at Soesterburg. Hawker Siddeley repurchased it in 1971 and the aircraft was finally refurbished to a Hunter T.66E for India, delivery being made in December 1973. George Pennick

No. 738 NAS, equipped with Hunter GA.11s, moved to Brawdy on 1 January 1964 and, while there, was selected to provide a four-aircraft aerobatic display team, with the appellation Rough Diamonds. Seen in formation, the Squadron's Pegasus badge is carried on each aircraft's nose, with the team leader, in XE680/'789', distinguished by additional dayglo paintwork on his aircraft's nose and spine. All four aircraft were converted F.4s and, following the team's disbandment in 1969, WT804/'782' became a member of the later-formed Blue Herons, while WV257/'790' was refurbished by Hawker Siddeley, to Swiss Hunter Mark 58A, J-4125. Aeroplane Monthly

reconnaissance base for the rest of the decade, controlled by the Tactical Operation Centre and operating over an area ranging from the Mediterranean to Norway. The two squadrons each had a separate team of Army Ground Liaison Officers, who worked with a Mobile Field Photographic Unit. The units processed the film at the end of each sortie, after which experienced photographic interpreters evaluated the frames and passed their observations into the NATO system.

The Hunter FR.10 quickly became accepted as the consummate low-level, high-speed visual reconnaissance aircraft and the annual NATO competition for this class of aircraft, *Royal Flush*, saw the two squadrons frequently beating American, French and German participants, by virtue of the Hunter's superior flexibility and manoeuvrability under operational conditions. A flight from No. 2 Squadron deployed to El Adem, fifteen miles south of Tobruk, in October 1963, to join in the British Joint Services' Exercise *Triplex West*, held to evaluate the practicality of reinforcing the Mediterranean Theatre from the United Kingdom at short notice.

A year later, when the Yemen crisis escalated, exercises were replaced by reality. No. 1417 Flight operated as an intrinsic part of the Khormaksar-based Tactical Wing, equipped with Meteor FR.9s. The Hunter FR.10, having proved its superiority over other contemporary photo-reconnaissance types in NATO, was scheduled to replace the Tactical Wing's Meteors, and three of the Flight's complement of four aircraft, among them XE589, went to Khormaksar as an element of the RAF's Aden Strike Wing, in time for the Radfan operations. Many hundreds of target photographs were produced by the FR.10s, to supplement the rather meagre maps of the area and thereby reduce the time to track down ground targets. The Flight also kept Headquarters aware of any likely reinforcements destined for the dissident bands and post-engagement positions were filmed for assessment by the ground forces.

By the middle of June 1964, when the Radfan risings had abated, No. 1417 Flight's Hunter FR.10s had flown nearly 120 sorties, during which many thousands of frames had been exposed, while Aden cannon firing had accounted for nearly 8,000 rounds of ammunition. The Flight encountered the same climatic problems as the Hunter FGA.9s, which were amplified by the steady, low-level flying requirements necessary to obtain

useful photographic records. Hunter FR.10s of No. 1417 Flight left the Middle East and returned to the UK for disbandment. Much later, in 1981, the Flight was re-formed and equipped with Harriers, prior to deploying to Belize in Central America. A number of FR.10s were to undergo refurbishment yet

again, for overseas customers. Thts will be detailed in a later chapter.

The final Mark of Hunter to be operated by British armed forces, resulted from a Royal Navy demand for a single-seat weapons trainer to augment their existing T.7 and 8s. In 1961, a contract was issued

Coltishall's Battle of Britain Air Show, on 18 September 1971, saw Hunter FR.10 XE626/'9', of the No. 79 Squadron component of No. 229 OCU. Hawker Siddeley purchased the aircraft in August 1972, by which time it had flown over 1,800 hours. Two years later it was delivered to Kenya, as a Hunter FGA.80, numbered 803. George Pennick

XF977 was originally built at Blackpool, as a Hunter F.4 which first flew on 17 May 1956. Early in 1962, it was returned to Hawker Siddeley and converted to GA.11 standard, to meet the Admiralty requirement for a single-seat weapons training aircraft. It first arrived at No. 739 (Training) Squadron, Lossiemouth, on 2 October and later went to Short Brothers at Belfast, to be one of the few fitted with reconnaissance camera in the nose, re-designated Hunter PR.11As. It is seen here in this configuration as '735', on the strength of FRADU at RNAS Yeovilton, firing a salvo of 2in spin-stabilized, unguided, folding-fin RPs, from rocket pods on its outboard pylons. Author's collection

A rather untidy line-up of assorted Hunters at Greenham Common, on August 1, 1976. In the foreground are
five GA.11s, of Airwork Services' operated FRADU, beyond which is a Yeovilton-based T.8, which also has
a Harley light fitted in the extreme nose. Beyond stands an A&AEE T.7, with an ETPS two-seater in
'raspberry ripple' behind and WB188 is parked ahead of the whole line. WT804/'831' was a previous
member of the Rough Diamonds. George Pennick

WT806, first flown on 31 March 1955, was opne of the last Hunters built in Kingston's first batch of F.4s.
It suffered damage during a high-g turn and had to be returned to Hunter for rebuilding. In 1962, it was
converted to GA.11 standard and is seen taxiing at the Mildenhall 1980 Air Fete, as a member of the Blue
Herons **aerobatic team.** Author's collection

Hunter GA.11 WT711/'833', photographed in April 1997, has been standing behind Air Atlantique's T.2s at Baginton, for some time – not too apposite though, as it was originally built at Kingston. The origin of the double diamonds and 'D's on the fin, has not been established. Author's collection

by the Admiralty, to Hawker Siddeley, for the conversion of forty F. 4 aircraft and the designation Hunter GA.11 was allocated to the new naval aircraft. The TACAN navigation system installed in the T.8 was required for the GA.11, as was the fitting of an airfield arrestor hook, while the Aden cannons and their associated removable pack were to be discarded.

RAF and Hawker inventories were examined to determine which F.4s had the lowest airframe hours and the selected aircraft were transported to Kingston-upon-Thames for refurbishment, the first arriving towards the end of the year. An ex-No. 43 Squadron aircraft, XE712, was the first GA.11 to be completed, delivery to the A&AEE for acceptance trials being made on 6 April 1962. On completion of the trials, XE712 went to No. 738 Naval Air Squadron (NAS) at Lossiemouth until 1 January 1964, when the squadron moved to Brawdy due to congestion at the Scottish airfield. The GA.11s

were finished in a smart glossy epoxy paint scheme of Extra Dark Sea Grey upper surfaces and white below, although a few, including WT809, had a white dorsal spine. No. 764 NAS also operated the aircraft at Lossiemouth, with its main task being the training of Air Warfare Instructors.

About two dozen of the Mark 4s selected for conversion were fitted with pre-Mod 228 wings and, as such, could only be fitted with inboard pylons. The balance of the contract, with the stronger wings, had provision for four pylons, those outboard equipped for practice bombs or transferrable with a cluster of rocket projectile rails. Some Naval GA.11s followed the T.8C in having provision for a Harley light in the nose for tracking when the aircraft was serving as a target. The FAA operated its single-seat Hunters on a variety of weapon-training programmes, while they also conducted experimental trials with a view to either the Philco Sidewinder or Martin Bullpup air-to-air

missile systems being installed on the aircraft, but these did not come to fruition. Several aircraft went to Short Brothers at Belfast, to be fitted with reconnaissance cameras, on the lines of the RAF FR.10 (but without armament), and in this configuration were re-designated PR.11s.

The Admiralty planned to increase its strength of GA.11s, but this was thwarted by the Treasury's decision to curtail further purchases of the aircraft and, consequently, a small number of standard Hunter F.4s were transferred to the FAA for a limited period. Eventually, GA.11 operations were mainly confined to the Fleet Requirement Unit (FRU) and the Air Direction Training Unit (ADTU), which were amalgamated to form the Fleet Requirement Air Direction Unit (FRADU), based at RNAS Yeovilton in Somerset. The FRADU contract was operated by Airwork Services Limited, using the aircraft for radar calibration flights, as well as simulated air attacks on Naval units out of

Portland and Portsmouth. In 1965, the Fleet Air Arm proposed forming an official aerobatic team and No. 738 Squadron was selected to work up a display programme. A four-aircraft formation was selected, using GA.11s and named the *Rough Diamonds*, which were based at RNAS Brawdy. Their Hunters flew in standard FAA colours apart from the leader, who carried dayglo bands on the nose and spine. The team was disbanded in 1969, but six years later, in 1975, several civilian pilots at Yeovilton's FRADU thought it was about time that the air branch of the

Senior Service should have an aerobatic team again. Serviced by Airwork Limited, a flight of GA.11s was formed and, being based on HMS *Heron*, was named the *Blue Herons*. It was unique in being a service aerobatic team managed by a civilian organization, but sadly they succumbed to the dictates of the auditors in 1980.

Without their Aden cannon and link-collector boxes, the Royal Navy single-seat Hunters looked very sleek – especially when they flew, as they sometimes did, without underwing pylons. They came nearest in semblance to the original

P.1067 prototypes, apart from the ventral airbrake. But even with its excrescencies, the Hunter always was – and is – a good-looking aeroplane and its virtues go much deeper than mere appearance.

UK Squadron Service

Royal Air Force
(Mark 1) Nos. 43, 54, 222 and 247;
(Mark 2) Nos 257 and 263;
(Mark 4) Nos 3, 4, 14, 20, 26, 43, 54, 66, 67, 71, 74, 92, 93, 98, 111, 112, 118, 130, 222, 234, 245 and 247;
(Mark 5) Nos. 1, 34, 41, 56, 208, 257 and 263;
(Mark 6) Nos. 1, 4, 14, 19, 20, 26, 43, 54, 56, 63, 65, 66, 74, 92, 93, 111, 208, 247 and 263;
(Mark 9) Nos. 1, 4, 8, 20, 28, 43, 45, 54, 58 and 208;
(Mark 10) Nos. 2, 4, 8 and 79.

Royal Navy (Fleet Air Arm)
(Mark 8) Nos. 700, 736, 738, 759, 764, 800 and 899;
(Mark 11) Nos. 738 and 764.

The four-Hunter GA.11 Fleet Air Arm Blue Herons aerobatic team, formed in July 1975 and flown by Airwork Services' pilots, constituted the first time in the world that a team of civilian pilots flew military jet aircraft, to represent a Service. The team won second prize in the Shell Trophy Competition at the Greenham Common-staged International Air Tattoo and were outright winners in the following year's event. RNAS Yeovilton

(Below) Hunter GA.11 WW654/'833', a member of the 1976 Blue Herons team, shows the stylized heron painted on the outer face of its drop-tanks. This aircraft, originally a product of Blackpool's first F.4 batch in March 1955, was converted to Admiralty requirements in September 1962 and was new to the aerobatic team when photographed at Greenham Common. George Pennick

CHAPTER FOURTEEN

Further UK Operators

It is indicative of the Hunter's value, that nearly every government establishment had aircraft of various Marks on their inventory at some time. Furthermore, several RAF units flew examples, although their use was not directly connected with the unit's role.

Operational Conversion Units (OCUs)

The larger of the two Operational Conversion Units engaged in the training of Hunter pilots was No. 229 OCU. At the end of World War II, there were many Operational Training Units (OTUs) in existence, among them No. 61 OTU which, since June 1941, had been a fighter training unit until it was disbanded in June 1947 and some of its aircraft entered the inventory of a newly formed No. 203 Advanced Flying School (AFS), in the same month. Two years later, No. 203 AFS was re-designated No. 226 Operational Conversion Unit. With the acceleration of Vampires and Meteors entering front-line squadrons, the requirement to supply fully-trained day fighter pilots to operational standard, was too much for one unit to meet. It was therefore decided, in1950, that No. 226 OCU, at its Stradishall base in Suffolk, would concentrate on pilot conver-

sions for Meteor squadrons, while a new No. 229 OCU handled Vampire squadron needs.

No. 229 OCU transferred to Chivenor on 28 March 1951, and in 1954 became the unit to produce pilots for the new Canadair-built Sabre, filling the gap in RAF Fighter Command until British transonic fighters were available. These appeared the following year and Hunter F.1s started landing at Chivenor in April 1955, one of the earliest arrivals being WT575, the twenty-first production aircraft, which had previously spent nine months at A&AEE, Boscombe Down. Further F.1s came from No. 5 Maintenance Unit and the first twelve-week Hunter pilot conversion course started on 15 May.

Hunter F.6, XK149, from Kingston's last single-seat production batch, served with Nos 1 and 54 Squadrons, before becoming '44', as a No. 79 Squadron component of No. 229 OCU, in the 1970s. It was photographed at a Lakenheath Open Day on 14 May 1988, in company with fellow-squadron aircraft '30' and Lightning F.3 'Q', of No. 5 Squadron. George Pennick

Landing at Chivenor on 1 August 1974, Hunter F.6 XK141/'51' of No. 229 OCU, carries the markings of No. 234 'shadow' Squadron, which only operated Hunters from May 1956 to July 1957 and they were F.4s. The fact that the aircraft is in such pristine condition, bears witness to its recent service at No. 5 MU Kemble. Peter J. Cooper

Seen being towed past Trident 4R-ACN of Sri Lanka's Air Lanka, at de Havilland's Hatfield airfield on 5 July 1969, No. 229 OCU Hunter F.6 XF420/'29' shows signs of recent gun firing. George Pennick

Fresh courses started every three or four weeks and this set the pattern for many years. New and ex-squadron aircraft joined the OCU and every Mark of RAF Hunter was used at some time. The Unit became the largest user of the type and seven 'shadow squadrons' – Nos. 63, 79, 127, 131, 145, 229 and 234 – were allocated, should the number of front-line squadrons need reinforcing, and the crests of many of these squadrons were applied to aircraft at the Unit. Over nineteen years of operations made No. 229 OCU the longest-serving RAF Hunter unit and its workload was very intensive. I well remember sitting, with my camera, in the sand dunes of Croyde Bay, about three miles from the threshold of Chivenor's operating runway, one summer day. There seemed to be a continuous stream of Hunters coming out of the base. My dog barked his disapproval of every one – he never shared my aeronautical leanings!

Hunter F.4, XF941, flew with No. 234 Squadron markings, as did T.7 XL575. The

Taking off on 1 August 1974, Baginton-built Hunter F.6 XG164/'64' was the only No. 229 OCU aircraft flown in the high-visibilty colours adopted by No. 4 FTS. It is believed that this aircraft was later transferred to the FAA. Peter J. Cooper

Alconbury Open Day, 3 August 1991, saw Hunter T.7A XL616/'D', from No. 237 OCU, in the static display, with No. 111 Squadron markings on its nose. The aircraft served with the Unit on future Buccaneer aircrew requirements, being fitted with some of that aircraft's instrumentation. George Pennick

F.6, XF383 carried No. 145 Squadron's crest, while XE608, another Hunter F.6, flew with the markings of No. 63 Squadron, from the Day Fighter's Conversion Squadron (DFCS). When that unit disbanded at West Raynham, in 1965, its aircraft formed No. 229 OCU's Weapons Instructor Flight. No. 79 Squadron operated some FR.10s and on its disbanding on 30 May 1970, it is known that XG168 joined the Chivenor-based conversion unit.

Because Chivenor, on its own, was unable to handle the RAF's increasing requirement for Hunter aircrew, in 1956 No. 233 OCU was formed at Pembrey, five miles west of that heart of Welsh rugby, Llanelli. About two dozen Hunter F.1s were used, the majority coming from the first two production batches, representative aircraft being WT615, WT620 and WT634 from Kingston/Langley, while WW604, WW605

Landing at Mildenhall on 8 June 1984, Hunter T.7 WV372, of No. 237 OCU, Honington, was a Kingston-built
F.4, which suffered fire damage when the jet-pipe parted company with its Avon, in November 1956. The
conversion to two-seat configuration was made during repairs, following which it served at Jever and
Gütersloh during the 1960s. In 1977, the aircraft moved to No. 4 FTS, before going to Honington for
Buccaneer aircrew familiarization. George Pennick

Hunter T.7A XL614/'O' was a regular participant in Air Show static displays, during the latter half of the
1980s and was photographed at Wattisham on 24 June 1989, by which time the OCU emblem had been
moved from the nose to behind the cockpit. Having first flown as a Mark 7, on New Year's Day 1959, in the
hands of Hugh Merewether, it was converted to 7A standard and served with No. 402 Weapons Training
Squadron at Sylt, before joining No. 237 OCU at Honington in 1971. George Pennick

and WW609 came from the Blackpool lines. No. 233 OCU lasted barely a year as a Hunter unit, but on 1 January 1970 it reformed as the principal OCU for Harrier pilots – covered later in this chapter.

A third Hunter-operating unit was constituted at Honington, in Suffolk, in 1971. This was No. 237 OCU, with an entirely different agenda from the previous two. The Blackburn (later Hawker Siddeley) Buccaneer S.2 had come into service, when sixty-two ex-Fleet Air Arm aircraft were transferred to the RAF's Nos. 12 and 15 Squadrons at the base. The Buccaneer was not fully dual-controlled, consequently the OCU was formed, using both ex-RAF and -FAA two-seat Hunters, to fulfill the new type's aircrew requirements. Some of the Hunters were modified to carry Buccaneer instrumentation, with T.7s XL568 and XL601, plus TACAN-equipped T.8B XF967, being representative of the Unit's aircraft. No. 237 OCU lasted for twenty years, during which time it moved from

Honington to Lossiemouth, where it was disbanded in 1991. Two years later, at least five assorted two-seaters remained operational there, training future Maritime Buccaneer Wing pilots – and among them being the new-build T.7 XL568, first flown on 6 March 1958 and converted as one of the four Hunter T.7As in 1963.

Central Fighter Establishment (CFE)

Shortly after the end of World War II, the CFE moved from Tangmere to the Norfolk airbase of West Raynham. The Establishment was a large organizaton, responsible, not only for evaluating the tactical and operational abilities of new fighter aircraft but also for the training of leaders for fighter squadrons. In the mid-1950s, it comprised the Air Fighting Development Squadron (AFDS), the Day Fighter Leader School, to be renamed the Day Fighter Combat School

(DFCS), an All Weather Development Squadron (AWDS), a Signals Squadron and the Instrument Rating Flight.

A vast miscellany of different types of aircraft operated from West Raynham and the AFDS is said to have had, over the years, every Mark of Hunter on its inventory at some time, although there is some doubt about the FR.10 and the single Mark 12 did not come into contact with the Establishment, as it was not a service aircraft. The first two Hunters to be retained by the AFDS were the twenty-third and twenty-fourth production F.1s, WT577 and WT578, both delivered on 5 July 1954. Later in the same year, the first service Sapphire-powered F.2, WN895, passed through the DFCS before going to No. 263 Squadron, while WN911 was the first F.2 operated by the AFDS. Two-seat Hunters began arriving in the autumn of 1958, three of the earliest being T.7s XL591 and XL593, both delivered in September, and XL595 a month later.

Evaluation of the Hunter's operational proficiency, with all its various armaments, was undertaken at West Raynham by the CFE. Typical of weapon layouts examined, were the twenty-four 3in (76.2mm) rocket projectiles carried by F.6 XG128, flying with the Mod 228 wings before the retrofitting of leading-edge extensions. The 36 R.P load, demonstrated by a late production F.6 at the 1957 SBAC Display, was not cleared for operational use by the RAF. *Aeroplane Monthly*

A small aside in West Raynham's history with the Hunter took place shortly after the 2,000yd (1,829m) runway had been resurfaced. When the runway was wet there had been a spate of Hunters landing, applying the Maxaret brakes, but carrying on down its full length and going off onto the rough grass at the end. Squadron Leader Ron 'Jock' Harvey of the RAE Aero Flight was sent to investigate, as other Hunter bases were not experiencing any similar problems. He found that the new runway surface was very smooth but with indentations that were not allowing the water to drain away. He introduced the procedure, on landing, of pulling the stick fully back after the brakes had been applied, thereby using the elevator to increase the downforces on the tyres (long before Formula One racing cars used rear spoilers). The

landing accidents at West Raynham in wet conditions were eliminated.

In 1959, both the AWDS and AFDS moved further east across Norfolk, to Coltishall, their attentions being turned to getting the new English Electric Lightning operational. The Hunters of the DFCS remained until October 1962, when the CFE at West Raynham was closed.

No. 4 Flying Training School (FTS)

It was in April 1921 that No. 4 FTS was initiated and for twenty years it functioned with various RAF biplanes, in the Middle East. Following World War II, it had periods of flying in the old Southern Rhodesia (now Zimbabwe), then in the UK with the

Vampire T.11, followed by the Gnat T.1. The School became established in 1958 at Valley, on the Isle of Anglesey where, from 1967, Hunter F.6s became the principal type operated, XF384, XF420 and XG274 being representative of them. Two-seat T.7s, which eventually became the School's most numerous Mark, also came onto the inventory, with new-builds XL567 and XL622 being among them, so that the FTS usually had about two dozen aircraft available for advanced pilot training at any one time.

In 1971, a new colour scheme was devised to make training aircraft more visible and Valley's aircraft started to appear in this red/white/ Light Aircraft Grey livery. Two years later, the FTS formed an aerobatic team of F.6s called the *Dragons*, resplendent in the high-visibility scheme.

Valley-based No.4 FTS's No. 3 Squadron received a new red, white and Light Aircraft Grey colour scheme in the early 1970s. Of the aircraft shown in this line-up, taken in July 1973, XF509/'73' had been used in 1963 as a chase plane at Filton, for early flight trials of the Fairey FD.2 WG774, after its conversion to the BAC 221.

Nos. 1 and 2 Tactical Weapons Units (TWUs).

The Tactical Weapons Unit, formed in 1974 at Brawdy, was considered a transition unit to gradually phase pilots between No. 4 FTS and the Operational Conversion Units. Its programmes covered weapons training and operational tactics, as well as the techniques of operating at low level. As the Unit received its F.6s, 'in-house' conversions were made to install the

1978, the TWU was divided into two separate Units, Brawdy re-equipping with another product of the Hawker Siddeley drawing boards, the Hawk. The Hunters flew up to Scotland, where No. 2 TWU was formed at Lossiemouth, staying for another two years before moving again to Chivenor, and also receiving Hawks. Representative Hunter F.6s at Brawdy were XE608, XE627 and Baginton-produced XG154, with T.7 XL572 also known to have served there. The Hunters that went to Lossiemouth

every single aspect of military, together with a lot of civil, aviation in Britain has come into contact with the A&AEE at some time. All aspects of the Hunter's evaluation as an RAF aircraft transpired through Boscombe Down, consequently very many individual airframes passed through a myriad of testing programmes.

Numerous Hunters were put on charge to the Establishment over the years, to be used as flying test vehicles for service equipment and armaments, not directly associated

Several Hunter F.6s were gradually updated to virtual FGA.9 standard, but still retained the earlier Mark designation – XG160/'22', from No. 1 TWU at Brawdy, photographed at RAF Wattisham on 8 August 1981, being an example. George Pennick

tail-parachute, as fitted on the two-seaters and F.9s that were also in service at Brawdy. A more major one-off conversion was conducted on Hunter F.6 XE606, which had a set of Mod 228 wings fitted, following which it became the sole Mark 6A.

Nearly seventy Hunters were in use when the TWU was at full strength, with Nos. 63, 79 and 234 'shadow squadrons' available, should a time of crisis arise. The geographical location of Brawdy, on the south-west coast of Wales, was not exactly conducive to all-year-round flying. Courses overran their due completion dates and the supply of qualified pilots to operational squadrons slowed down. Therefore, in

included F.6s XE582, XE624, plus another Armstrong Whitworth product, XG155, while T.7s XL583 and XL619 are known to have been on charge to No. 2 TWU.

Aircraft and Armament Experimental Establishment (A&AEE)

The Establishment's title was bequeathed on 20 March 1924, when it operated from Martlesham Heath in Suffolk. The move to Boscombe Down in Wiltshire coincided with the outbreak of World War II and

with the type *per se*. Such an example was XE601, assigned to the Comptroller (Air), Ministry of Supply, in the second batch of 100 Kingston/Langley-built F. 6s, without the wing leading-edge extensions and first flown on 2 May 1956. Many modifications were incorporated over the years, including the fitting of a Mod 228 wing, with a view to the testing of various armaments, including rocket pods, free-fall bombs and the ballistic analysis of unguided weapons. It is known to have been repainted in the 1970s in a new Light Aircraft Grey and red colour scheme, and was displayed in a revised ETPS colour scheme at the 1995 Fairford International Air Tattoo.

Nearly forty years of continuous operation with the same unit is displayed, as the A&AEE's Hunter F.6 crosses the threshold at Fairford's 1995 International Air Tattoo. Author's collection

Empire Test Pilots' School (ETPS)

Another resident of Boscombe Down is the ETPS, which was formed there as 'The Test Pilots' School', in a collection of Nissen huts. Course No. 1 ended on 29 February 1944 and, later in the year, the official name 'Empire Test Pilots' School' was registered, reflecting the growing number of students from the colonies. The School moved to Cranfield in 1945 and to RAE Farnborough in 1948, before returning to Wiltshire in 1968.

Several single-seat Hunters have been on charge to the ETPS, including the eighteenth production F.1 WT572, F.4 XF970 and the third of Baginton's only F.6 production batch, XF375. In the early 1980s, a vivid new red, white and blue colour scheme was applied to the School's permanent aircraft, the scheme colloquially known as 'raspberry ripple'.

Currently T.7s XL564 and XL612 are on the strength of the School's fixed-wing fleet and are believed to be the only two swept-wing aircraft in the world that are routinely intentionally spun, erect and inverted. They are fitted with telemetry data transmitters and special head-up 'spin panels', supplementary to the conventional instruments, positioned on the eyeline of each pilot, to give positive information on the direction of spin. Inverted spinning can be very disorientating, even

to experienced pilots. The panels give both the tutor and student direction of turn, with left-or-right-roll, back-up red and green lights, plus a single-needle altimeter, calibrated from 40,000ft (12,192m) to 10,000ft (3,048m). A female recorded tape advises 'recover now' at 25,000ft (7,620m) and 'eject now!' at 10,000ft (3,048m). Three gauges also indicate the position of the ailerons, rudder and the aircraft's angle-of-attack. These Hunters are only flown on the course, after the ETPS student has completed five spinning flights in the School's Jet Provost and Hawk aircraft.

Royal Radar Establishment (RRE)

Possibly one of the most enigmatic of all British aviation research establishments, which, from the 1940-titled Telecommunications Research Establishment (TRE) and 1953-retitled Radar Research Establishment (RRE), was granted the 'Royal' title in 1957. In the same year, flying by the Radar Research Flying Unit (RRFU), which had operated out of Defford near the Worcestershire market town of Malvern, was transferred to Pershore in the same county. One of the first Hunters to touch down at RRE Defford was the third production F.1, WT557, on which the type's radio trials were conducted.

Some Hunter F.4s were used by the Establishment in the mid-1950s, WV325 known to have been one of them. At least two F.6s, WW594 and WW598, from the first seven-aircraft Kingston production batch, were employed in the RRE's evaluation of Red Steer, which was shared with Vampire WP240. Red Steer was a development of the AI20 radar, perfected for installation as the V-bomber force's tail warning system.

Royal Aircraft Establishment (RAE)

Based at Farnborough in Hampshire since April 1918, the RAE expanded to the ex-World War II airfield at Thurleigh in Bedfordshire in the early 1950s, this later to become RAE Bedford and remain the Establishment's only experimental flying base.

Connection with Hunter development possibly began with WT571, the seventeenth production F.1, before it had experimental area-rule bulges fitted (referred to in a later chapter). RAE's Aero Flight received the aircraft on 9 April 1954, for the type's general handling assessment as a fighter, this being undertaken by the Flight's Sqd Ldr Harvey. Another early Hunter/Farnborough association was made when WT570 arrived for testing of the fully power-operated ailerons, in July 1954. The sixth production F.2, WN893, was one of the first Hunters to be specifically

XL612 was one of the forty-five new-build Hunter T.7s that came from Kingston and was first flown by Frank Bullen on 12 December 1958. After RAF service at Sylt and Leuchars, the aircraft went on charge to the ETPS in 1983, where it is used for the deliberate spinning and recovery section of a student's course. When seen arriving at Fairford's International Air Tattoo in 1995, it displayed the fact that, in a recent overhaul, an ex-RAF camouflaged fin had been fitted. Author's collection.

The third of the first batch of seven Hunter F.6s, WW594 was designated the P.1109A. It was used as the aerodynamic and flight-test aircraft for the AI20 radar adapted as a guidance system for the DH Firestreak air-to-air missile, with much of its time being spent at the RRE in the late 1950s. Although the electronic side of the system was installed, missiles were never fitted on this aircraft, which is arguably the best looking of all Hunter variants. In 1961, it was converted to FR.10 standard and, fourteen years later, was refurbished yet again, as an FGA.70 for Lebanon, with their serial L.282. Hawker Aircraft

WW598, first flown on the last day of 1955, was the last of the first seven F.6s and it too was modified to P.1109 aerodynamic standard. It spent nearly twenty years with the RAE at Farnborough and Bedford, as a member of the Establishment's High Speed Flight, during which time it participated in a series of tropical low-level gust research programmes. In 1975, this aircraft was also converted to FGA.70 configuration for Lebanon and was delivered with the serial L.280. Author's collection

A late production F.6 from Kingston, XG290 was first flown on 20 November 1956 by David Lockspeiser and, following delivery to the A&AEE, had an undisclosed history. A rare photograph was taken when it was fitted with a nose probe, for an RAE Bedford research programme. RAE Bedford

allocated to the Establishment, where it arrived in August 1954 and, so far as is known, remained.

XE531, the single Mark 12, built for the RAE to evaluate the projected TSR-2 radar, was delivered to Farnborough on 8 February 1963. Following the annihilation of the TSR-2, much of its life was spent at the Establishment and, in fact, ended there, when the unique aircraft crashed while taking off on 17 March 1982. Hunter T.8 XF321, received in 1976, was also a long-serving RAE aircraft until it crash-landed in July 1985, while yet another two-seater, T.8M XL602, became an RAE-operated test-flying airframe for the Harrier Blue Fox radar system, in the early 1980s.

Central Flying School (CFS)

One more RAF unit with a long history is the CFS, formed at Upavon in Wiltshire on 19 June 1912. The Cotswolds' plateau at Little Rissington received the School, from Hullavington, in May 1946 and it remained there for thirty years, with the task of training instructors.

Within the School is the Handling Squadron, whose brief is to compile Pilot's Notes for operational aircraft and, in the course, uses representative Marks of each type. The majority of Hunter Marks passed through the Squadron, with F.4 XF943, which carried the CFS Type Flight crest and F.6 XK148, this having been transferred to the School from Boscombe Down. Although the Hunter was not involved, the CFS has also been responsible for the operations of the RAF Display Team *Red Arrows*.

Station Flights

Many RAF bases, both in the UK and overseas, operated a small flight of single, or occasionally two, aircraft unassociated with the role of the base's main squadrons. The Flights were maintained to provide inter-unit personal communications by senior officers, on a more economic basis than using the squadron's front-line aircraft – the use of a Vulcan to convey a single officer to another station would be guaranteed to raise questions relative to tax-payers' money! Colloquially, the Flight's aircraft were known as 'squadron hacks'.

The two-seat Vampire T.11 and Meteor T.7 were the mainstay of these Flights for many years, but the availability of Hunter T.7 aircraft in the late 1950s and 1960s, together with some single-seat F.4s, saw the earlier types struck off charge. In the Middle East, Nos. 8 and 43 Squadrons, based at Khormaksar, used T.7s XL615 and XL613 respectively. In Germany, over the years, Gütersloh held XL619 and XL618, the latter transferring to Jever where it joined XL622 and F.4 XF315, while the Geilenkirchen Station Flight operated another F.4, XF950. At Oldenburg, F.4 WV260 was on its Flight's charge and RAF Sylte used several similar Marks, including XF370.

In the UK, the Wattisham Station Flight is known to have used Hunter T.7 XL600, Linton-on-Ouse operated F.4s WV392, WV393 and WT809, at various times,

while the Middleton St George Flight had Baginton-built F.4 XG165. It is believed that current service expenditure cuts have eliminated the Flights altogether.

Fighter Weapons School (FWS)

Formed at Leconfield in Yorkshire on 1 January 1955, the School was a retitling of the Central Gunnery School, which had existed at the airfield for ten years. The School was charged to supply operational squadrons with qualified Pilot Attack Instructors.

An early F.1 on charge to the School was WT614. The eighth F.4, WT708, together with other F.4s, WT739, WV264 and WV376, is known to have served with them until the FWS was disbanded three years later, on 3 March 1958.

Harrier Conversion Unit (HCU)

When the RAF started receiving the Hunter's successor from Kingston, the Harrier GR.1, which had endured a rather prolonged gestation from the Hawker P.1127, via the Hawker Siddeley Kestrel, RAF Wittering in Cambridgeshire was established as the UK operating base with No. 1 Squadron. Parallel with this, No. 2 Squadron was set up at Wildenrath in Germany. At Wittering, the HCU was formed on 1 January 1969, to convert experienced operational pilots onto the Harrier and exactly one year later the title No. 233 Operational Conversion Unit was resurrected and bestowed on the Unit.

Several ex-squadron Hunter FGA.9s had formed the basis of the HCU, to be used by

instructors, who formated with Harrier pilots in the early flights on their new aircraft. Only one aircraft, XF430, has been verified as serving with the HCU and the Unit was run down as No. 233 OCU became more established. The ultimate fate of HCU aircraft has not been confirmed.

Martin Baker Limited

On Wednesday 24 July 1946, Bernard 'Benny' Lynch literally took his life in his hands when he made the first live ejection from a flying aircraft in Britain. The aircraft, Meteor Mark III EE416 and its Martin-Baker Mark 1 seat, are displayed in the London Science Museum, standing as symbols of the pioneering work that has enabled over 6,500 aircrew to walk away from disaster.

Martin-Baker ejection seats were installed in every Mark of Hunter, the single-seat aircraft being fitted with either the Type 2H, with thigh guards, or Type 3H featuring a leg-restraining harness. The pulling of the firing blind initiated canopy jettisoning in both types. Two-seat Hunters had the Type 4H seat as standard and trials of future production seats were conducted on the Avon RA.28-powered, second prototype P.1101, XJ627, the type that was expected to form the basis for the Hunter trainer.

Being on loan from the Hawker Siddeley Group, the aircraft was delivered from Dunsfold to the Martin-Baker airfield at Chalgrove in Oxfordshire, the scene of 'Benny' Lynch's pioneering ejection, on 19 November 1958. It had previously spent seven months at the A&AEE, following its

XJ627, the second prototype P.1101 and powered by a 200-series Avon RA.28, was the Hunter trainer that the RAF thought it was going to receive. First flown on 17 November 1956, it was employed at Boscombe Down, before being delivered to Martin-Baker for a ten-year period of ejector-seat trials. In September 1968, the aircraft was returned to Hawker Siddeley and converted into a T.72 for Chile, with their serial number 721. Author's collection

maiden flight on 17 November 1956, and was now resplendent in a new blue and white colour scheme, carrying the Hawker Siddeley Group logo either side of the nose. During the ten years that XJ627 served with Martin-Baker, many high-speed and low-level trial ejections were made and they fabricated a metal protective shield for installation between the two seats. For test-firing flights, which were made from the right-hand side of the cockpit, the Plexiglass was removed from the canopy on that side and the trajectory of the ejecting seat only just missed the central frame member.

on the AI23 radar trials programmes conducted for the forthcoming Lightning. When a second piece of equipment, the Pilot's Attack Sight (PAS) development of the standard gyro gunsight, was produced as part of the overall Airborne Interception Radar and Pilot's Attack Sight System (AIRPASS) for the supersonic interceptor, Hunter T.4 WT736 was allocated to join the FFU, to assist in the flight trials.

Having served with Rolls-Royce at Hucknall as a trials aircraft for the Avon 121, WT736 was collected from the

craft, but the Hunter did become a bit of a problem for the Unit. It periodically developed faults in the fuel system, often due to failure of the booster pump, which meant that Houston sometimes could not select fuel, despite their being plenty on board. Leuchars received several unscheduled arrivals by the aircraft, for the problem to be sorted out.

WT736 carried out its last trip for the Ferranti Flying Unit in November 1958, following which it flew down to the CFE at West Raynham for their PAS evaluation trials and thereafter ceased associa-

A product of Kingston's first batch of Hunter F.4s, WT736 first flew on 4 February 1955 and went to the FFU, from Hucknall, the following year. It is seen on Ferranti's Turnhouse hardstanding and is remembered as being plagued with faults in its fuel system. The aircraft was scrapped in November 1964, after only just over 385 flying hours. Author's collection

Ferranti Limited

Now titled GEC Ferranti, the original company commenced operating the Ferranti Flying Unit (FFU) at Turnhouse airfield, five miles outside Edinburgh, on 8 August 1952, with an ex-RAF Dakota C.3 TS423. The FFU was the airborne proving unit for the company's Trials and Installation Division (TID), which worked in close collaboration with both the RRE and RAE. Several Canberras and Meteors joined the FFU at various times

engine-maker's airfield in November 1956 by an ex-No. 222 Squadron pilot, Flying Officer Len Houston, who, having already completed his ETPS instrument rating in October, had joined the FFU in the same month. The PAS was installed in the Hunter early in 1957, following which the aircraft was flown to Boscombe Down for 'A' Flight pilots to conduct live firing trials. WT736 undertook many PAS trial flights for the FFU, who used what is believed to have been the longest serving Meteor, NF.11 WD790, as the target air-

tion with Turnhouse. Len Houston was scheduled to fly the Unit's first Lightning, XG312, and the FFU was forced to base these operations at Warton as the Turnhouse runway was 500ft (152.4m) too short for regular operations with the aircraft. As XG312 did not arrive with the Unit until 9 May 1959 and as Houston had been flying the Meteor for the past few months, he had to go to Farnborough to re-acquaint himself with a high-performance swept-wing aircraft – and, naturally, it was another Hunter.

CHAPTER FIFTEEN

Overseas Production

There is no doubt that the advent of the MiG-15 in the air forces of the Warsaw Pact, caused a considerable stir among NATO ranks. The Organization's front-line defences were based on the Vampire, Venom and Meteor, plus a smaller number of F-84 Thunderjets, all of which were, being charitable, bordering on obsolescence. European members of the Treaty were drifting towards dependence on the support already being provided by the North American continent, which, in itself, was not an ideal situation for anyone, either side of the Atlantic.

The North Korean invasion of South Korea on 25 June 1950 had shattered post-war complacency and this, coupled with a worsening of relations with the Communist bloc, had generated a sudden flush of orders to the European aircraft industry, for which it was financially unprepared. This situation initiated a United States Congress move to pass the Offshore Procurement (OSP) Bill, whereby America would provide the funding, thereby enabling Allied companies to meet the demands made upon them.

On 10 July 1952, Neville Duke flew the P.1067 prototype WB188 at the Brussels Air Show. The display enhanced the existing opinion that this aircraft should be in the forefront of NATO's considerations for a next generation interceptor. A US Air Force evaluation team, including such luminaries as Major General Albert Boyd, Colonel Frederick J. Ascani, Lieutenant Colonel Richard L. Johnson plus Major Charles E. Yeager, had been briefed to opine on the various aircraft being considered for OSP funding and Dunsfold received a deputation on 22 October 1952. Both WB188 and WB195 were flown by American pilots, following which glowing

A fine photograph of the prototype P.1067 WB188, whose demonstration in the hands of Neville Duke, at Brussels, laid the foundation for American Off-Shore Procurement contracts being placed for Belgian and Dutch Hunter production. Author's collection

testimonies were given, including the consideration that they handled 'as well as any aircraft in the world today'.

While the Hunter did not feature in the original October 1952 OSP orders, a second group of contracts was placed in April 1953, which not only covered production for the RAF but made finance available for licensed manufacture by continental

Licensed Production in Belgium

In 1954, an agreement was signed whereby 112 Hunter F. Mark 4s would be licence-built by Avions Fairey in Brussels and SABCA, the production to commence in 1955, with completion the following year. The Belgian serial numbering

Devils) aerobatic display team for a long time. From 1957 to 1965, they flew five overall-red Hunter F.6s at air shows all over Europe and revelled in their aircraft's agility. The *Musée Royal de l'Armée* displays F.4 ID-46, which, for some reason, is marked as IF-70 – in reality, an F.6 which was repurchased by Hawker Siddeley and converted to an FGA.57 for Kuwait.

Four of the 112 Hunter F.4s produced in Belgium, for the BAF, taxiing in line-astern. The aircraft carry the unit code of the 7th Ecole de Chasse, the country's Hunter OCU based at Chievre, plus a white horse motif on their red nose trims. Author's collection

countries for their own air forces, which were an integral part of NATO. OSP contracts were signed for sixty-four Hunters to be built in Belgium and forty-eight in Holland, the aircraft to replace the Meteor F.8s currently in service with the Belgian and Royal Netherlands Air Forces. The two countries had followed the tribulations of earlier Marks and the funding related to the Hunter F.4, with provision for two inboard wing drop-tanks, plus the two rear fuselage tanks being replaced by wing bag-tanks. Both countries increased their required numbers by individual local funding, but the OSP finance enabled production lines to be established for further later Marks.

system featured two letter prefixes followed by the number, positioned similarly to RAF aircraft, and the Mk4s ran from ID-1 to ID-112. They served with the *Force Aérienne Belge/Belgische Luchtmacht/* Belgian Air Force (BAF) 1st Wing at Beauvechain, 7th Wing at Chièvre and 9th Wing at Bierset. Manufacture of 144 Hunter F. Mark 6 aircraft followed the last Mk4, keeping the production lines open until late 1958. Serials of the later Marks ran from IF-1 to IF-144 and only the BAF's 7th and 9th Wings received them, the 1st Wing replacing its Mk4s with the twin-engined Avro Canada CF-100 all-weather fighter. Belgium's Air Force has operated *Le Diables Rouges* (The Red

It has been said that Belgium's experience with the Hunter left something to be desired. Some of them suffered from a lack of reliability, which could not always be rectified by Hawker Aircraft due to their commitments for the RAF. Many of the aircraft were taken out of service to be put in storage and relations between Hawker and the Belgian Government became worse when ninety-four Hunters were bought back by the aircraft manufacturer, for a scrap-metal unit price. A subsequent payment made by Hawker, when the aircraft had been converted and resold, was considered to be only a token on their part.

Belgium produced a total of 256 Hunters of the two Marks, the first sixty-four having

Belgian Hunter F.6, IF-93, was photographed at B111/Ahlhorn, during a NATO exercise in 1961. The aircraft was bought by Hawker Siddeley in 1964 and converted to Hunter FGA.59A, serial 698, for Iraq.
D. Meward via George Pennick

been paid for by the United States, under the OSP Bill. As mentioned, ninety-four were repurchased by Hawker Aircraft and five (IF-12, IF-33, IF-47, IF-82 and IF-102) are known to have been lost through accidents. The subsequent history of two repurchased aircraft has been well documented. The centre and rear fuselage of Mark 6 IF-19 were married to the wings, fin and

rudder of another Mark 6, IF-67. An ex-RAF ground display two-seat front fuselage was grafted on, for the whole airframe to be given the Avon RA.28 from a Baginton-produced F.6, XF378, which had become something of a 'hangar queen' since it had suffered fire damage. The whole amalgam was registered in August 1959 as Mark 66A G-APUX and employed as a private-

venture demonstrator by Hawker Siddeley, sometimes fitted with two 350-gallon (1,592.5-litre) under-wing ferry tanks. This was the aircraft in which 'Bill' Bedford made his memorable inverted spinning demonstrations at the 1959 SBAC Display referred to in Chapter 11.

In 1963, G-APUX made a sales tour of the Middle East, following which it was

For Wethersfield's Open Day on 17 June 1961, Hunter F.6, IF-61/W-OV flew over from Chievre for static display. The 7th Ecole de Chasse had adopted the 'OV' unit code by this time, with red and white checks on their wing tips. George Pennick

leased to Iraq for a year, repainted in the country's military colours. The following year, a similar lease was made to Jordan and, in 1965, it spent another twelve months in the Middle East, this time in Lebanese military colours, all three countries having used the aircraft for training purposes, pending receipt of their own individual orders for two-seaters. Eventually G-APUX returned to Hawker Aircraft, where once again it was refurbished and, in 1967, became part of an order for the *Fuerza Aérea de Chile* (Chilean Air Force), as a Hunter T. 72, with that county's serial J-718. The fate of the remaining fifty-seven has not been confirmed.

Licensed Production in Holland

Parallel to the Belgian negotiations, Hawker Aircraft signed an agreement with Fokker-Aviolanda of Amsterdam, for the company to build, under licence, ninety-six Hunter F. Mark 4 aircraft, the US paying for forty-eight of them under OSP Bill funding. Finance for the balance and subsequent orders came from Holland's internal budgeting.

Construction took place during 1955-56 as in Belgium, the aircraft operating with units of the *Koninklijke Luchtmacht* (Royal Netherlands Air Force (RNethAF)), these being Nos. 324 and 325 Squadrons based at Leeuwarden and No. 327 Squadron at Soesterberge. The RNethAF Mk4s carried serial numbers running from N-101 to N-196, which were displayed in large form either side of the front fuselage, and the Dutch camouflage scheme roughly followed RAF Fighter Command's style (as did the Belgian Air Force Hunters). No. 322 Squadron of the RNethAF also received a number of Hunters in 1960, to be embarked on the Dutch aircraft carrier *Karel Doorman*, in response to a threatened confrontation

The Hunter F.4 aerobatic team that represented the RNethAF in several formation competitions organized by NATO, in the late 1950s. Author's collection

RNethAF Hunter F.4, upgraded to F.6 standard, N-189/Y9-19 of No. 323 Squadron, at Cazaux air base in France. It was participating in the annual air-to-air firing competition for the Guynemer Trophy, organized at the Cazaux firing range, by the NATO Allied Air Forces, Central Europe. The competition consisted of camera-gun attacks on other aircraft and cannon/machine gun runs at target drogues. Author's collection

(Above) **Hunter F.6, N-216, from the RNethAF No. 325 Squadron, based at Soesterburg, photographed on 19 April 1968. Three months later, it was purchased by Hawker Siddeley and converted into a Mark 56A, A1015, for the Indian AF, delivery being made on 10 March 1970.** George Pennick

between Indonesia and the rather small Netherlands forces on Dutch New Guinea. Two years later, the crisis had abated, but what became of the Hunters sent out there has not been confirmed.

Early in 1957, production commenced on a follow-up contract for Fokker to build ninety-three Hunter F. Mark 6s, their serial numbering to be from N-201 to N-293. Production was completed in 1958 and the aircraft progressively replaced the F.Mark 4s. A total of six Squadrons eventually received Hunters of the two Marks, these being Nos. 322, 323, 324, 325, 326 and 327. From 1963, the Royal Netherlands Air Force started re-equipping with the Lockheed F-104G Starfighter, but No. 325 Squadron retained its Hunters until 1966, when it replaced them with Northrop NF-5s. Twenty Hawker-produced Hunter T.7s were also purchased by the RNethAF, ten of which were aircraft from a cancelled Air Ministry contract, for which serials XM117 to XM126 had been allocated, and ten specifically built for Holland. The two-seaters were numbered N-301 to N-320, delivery being made between April 1958 and February 1959. They served with a RNethAF Hunter Operational Conversion Unit, based at Twente.

Commencing in 1964, Hawker Siddeley bought a total of forty-seven Fokker-produced Mark 6 aircraft, after they had

Hunter F.6s of No. 325 Squadron, RNethAF, with the Soesterburg scorpion badge on their fins, were equipped to carry Sidewinder air-to-air missiles on the outboard pylons. Of this formation, both N-271 and N-274 were bought by Hawker Siddeley in 1968, for conversion to Hunter Mark 56As, A1011 and A1012 respectively. N-249 was purchased four years earlier and converted to a two-seat Jordanian T.66B, number 716. Author's collection

finished service with the RNethAF and also repurchased ten of the original twenty Kingston-built T.7s supplied at the end of the 1950s. All were refurbished and sold to various overseas Air Forces. At the *Militaire Luchtvaart Museum*, F.4s N-122 and N-144, F.6 N-258, plus T.7 N-305, are

all on display, while the *Aviodome* at Schiphol has a Hunter airframe composed of various elements of Danish and RAF aircraft, carrying the RAF serial WV395, which in reality, suffered an in-flight fire and, after landing, was repurchased by Hawker Aircraft.

The Nationaal Lucht-en Ruintevaartlaboratorium (NLR)/National Air and Aerospace Laboratory – Holland's
equivalent to Farnborough and Boscombe Down – flew a Hunter T.7 for many years, the aircraft being
ex-RAF XM126 and allocated the RNethAF serial N-320 when delivered to Holland on 26 January 1959.
Later, the aircraft was placed on the Dutch civil register as PH-NLH, painted in a vivid white, orange
and blue livery, the scheme dictating the use of a matt-black anti-dazzle panel ahead of the windscreen.
Blade aerials and Bendix ADF blister are evident, together with a fin-tip trailing aerial, while the inboard
port-side pylon carries an electronic pod. The nose-probe installation was a later modification, and
high-altitude nuclear radiation samplers are known to have been fitted on the inboard pylons, for various
research programmes. The NLR had operated another T. 7, N-315, prior to receiving N-320.
Author's collection

CHAPTER SIXTEEN

The Export Saga

Hawker Aircraft Limited always had a good sales and marketing philosophy. They designed and constructed good aeroplanes. Sell them! This sound, commercial reasoning permeated through the entire company. The design team believed in what they created and the sales organization believed in what they were selling.

the Hunter F.4 as its standard interceptor. Three years later, a Swiss team evaluated the Hunter Mark 6 against the Mystère IVA, Canadair F-86, Czech-built MiG-15, Saab J-29 and its indigenous P-16, the Hawker aircraft coming out the winner by several lengths. Finally, also in 1957, India placed a substantial order for aircraft based

Abu Dhabi – Hunter Mark 76, 76A and 77

In the latter half of the 1960s, many Royal Air Force units in the Middle East were closed down and British influence in the area closed with them. The United Arab Emirates Air Force (UEAF) was formed

Some of the early Swiss production Hunter F.58s, carrying the first Partouille Suisse logo, in company with the Blue Herons from Yeovilton. Further down the line, are a pair of German F-104Gs, an RAF Jaguar, two Phantoms from No. 64 Squadron, two Lightning F.3s, an F-15 and a pair of Buccaneers. Author's collection

It was this dedication, in the years leading up to World War II, that placed the company in the position where it was able to accept all that was demanded when hostilities commenced. It was also this dedication, which was perpetuated when the company became Hawker Siddeley, that made the Hunter the commercial success that it was.

While the recipient countries are presented here in alphabetical order, it is expedient, at this point, to mention three orders that were influential in the history of Hunter exports. In 1954, Sweden chose

on the F.6. Such orders had a considerable effect on several other countries contemplating looking to Kingston-upon-Thames for their new aircraft.

One further point that becomes evident in detailing the export of Hunters, is the effect that cancellation of RAF orders had on Hawker Aircraft Limited. Potential orders from overseas customers had the company scrambling through Maintenance Units and the air forces of earlier foreign operators, just to get hold of airframes that could be purchased for refurbishment, to meet the new orders.

and a substantial contribution was provided by the original Abu Dhabi Air Force, when they created a Sharjah-based ground-attack squadron in 1970. The elements of this squadron were formed by an order under Contract No. HSA/69/AD/082, placed with Hawker in February 1969, for ten single-seat and a pair of two-seat Hunters. Seven of the single-seaters were converted to FGA.9 standard and designated Mark 76s, the three remaining being brought up to FR.10s, to be designated Mark 76As, all ten being ex-RAF airframes. The two trainers were repurchased by Hawker, from the

The first civil-owned Hunter, G-HUNT was built at Kingston in 1956, as Mark 51 E-418, for the Royal Danish Air Force, and was bought by Hawker Aircraft in 1975. It was restored by former BAe engineer Eric Hayward for Spencer Flack, who was the owner when it flew at Mildenhall in 1980, piloted by the late Stefan Karwowski, and the aircraft was subsequently purchased by Michael Carlton. Following Carlton's death in an African flying accident during 1986, G-HUNT was sold to the Combat Jets Flying Museum in the USA.
Author's collection

(Right) Besides G-HUNT, Spencer Flack also owned Hawker Fury FB11 G-FURY, which he is flying in formation with Stefan Karwowski, at Mildenhall, in 1980. Author's collection

twenty T.7s originally supplied to the RNethAF, and were designated T.Mark 77s in the Abu Dhabi Air Force.

The aircraft concerned were F.4s WV389, WV402, XF362, XF367, XF935, XG341 and F.6 XE589, all becoming Mark 76s. The three Mark 76As were originally F.4s WV400 and XF971, plus F.6 WW592, while the two T.77s were T.7s N-301 and N-312 in the RNethAF. In 1975, the aircraft were transferred to the *Al Quwwat Aljawwiya Almalakiya* (Royal Jordanian Air Force), following that country's losses in the 1973 Yom Kippur war.

Chile – Hunter Mark 71, 71A and 72

The *Fuerza Aérea de Chile* (Chilean Air Force (CAF)) was seen as a potential customer by several countries and negotiations commenced in 1964, for the supply of modern ground-attack and trainer aircraft. Hawker emerged victorious in 1966, receiving an order for fifteen Hunters, to be refurbished to FGA.9 standard, under Contract No. HSA/66/C/066, with delivery to be completed by June 1968. The contract also covered the conversion of three airframes to FR.10 standard, delivery to be made three months later.

A follow-up order, under Contract No. HSA/69/C/084, for nine further FGA.9-type aircraft, was fulfilled by September 1971 and a third order for four additional aircraft of the same type, was completed in January 1974. All the fighter/ground-attack aircraft were designated Mark 71s by Chile. The original contract was amended to include the supply of three Hunters converted to FR.10 standard and an additional order for three more FR.10s followed, all six being delivered by February 1974 and titled Mark 71A in the CAF. One more addition was later made to each of the two contracts. These covered two batches, each of three two-seat Hunter trainers, the last joining the CAF in February 1974 and all six being known as T.Mark 72s. Chilean Hunters were fitted with the 'big Avon', in their case, the Avon 207 (RA.28-rated) at 10,000lb (4,536kg) static thrust.

The Hunters served within the CAF *Grupos de Aviacion No. 8*, based at Antofagasta in the north of the country, but were affected by a political arms embargo lasting from 1974 to 1980 and spares became in very short supply – much to Hawker's chagrin, having fought so hard to win export orders for the UK. Since 1980, the *Aguila* updating programme by the CAF has seen the aircraft fitted with Caiquen II radar warning receivers, Eclipse chaff/flare dispensers, American-standard cockpit instrumentation and provision for carrying the Israeli-built Shafrir air-to-air missile.

The Chilean orders were fulfilled by refurbishing ex-RAF aircraft, a prototype, a former demonstrator, plus Hawker's repurchasing of Belgian and Dutch-produced airframes. The following aircraft are confirmed as having been concerned in the contracts:

Mark 71s included: ex-F.4s WT801, WW653, XF302 and XF323; ex-F.6s XE557, XE561, XE580, XE625, XE644, XF447, XF512, XG199, XG232 and XJ713; ex-RNethAF N-201, N-210, N-220, N-232, N-262, N-266, N-270, N-273, N-276 and N-277; ex-BAF IF-44, IF-106, IF-108 and IF-141.

Mark 71As included: ex-F.4s WV326, XF317 and XF982; ex-F.6s XF453, XJ717 and XK148; ex-RNethAF N-202 and N-224; ex-BAF IF-19.

Mark 72s included: ex-F.4 XE704; ex-Mark 66 demonstrator G-APUX; ex-P.1101 second prototype XJ627; ex-RNethAF N-202 and N-224.

Denmark – Hunter Mark 51 and 53

It was decided in the Spring of 1954, to replace the Meteor F.8s serving in the *Kongelige Danske Flyvevaben* (Royal Danish Air Force (RDAF)), with Hunter F.4s. Contract No. HAL/54/D/017 was signed on 3 July 1954, for Hawker to build thirty new aircraft, given the RDAF designation

Mark 51, with serials E-401 to E-430. The first aircraft had its maiden flight, in the hands of David Lockspeiser, on 15 December 1955 and was delivered, together with E-402, on 30 January of the following year. On 11 November 1955, WW591, a brand new F.4, had gone to Denmark for evaluation and it was retained to enter service with the RDAF on the same day as the first two new-build aircraft arrived. E-430, the last Hunter built under the contract, was delivered on 18 August 1956 and all thirty-one aircraft served with Esk 724. Originally fitted with Avon 115 (RA.7-rated) engines, the RDAF aircraft were modified in line with experience gained on RAF Hunters, to eradicate engine surge when the Aden cannon were fired.

In 1958, Contract Nos. HAL/56/D/026 and HAL/57/D/024 were signed, each covering the manufacture of a Hunter T.7-type aircraft (apart from the absence of wing leading-edge extensions), for designation as Mark 53s in the RDAF, with serials EP-271 and EP-272. Both were delivered at the end of the year and, much later, in 1968 and 1969, Denmark purchased two additional T.7s from the RNethAF, all four trainers serving with Esk 724.

Economic restraints in 1966 brought about a reduction of the RDAF's strength, plus an inability to buy spares for their Hunters. Consequently, some Mark 51s were stored, while others became 'hangar queens' for the aircraft that were still flying. Esk 724 was eventually disbanded on 31 March 1974 and Hawker Siddeley repurchased twenty airframes for their refurbish-

Kingston-built Hunter F.51, E-412 of Esk 724, Royal Danish Air Force, taxiing at Soesterburg in that air force's 1968 style of camouflage and markings. This aircraft was repurchased by Hawker Aircraft in March 1976, with over 3,000 hours 'on the clock'.
George Pennick

The first of two T.53s ordered by Denmark in 1958, which were not fitted with leading-edge extensions,
ET-271 lands at Bentwaters, on 17 September 1971. George Pennick

Originally built at Kingston, as a Hunter T.7, for the RNethAF. When Denmark purchased this two-seater
from Holland, in 1968, it became T.53 ET-274 and is shown in the RDAF olive-drab finish, with low-visibilty
national markings, introduced in the early 1970s. R. Hobbs

ment programme. These are known to have included: Mark 51s E-402 and E-403, E-407 to E-409, E-412, E-418 to E-421, E-423 to E-425, E-427 and E-430. Both the Hawker-built Mark 53s were also repurchased but the fate of the two ex-RNethAF aircraft has not been confirmed. E-401 is displayed at *Flyvevabnets Historiske Samling*, where the cockpit of E-426 is sometimes shown, alternating with *Egeskov Veteranmuseum*.

as such, received American military equipment, including a number of F-86F Sabres. India saw its IAF superiority threatened and turned to Hawker Aircraft Limited for the supply of Hunter F.6s, this being the first order for the Mark from overseas.

In September 1957, Contract No. HAL/57/I/034 was signed, for 160 Hunter F.6 aircraft, to be supplied to the IAF, as the Mark 56. Delivery was to be completed by

began early in 1958, the aircraft being fitted with four 100-gallon (455-litre) drop-tanks. The first new-build aircraft, BA249, had its maiden flight on 4 July 1958, with Duncan Simpson at the controls, although the second, BA250, preceded it, when David Lockspeiser first flew this aircraft on 26 June. India's premier Hunter to be received on home tarmac, was BA242, which arrived on 8 August, 1958. IAF

The Indian Air Force was the first overseas customer for the Hunter F.6, their original order being for 160 aircraft, designated the Mark 56, in the IAF. A product of this order was photographed in 1958, on a rather neglected-looking taxi-way, with an ultimate load of thirty-six 3 in (76.2mm) rocket projectiles – such an armament only being used for short-range missions, due to its induced drag. Author's collection

India – Hunter Mark 56, 56A, 66, 66D and 66E

The turbulent separation of the old Indian sub-continent at the end of the 1940s initiated a fifteen-month conflict between the new Pakistan and the remaining India. The new Indian Air Force (IAF) operated a mixed-bag of British-built piston-engined and first-generation jet aircraft, which were augmented in 1953 by the first of seventy-one Dassault Ouragans. Pakistan became a member of the South-East Asia Treaty Organization (SEATO) in May 1954 and,

the end of 1960, with serials running from BA201 to BA360, all the aircraft to be modified to have gun-blast deflectors, tail parachutes and the ability to operate with 230-gallon (1,046.5-litre) drop-tanks. The first thirty-two aircraft (BA201 to BA232) were to be diverted from a cancelled RAF order and a further sixteen (BA233 to BA248), would be modified RAF aircraft. The contract was to be completed by 112 new-build aircraft, numbered BA249 to BA360.

BA201 first flew on 11 October 1957 and, following conversion training at Dunsfold by a party of IAF pilots, deliveries

Hunters joined Nos. 7, 17, 20 and 27 Squadrons, the last Mark 56 arriving in November 1960. The September 1957 contract also covered the construction of sixteen, later increased to twenty-two, new two-seat Hunters, based on XJ627, the second prototype P.1101, fitted with twin-Aden cannon and powered by Avon 203 or 207 (RA.28 rating) engines. Indian two-seaters were designated T.66, with serials BS361 to BS376 and BS485 to BS490 allocated. Deliveries ran in conjunction with the Mark 56 aircraft, from February 1959 to the end of 1960.

Four follow-up orders for single-seat Hunters were received by Hawker Aircraft, all of which were fulfilled by existing aircraft, refurbished to FGA.9 standard and designated Mark 56As in the IAF. The first, in 1965, under Contract No. HSA/65/I/061, covered thirty-six aircraft, thirty-five ex-BAF and one ex-RNethAF, given the serial

aircraft, to be called T.66E. Ex-RAF F.6s were reconfigured to meet the order, the IAF serials S1389 to S1393 being allocated, and delivery was to be completed by December 1973. Two Hunter trainers served with each of the four operational squadrons, the balance forming a Hunter OCU at Ambala.

XF499 to XF501, XF503, XF505, XG150 and XG163.

Mark 56A, first order, ex-BAF F.6s IF-1, IF-3, IF-4, IF-7, IF-13, IF-16 to IF-18, IF-36, IF-43, IF-50, IF-62, IF-64, IF-66, IF-77, IF-78, IF-85, IF-89, IF-91, IF-98, IF-104, IF-110, IF-113, IF-115 to IF-117, IF-120,

India was the first customer for the Avon RA.28-powered two-seat Hunter. Given the designation T.66, BS361, the first of the sixteen new-build aircraft ordered, is shown on a dull day, prior to delivery to No. 17 Squadron, Indian Air Force, on 21 April 1959. RAF Museum

numbers A459 to A494. In 1967, Contract No. HSA/67/I/001, Part 1, for eight ex-RAF aircraft (IAF serials A936 to A943), was followed in the same year by Part 2, for three more ex-RAF aircraft, A967 to A969. In 1968, Contract No. HSA/68/I/077 called for six additional aircraft, one being ex-RAF, the balance ex-RNethAF, serials A1010 to A1015 being allotted.

India also issued two follow-up orders for two-seat Hunters. On 10 March 1966 Contract No. HSA/66/I/067 called for twelve Hunter trainers, these being ex-RNethAF single-seat airframes, converted to two-seat configuration, for the contract. Designation T.66D was given to the aircraft, with serials S570 to S581 and deliveries were to be made over sixteen months from May 1966 to September 1967. Seven years later, the second two-seat follow-up order was received by the then Hawker Siddeley Aviation, this being for five

War broke out again between India and Pakistan in 1965, with yet another in 1971. Hunters came into conflict with F-86F Sabres, F-104s, MiG-19s and Mirage IIIEs, acquitting themselves quite well in air-to-air combat, but really excelling in the ground-attack role. It is believed that thirteen Hunters were lost in the 1965 hostilities, plus a further six in 1971. In a more peaceful vein, the IAF formed an aerobatic team in the early 1980s, with the title *The Thunderbolts*, equipped with Mark 56A aircraft and flown by pilots from the Hashimara-based No. 20 Squadron.

The original diversions and later refurbishing programmes, are confirmed to have concerned the following aircraft:

Mark 56s, first thirty-two, cancelled RAF F.6s allotted serials XK157 to XK224; next sixteen, ex-RAF F.6s XE537 to XE540, XE547, XE549, XE600, XF463, XF497,

IF-123, IF-124, IF-127, IF-128, IF-131, IF-132, IF-137 and IF-144; ex-RNethAF F.6 N-209.

Mark 56A, second order, ex-RAF F.6s XF521, XG129, XG170, XG186, XG189, XG190, XG201 and XG211.

Mark 56A, third order, ex-RAF F.6s XE620, XJ646 and XJ691.

Mark 56A, fourth order, ex-RAF F.6 XF446; ex-RNethAF N-213, N-216, N-252, N-271 and N-274.

Mark 66D, ex-RNethAF F.6s N-203, N-204, N-208, N-212, N-214, N-218, N-223, N-230, N-250, N-261, N-265 and N-269.

Mark 66E, ex-RAF F.6s WW596, XE556, XE585, XF459, and XJ694.

Iraq – Hunter Mark 59, 59A, 59B and 69

As one of the largest oil exporters in the Middle East, the country has always maintained a considerable military capability and in the mid-1950s, the Iraqi Air Force (IrAF) was mainly reliant on British aircraft. Following the 1956 Arab-Israeli war, when the superiority of the *Heyl Ha'Avir* (Israeli Air Force) was made so apparent, several Arab countries involved in the conflict engaged in a programme of modernizing their air forces. In 1957, Iraq purchased fifteen ex-RAF Hunter F.6s, in a direct Whitehall/Baghdad negotiation, conducted with US funding. The Hunters, which retained their RAF Mark number, formed a Habbaniyah-based operational squadron, the pilots having passed a course at No. 229 OCU at Chivenor.

As the aircraft gave such good service in the IrAF, Iraq placed an order, with Hawker Siddeley, in 1963, for twenty-four FGA.9-type Hunters, to be designated the Mark 59 and delivery completed by May 1965. Contract No. HSA/63/I/060 covered the order, which was accomplished by converting twenty-two ex-BAF and two ex-RNethAF F.6 aircraft, to full FGA.9 standard. While these conversions were in hand, Kingston received another order for eighteen additional aircraft to be delivered by May 1967, under Contract No. HSA/ 65/I/062. This second order involved conversion, to full FGA.9 quality, of sixteen ex-BAF and two more ex-RNethAF airframes, Mark 59A being applied to the aircraft.

Kingston-built Hunter F.6, XK146, was the fourth of the original fifteen ex-RAF aircraft purchased by Iraq, with funding provided by the United States. With the IAF number '403', it was delivered in December 1957, with Mod 228 wings, as a constituent of Iraq's first Hunter squadron. Author's collection

One year later, Contract No. HSA/65/I/062A covered the production of four more aircraft, designated Mark 59B, by the conversion of four ex-RNethAF F.6s, to FGA.9 standard, all to be received in Iraq by September 1966. The grand total of forty-six ground-attack Hunters made the IrAF the largest operator of the type among Arab countries. They carried out many operations in local tribal hostilities, as well as being used in small numbers in both the 1967 Six-Day and 1973 Yom Kippur Wars, but when the conflict with Iran broke out, in 1980, the ground-attack role had been taken over by Iraq's Soviet-produced Su-7B and Su-20 aircraft and the Hunters were confined to OTU activities. Iraq also ordered three two-seat Hunters in 1963, designated T.69. Contract No. HSA/63/I/054 was signed, for the aircraft to be supplied by conversion of three ex-BAF F.6s and delivery was made during the following year. The IrAF operational activities of their T.69s has not been confirmed.

The IrAF Hunters employed the following original aircraft:

The original ex-RAF aircraft supplied with US funding, F.6s XJ677 to XJ679, XJ681, XJ682, XK143 to XK147, XK152 to XK156.

Mark 59, ex-BAF F.6s IF-6, IF-10, IF-11, IF-14, IF-20, IF-21, IF-24, IF-27, IF-28, IF-32, IF-48, IF-75, IF-79, IF-80, IF-88, IF-94, IF-107, IF-114, IF-122, IF-126, IF-140 and IF-142; ex-RNethAF F.6s N-234 and N-247.

Mark 59A, ex-BAF F.6s IF-8, IF-9, IF-22, IF-25, IF-29, IF-31, IF-54, IF-59, IF-71, IF-72, IF-74, IF-87, IF-93, IF-99, IF-135 and IF-138; ex-RNethAF F.6s N-253 and N-255.

Mark 59B, ex-RNethAF F.6s N-205, N-221, N-259 and N-263.

Mark 69, ex-BAF F.6s IF-68, IF-84 and IF-143.

Jordan – Hunter Mark 66B, 73, 73A and 73B

A year after Iraq received the fifteen ex-RAF Hunter F.6s, both Lebanon and Jordan were each recipients of similar aircraft, transferred from the RAF. The *Al Quwwat Alijawwiya Almalakiya Alurduniya* (Royal Jordanian Air Force (RJAF)), with encouragement from their qualified-pilot ruler, His Majesty King Hussein, engaged in a great effort of modernization. In 1958, as a gesture to lay the foundations for an update of equipment, Britain supplied twelve ex-RAF Hunter F.6s, which became a part of the RJAF's No. 1 Squadron, based at Mafraq.

A year later, Hawker Siddeley received its first order from Jordan for the supply of three two-seat trainer Hunters, to the standard of the Indian Mark 66, based on the second prototype P.1101. In the RJAF, the trainers, designated T.66Bs, were scheduled for delivery from 1960 onwards, the aircraft delivered on 4 July 1960 being

Jordan received two Hunter FR.10s, one, Baginton-built XF426, being a straight transfer from the RAF, given the number '853'. The other, shown here, was a conversion of Kingston-built F.6, XG262, which received the Jordanian serial '712', when delivered early in 1961. It is believed both FR.10s were among the aircraft passed on to the Sultan of Oman's Air Force. *Author's collection*

The last order from Jordan was for these three Hunter FGA.73Bs, which were delivered in 1971. Two were conversions from ex-RAF F.4s and one, an ex-RNethAF aircraft, but which is which is impossible to tell from this view of them standing in front of a Dunsfold T.2 hangar. *Aeroplane Monthly*

Having served with the RNethAF and the RDAF, this Hunter T.7 was, as G-BOOM, the first of the Mark to go on the British civil register. The aircraft has had a succession of owners, at the time of writing being a part of the Royal Jordanian Historic Flight, and is seen at Waddington, in 1996, in the colours of an aircraft of No. 1 Squadron, RJAF.
Author's collection

the last new-build Hunter off the Kingston lines. Ex-RNethAF F.6 airframes formed the bases of the two remaining T.66Bs, with Contract Nos. HSA/65/J/063 and HSA/67/J/070 covering the conversions. The much-travelled G-APUX demonstrator trainer also spent a year with the RJAF No. 6 Squadron OCU, before returning to Hawker Siddeley. Also in 1960, ex-RAF Hunter FR.10, XF426, was transferred to the RJAF, while an F.6 was converted to

the same configuration and delivered the following year. An aerobatic team, called *The Hashemite Diamond*, flying an unconfirmed number of aircraft, started giving displays in the early 1960s, to local states.

No. 2 Squadron of the RJAF was formed in 1962, by the transfer of a further twelve Hunters from the RAF, later to be augmented by the conversion of eight ex-RAF F.6s to FGA.9 standard, these to become Mark 73s. At the start of the Six-Day War

of 1967, the RJAF suffered from the results of its only early warning radar station, at Ajlun, being eliminated by the Israeli Air Force. A further attack on the RJAF base at Mafraq destroyed the majority of its aircraft, and Jordan was left with only two Hunters at the end of the conflict.

Neighbouring Saudi Arabia gave Jordan three of its single-seat Hunters in 1968, while four RAF FGA.9s were also transferred to the RJAF. Replacement aircraft were ordered from Hawker Siddeley, four further FGA.9 standard Hunters, termed Mark 73A in the RJAF, to be produced by the upgrading of four ex-RAF F.6s. A second order for eight additional Mark 73A aircraft was followed by a third, for three Mark 73B aircraft. All were ground-attack variants, produced by the conversion of a mix of ex-RAF and -RNethAF aircraft, delivery being completed in 1971. Hunters were gradually phased out of the country's front-line service, their squadrons re-equipping with Northrop F-5 aircraft, while the OCU received Cessna T-37s in 1974. The next year, Jordan passed all its Hunters to the Air Force of the Sultan of Oman.

The rather protracted equipping of the RJAF with Hunters, involved the following confirmed aircraft:

1958 RAF transfer, F.6s WW597, XE543, XE551, XE558, XF373, XF379 to XF381, XF444, XF452, XF496 and XF498.

1960 RAF transfer, FR.10 XF426. Same year conversion to FR.10, F.6 XG262.

1962 RAF transfer, F.6s XF415, XF417, XF423, XF518, XG132, XG171, XG187, XG257, XG263 and XG267 to XG269.

Mark 66B, one new-build, ex-RNethAF N-249 and N-283.

1967/8 RAF transfer, FGA.9s XF454, XF514, XG298 and XK150.

Mark 73, F.6s XE603, XE645, XE655, XF520, XG137, XG159, XG231 and XG255.

Mark 73A/1969, F.6s XF389, XG234, XG237 and XJ645; 1971, F.4s WV325, WV407, WV408, XF364, XF936, XF952, XF968 and XF987; ex-RNethAF N-264.

Mark 73B, F.4s WV401 and XF979; ex-RNethAF N-279.

Kenya – Hunter Mark 80 and 81

The Kenya Air Force (KAF), established with Britain's assistance following the country's independence in 1963, was officially inaugurated in June 1964 and equipped with two ex-RAF Chipmunks. A small mixture of Beavers and Caribou followed, but the attacking potential of

neighbouring Ethiopia, Somalia and Uganda prompted an order for six BAC Strikemasters, in 1970. A new main operational base was built at Nanyuki and early in 1974, the Kenyan Government placed an order with Hawker Siddeley for six ex-UK service Hunters. The required four single-seat aircraft comprised three F.4s and one FR.10, all ex-RAF and designated Mark 80s in the KAF, while the pair of two-seat trainers ordered were ex-FAA T.8s, titled Mark 81s.

Delivery on 24 June 1974 of the two Mark 81 trainers, numbered 801 and 802, together with a Mark 80 numbered 803, was followed in December by two more single-seaters, 804 and 805. The last Mark 80, KAF number 806, arrived at Nanyuki on 13 January 1975 and the Hunters operated until 1979, by which time only four remained airworthy. The KAF took delivery of the first of twelve Northrop F-5s in the same year and the Hunters were placed in storage, until purchased in 1981 by Zimbabwe, who based them at Thornhill.

The aircraft confirmed as being involved in the KAF purchase were:

Mark 80, F.4s XF309, XF972 and XF975; FR.10 XE626.

Mark 81, T.8s WT755 and XL604.

Kuwait – Hunter Mark 57 and 67

The Middle East and potential conflict are never too far apart and the Kuwait Air Force, having existed as an extension of the Government's Security Department since the 1950s, was officially formed in 1961. Protection of the country's oilfields was the main criterion, with adjacent Iraq known to have ambitions of ownership high on its own agenda. It is known that RAF assistance was given when requested, during local uprisings and on at least one occasion they suffered loss, this being on 16 July 1961, when Hunter F.6 XG134 crashed, killing the pilot.

In 1963, an order was placed with Hawker Aircraft for the supply of four ground-attack and two trainer Hunters, the transaction incorporated in Contract No. HAL/63/K/050. Kuwait Air Force designation Mark 57 applied to the four single-seat aircraft, which were produced by the conversion of ex-BAF F.6s to full FGA.9 standard and delivered in a period

commencing February 1965. The two Mark 67 trainers were also manufactured by conversion of former BAF F.6s and delivery coincided with the first Mark 57. Two years later another order was placed, for three additional Mark 67s, covered by Contract No. HSA/67/K/069, these being procured by conversion of two former RNethAF F.6 airframes and an ex-RAF FGA.9. Also in 1967, at least two RAF F.6s were transferred to the Kuwait Air Force, these being XE550 and XE618, although their length of stay and ultimate end has not been confirmed.

Kuwait had thirty-six Douglas A-4 Skyhawks on order and their arrival in 1975 saw the placing of the FGA.57s into storage, later to be delivered to Oman, where they joined the former Jordanian Hunters. The five T.67 aircraft continued giving good service for several more years, until they too were put in store and it is possible that Oman eventually received them, but this has not been verified.

The following aircraft are confirmed as forming the Kuwait purchases:

Mark 57, ex-BAF F.6s IF-26, IF-41, IF-69 and IF-70.

Mark 67, first order, ex-BAF F.6s IF-37 and IF-56.

Mark 67, second order, ex-RAF FGA.9 XE530; ex-RNethAF F.6s N-257 and N-282.

Lebanon – Hunter Mark 66C, 70 and 70A

Although having had little involvement in the ongoing discord between Israel and the Arab states, Lebanon has operated the *Force Aérienne Libanaise* (FAeL) since the 1950s. Hunters are possibly still on their inventory, the type being introduced in 1958, with the transfer of six ex-RAF F.6 aircraft, under a US Offshore Payment agreement.

In 1964, Hawker Siddeley received an order from the Lebanese Government and Contract No. HSA/64/L/059 was signed, for the supply of three two-seat Hunter trainers, to Indian T.Mark 66 standard. These would be titled T.Mark 66Cs in the FAeL, manufactured by the conversion of ex-BAF F.6 airframes. The contract also covered the provision of four FGA.9 standard single-seat Hunters, which would again involve refurbishment of Belgian-built F.6s, the aircraft to be designated Mark 70s. FAeL numbers L176 to L179 were applied on the FGA.70s and L280 to L282 on the T.66Cs, delivery of the contract being completed by September 1966, the same year that the Hunter T.66A demonstrator, G-APUX, was on a twelve-month secondment to Lebanon.

Israel made occasional incursions into Lebanese airspace and actually invaded the country in 1982, when some losses were sustained by the FAeL. To replace them, a further six ex-RAF Hunters, to FGA.9 standard, were supplied in 1975/6. One F.6, three FGA.9s and two FR.10s formed the bases of these aircraft, all of which were updated by the installation of Collins 618M VHF radios, requiring the fitting of a large blade aerial behind the canopy, the aircraft designated Mark 70As. A total of nineteen Hunters was accepted by Lebanon – not including G-APUX – and it is known that a substantial number still operated well into the late 1980s.

The following aircraft are confirmed as having been supplied to the *Force Aérienne Libanaise*:

1958 ex-RAF transfer, F.6s XE534, XE598, XF377, XF461, XF495 and XG167.

Mark 66C, ex-BAF F.6s IF-34, IF-60 and IF-112.

Mark 70, ex-BAF F.6s IF-86, IF-96, IF-101 and IF-129.

Mark 70A, ex-RAF F.6 WW598; FGA.9s XF430, XJ640 and XJ644; FR.10s WW594 and XF457.

Oman – No Mark numbers applicable

Britain assisted in the formation of the Sultan of Oman's Air Force (SOAF), on 1 March 1959, with the Sultan himself as Commander-in-Chief and Headquarters established outside the capital, Muscat. The previous two-year conflict with rebel forces instigated the SOAF's foundation, initially equipped with a few Percival Provosts and subsequently updated, on receipt of eight BAC Strikemasters. More unrest broke during the 1960s, encouraged by USSR and Communist China's influence replacing Britain's, following that country's withdrawal from Aden. In view of the country's geographical position on the Strait of Hormuz and Gulf of Oman, however, assistance in maintaining stability in the area has always been to Britain's advantage.

Arab States in the Middle East, together with Britain, offered support to the Sultan, the result of which was the SOAF's unique position of operating a considerable number of Hunters, without any initial association with Hawker Siddeley. Several RAF FGA.9s, formally operated in the Persian Gulf area, were transferred to Oman by the British Government, which, with ex-Kuwait Mark 57s and Jordanian Mark 73s, at one time gave the SOAF's No. 6 Squadron a strength of thirty-one Hunters at their Thumrayt base, some of them equipped to deliver a pair of AIM-9P Sidewinders from underwing pylons (a modification long wanted by the RAF, but never sanctioned). It is believed that several of the aircraft were only suitable as 'hangar queens' and the majority of actual airframes concerned has not been verified, but one that

has, is XG262, a former F.6, converted to FR.10 standard for the Royal Jordanian Air Force in 1960 and presented by King Hussein to the Sultan, in the mid-1970s.

Peru – Hunter Mark 52 and 62

Back in 1929, The Peruvian Naval Air Service and a Military Air Corps were amalgamated to form the *Cuerpo de Aernautica del Peru* which, in 1950 became the *Fuerza Aérea del Peru* (FAP). The country had joined the Organization of American States after World War II and, as such, was first equipped with Thunderbolt and Mitchell piston-engined aircraft. These were replaced with F-86F Sabres in the mid-1950s, and it is against this background that Hawker Aircraft's sale of Hunters to the FAP in 1955 must be viewed as a considerable triumph.

The replacement of Hunter F.4s by F.6s in RAF squadron service, meant that examples of the earlier Mark were available almost 'off-the-shelf'. Peru's order was for sixteen F.4s, with pre-Mod 228 wings and, of the total, thirteen had not reached front-line service. The three that had comprised one from North Weald's Station Flight, plus one each from Nos. 54 and 247 Squadrons. Therefore, the future Peruvian aircraft all had comparatively low flying hours and required little conversion for FAP service, where they became Mark 52s. Delivery was made by sea in May 1956, the aircraft joining *Escuadron Caza* 14, within *Grupo* 12 and numbered 630 to 645.

In 1959, Peru ordered a two-seat T.7 standard aircraft, which was supplied by conversion of the sixth production F.4,

With sixteen single-seat Hunters in its Air Force, Peru ordered a two-seat trainer, to be designated the T.62. The fifth Kingston-built F.4, WT706, was converted for this order and given the PAF serial '681', its maiden flight being made by Don Lucey, on 15 September 1959. A ventral blister covers the Bendix radio-compass aerial. Author's collection

WT706, which had previously served with the A&AEE at Boscombe Down on handling trials and was subsequently stored at a Maintenance Unit. This aircraft, numbered 681, became the sole Mark 62 in the FAP and its modifications included the fitting of a Bendix ARN-6 radio compass, requiring a small bulged aerial housing on the canopy fairing. It has been suggested that FAP Mark 52s also had this installation, but confirmation has not been obtained. Number 681 was received by the FAP in March 1960. By 1968, the Mark 52s, being replaced as interceptors by Mirage 5Ps, were re-assigned to a ground-attack role, for which, having pre-Mod 228 wings with only two pylons, they were not really suitable. In 1976, they were replaced by the Sukhoi Su-22, although a few were retained for operational training, together with the T.62. Dialogue was started at the 1966 SBAC Display, with a view to Peru purchasing updated F.6s, the number involved being between eight and sixteen aircraft. Once again, the shortage of Hunter airframes came into the equation, Chile already having an option on eighteen aircraft. On hearing of Peru's enquiries and knowing the paucity of available Hunters, Chilean representatives got their pens out, thereby ending any further Peruvian acquisitions.

The aircraft purchased by Peru are confirmed as:

Mark 52, ex-RAF F.4s WT717, WT734, WT756, WT758, WT759, WT765, WT766, WT768, WT773, WT774, WT776, WT779, WT796, WT800, WT803 and WW662.

Mark 62, ex-RAF F.4 WT706.

Qatar – Hunter Mark 78 and 79

Being one of the smaller Middle East countries, Qatar has kept a comparatively low profile during the troubled years in the region. As an oil-producing member of the Arab Organization for Industrialization, plans were made for the country, together with Saudi Arabia and the United Arab Emirates, to finance the licensed-production of British and French aircraft, plus engines, in Egypt. The withdrawal of Saudi Arabian funds ended the project and, although Qatar still subscribes to Egyptian manufacturing, it maintains a very small Qatar Emiri Air Force (QEAF)

based at Doha, which only has one runway. The QEAF operates with a few aircraft, nearly all British, flown by pilots seconded from the RAF.

When Abu Dhabi placed its first Hunter order with Hawker Siddeley, Qatar followed suit and Contract No. HSA/69/Q/083 was signed in June 1969, for the supply of three FGA.9 standard aircraft to be delivered by December 1971, as Mark 78s. The aircraft were produced by conversion of three ex-RNethAF F.6 airframes and the QEAF numbers QA10 to QA12 were applied. The contract also covered the supply of a two-seat Hunter, given the Qatari Mark 79 and this too came by refurbishing an ex-RNethAF aircraft, a Kingston-built T.7 diverted from a cancelled RAF batch. The T.79 was numbered QA13 and delivered at the same time as the three FGA.78s.

The aircraft were utilized for patrolling the Qatar coastline, the abilty of the FGA.78 aircraft to provide this role being greatly enhanced by their carrying four 230-gallon (1,046.5-litre) tanks on the Mod 228 wings. One aircraft has been lost due to an accident, but it is believed that the two remaining FGA.78s, plus the T.79, are still active in the Arabian Gulf area.

The aircraft confirmed as being purchased by Qatar are:

Mark 78, ex-RNethAF F.6s N-219, N-222 and N-268.

Mark 79, ex-RNethAF T.7 N-316.

Rhodesia – Hunter FGA Mark 9 applicable

The order placed in February 1962 for twelve Hunters, was one of the last made for aircraft by Premier Ian Smith's Government. They were to serve with the Royal Rhodesian Air Force (RRAF), as Hunter FGA.9s and the order was fulfilled by Hawker Siddeley's conversion of ten Kingston- plus two Baginton-built, ex-RAF squadron F.6s. Serials RRAF116 to RRAF127 were applied to the aircraft and delivery was made in December 1963, when they formed the major part of No. 1 Squadron strength at Thornhill.

With the Unilateral Declaration of Independence (UDI) made in 1965, followed in 1969 by the country proclaiming itself a republic, the Hunters became part of the new Rhodesian Air Force (RhAF).

Throughout a large part of the 1970s, they were heavily utilized on ground-attack sorties against guerrilla forces in Angola, Botswana, Mozambique and Zambia. When this is weighed against the fact that, since UDI, there had been a complete ban on trade between the UK and Rhodesia, resulting in the Hunters receiving no spares or service back-up, it indicates the very high standard of work put in by Hawker Siddeley, prior to the aircraft leaving Dunsfold.

The RhAF designed and manufactured indigenous specialized weapons for the Hunters to deliver in the difficult environment within which they operated, the results during anti-guerrilla raids proving very successful, and in the whole decade-long campaign anti-aircraft fire accounted for only two Hunters. Elections were held in 1979, whereupon a black-majority government was returned and, with Rhodesia being renamed Zimbabwe, the ten Hunters became on charge to the Zimbabwe Air Force (ZAF), who purchased four additional FGA.80s from Kenya. On 25 July 1982 Thornhill suffered a sabotage attack, which destroyed several Hunters, and by 1987 the remaining aircraft were withdrawn from service, as Zimbabwe started receiving the first of forty-eight Chinese-manufactured MiG-21s, renamed the Xian F-7.

The aircraft converted to FGA.9 standard for Rhodesia were:

Kingston-built F.6s XE548, XE559, XE560, XE613, XF506, XG294, XG295, XJ638, XJ716 and XJ718.

Baginton-built F.6s XF374 and XF504.

Saudi Arabia – Hunter Mark 60

Stemming from a small air arm in the 1920s, the Royal Saudi Air Force (RSAF) progressed via a mixture of advisers, plus aircraft, from Britain, Egypt, Italy, Jordan and the United States. Heightened tension in the region, together with threats to the country's air space from Egyptian aircraft based in North Yemen, prompted the establishment of the Saudi Arabian Defence Consortium, in January 1966. The British Aircraft Corporation, in conjunction with AEI and Airwork Limited, were contracted to supply a comprehensive air-defence network, including aircraft, missiles, radar and all ancillary systems, euphemistically known as the *Magic Carpet* arms deal. The principal aircraft involved in the deal were the Lightning and Strikemaster, but Hawker Siddeley was required to supply four Hunter F.6s, plus two T.7s, the latter to train RSAF interceptor pilots as an interim step prior to coming to grips with the English Electric monster. The single-seat Hunters were to be employed as deterrents against violation of the Saudi borders.

Contract No. HSA/66/S/064 was signed to cover the conversion of the six aircraft, the four F.6s being designated F 60s, with RSAF serials 60/601 to 60/604, while the T.7s retained their RAF Mark number (Mark 70 has been referred to in association with these aircraft, but as that Mark number had been allocated to the Lebanese FGA aircraft already delivered, it has to be discounted) and were given serials 70/616 and 70/617. All six Hunters

serials 835 and 836, were returned to Britain in 1974, where they received new RAF serial numbers.

The aircraft confirmed as being in the Saudi Arabian deal are:

Mark 60, ex-RAF, Kingston-built F.6s XE591, XJ712 and XJ715; Baginton-built F.6 XF450.

Mark 7, ex-RAF XL605 and XL620 (returned to UK in 1974 and respectively allocated new serials XX467 and XX466).

Singapore – Hunter Mark 74, 74A, 74B, 75 and 75A

Following Singapore's secession from the Federation of Malaysia in 1965, the Singapore Air Defence Command (SADC) was formed and orders were placed with British

would be designated FGA.74 and FR.74A respectively in the SADC, delivery to be made over the ten-month period from November 1970 to August 1971, for operating with No. 140 *Osprey* Squadron, from the Singapore air base at Tengah.

The contract was fulfilled by the conversion of ex-RAF FGA.9s to the required FGA.74 condition, while the SADC FR.74As came from stored ex-RAF FR.10 aircraft, the whole programme being comparatively easy compared with other refurbishment contracts. A follow-up order for twenty-two additional FR.10 standard aircraft, designated FR.74Bs, was a more complicated schedule, requiring the conversion of eight F.4 airframes, plus three FGA.9s. The remaining eleven aircraft had already been converted into RAF FR.10s and delivery was completed in October 1973, the aircraft complementing No. 141 *Merlin* Squadron. All these Hunters, like Oman's

From the second production batch of Hunter F.6s built at Kingston, XE605 was first converted to RAF FR.10 standard and later, in 1972, to one of twenty-two aircraft supplied to the Singapore Air Defence Command, as F.74Bs, the new serial being '523'. Three of these aircraft operated with No. 229 OCU at Chivenor and '523' is seen streaming its brake-chute, after an air-to-ground sortie over the Pembrey range, on 2 August 1974. Peter J. Cooper

were delivered in May 1966 and put into service straight away, one of the F.60s being lost in the following year. With the first of the Lightnings also arriving in 1967, the Hunters were withdrawn from RSAF inventories and passed over to the Royal Jordanian Air Force in 1968. The two T.7s, which had been given RJAF

aircraft manufacturers later in the decade. To complement Strikemasters ordered from BAC, Hawker Siddeley received its first directive, in 1968, to supply Hunters and Contract No. HSA/68/SG/078 was signed for the SADC to acquire twelve aircraft, converted to FGA.9 standard and a further four to FR.10 condition. These

FGA.9s, were equipped to carry Sidewinder air-to-air missiles.

Hawker Siddeley's order also covered the supply of four two-seat Hunters, which was later increased by a further five similar aircraft, the type numbers T.75 given to the first four and T.75A to the additional ones. Fulfilling these trainer orders once again

Alongside the Hunter F.74Bs at Chivenor, the SADC flew a pair of T.75s. Seen turning onto final approach, in November 1973, '500' shows signs of gun-firing over the range. This aircraft was built at Blackpool, as F.4, XE664, which became a T.8 for the FAA, in 1959, and was converted to a T.75 eleven years later.
Peter J. Cooper

illustrated Hawker Siddeley's problems in acquiring sufficient airframes. The T.75s came by the conversion of an ex-RAF F.4 that had already been rebuilt into the prototype T.8B, an ex-FAA T.8 and two Hawker-built T.7s for the RNethAF. T.75As came from the refurbishment of four ex-RAF F.4s and a further F.4, which had been converted to GA.11 standard for the Fleet Air Arm in 1963. The trainers had been delivered by November 1974 and all the SADC Hunters came onto the inventory of the newly-formed Republic of Singapore Air Force (RSAF) on 1 April 1975.

Singapore ordered a total of forty-seven Hunters, which carried the island's serial system numbers 500 to 546 and are known to have operated well into the 1980s, some of them being modified to have fuselage centreline stores-carrying abilities.

The aircraft confirmed as fulfilling the Singapore orders are:

Mark 74, ex-RAF FGA.9s XE615, XE652, XF456, XG251, XG260, XG296, XJ632, XJ642, XJ643, XJ680, XJ684 and XJ685.

Mark 74A, ex-RAF FR.10s XF437, XG205, XG292 and XJ689.

Mark 74B, ex-RAF F.4s WV258, WV331, WV364, WV366, XE679, XF360, XF369 and XF969; ex-RAF FGA.9s XG153, XG266 and XK142; ex-RAF FR.10s XE599, XE605, XE614, XF422, XF428, XF432, XF441, XF458, XF460, XJ633 and XJ714.

Mark 75, ex-NethAF T.7s N-303 and N-304; ex-FAA T.8 XE664; ex-FAA T.8B WW664.

Mark 75A, ex-RAF F.4s WV272, WV386, XF950 and XF970; ex-FAA GA.11 WT741.

Sweden – Hunter Mark 50

WT701, the first production Hunter F.4, was still being assembled at Langley, when the *Kungl. Svenska Flygvapnet* (Royal Swedish Air Force) (the prefix *Kungl./Royal* was deleted in 1974, but is applicable to this narrative) expressed its desire to have the type on its inventory. Negotiations between the Swedish Government and Hawker Aircraft came to fruition with the signing of Contract No.

HAL/54/S/016 on 29 June 1954. The company would build 120 F.4 standard aircraft, to which Hawker gave the Mark 50 identification and in the RSAF became the J-34. Swedish serial numbers 34001 to 34120 were allocated, 34001 having originally been laid down as Hunter F.4 WT770 for the RAF and sold to Sweden for type evaluation, delivery being made on 26 August 1955.

Hawker considered it expeditious to split production between Kingston and Blackpool for this very important order, so the first twenty-four were scheduled to be built at Kingston and the balance at the Lancashire plant. The aircraft were originally powered by Rolls-Royce Avon 113 or 115 (RA.7 rating) engines but these were later modified to surge-free 119/120s (RA.21 rating). They were fitted with F.4 Mod 228 wings, which were later modified to carry Sidewinder missiles (Sweden becoming yet another country to fit their Hunters with the missile that the RAF had been frequently requesting but were always told that the aircraft 'would be phased out within two years'. Hunters were still in squadron service in 1971!).

J-34s equipped four Wings/*Flygflottilj*, *F8* based at Barkarby, *F9* at Sare, *F.10* at Angelholm and *F18* at Tullinge, later commanded by Colonel D. Stenbek, who, as a Major, delivered 34001, the first J-34, from Dunsfold to Sweden. *F18* also had the distinction of forming the aerobatic team *Aero-Hunters* in 1962. Hunters, which gave good service in the RSAF and were popular with pilots, remained in operational service until the late 1960s, when the indigenous

Saab J-35 Draken took over and the J-34s were relegated to an OTU role. One aircraft, 34085, was allotted to *Svenska Flygmotor* as a trials airframe for their EBK56U afterburning system and given the designation J-34B. It was first flown with the modification on 6 May 1958, by Pilot Officer Lars Erik Larsson of the RSAF and, in subsequent test flights, improved the aircraft's climb performance by nearly 50 per cent. However, generally, it did not prove very

successful, being prone to flaming-out at altitude and the project was discontinued.

In retrospect, the finale of the Hunter in Sweden must have exasperated Hawker ranks – nearly all were cut up for scrap, although the company did manage to repurchase at least four, which were converted to fulfill an order from Switzerland. An undisclosed number were also saved for museums, 34016 known to be at the *Flygvapenmuseum Malmen* and 34070 at *Svendinos Bil Och*

The first production Hunter Mark 50 for Sweden, '34001', is just about as clean in profile as the P.1067, WB188, when that first flew. The Swedish aircraft, photographed in July 1955, does have the ventral airbrake, but lacks the anti-spin parachute carried on Neville Duke's prototype.
Author's collection

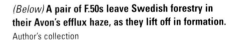

(Below) A pair of F.50s leave Swedish forestry in their Avon's efflux haze, as they lift off in formation.
Author's collection

Flygmuseum, while rumours have abounded for several years, of airframes being bought by groups in the USA.

Switzerland – Hunter Mark 58, 58A and 68

In terms of importance to Hawker Aircraft and the Hunter, the Swiss invitation, in 1957, for the company to enter their aircraft in a comprehensive evaluation programme, cannot be over-estimated. Having been neutral since 1815, Switzerland maintains a defence force that, coupled with its geographical assets, presents a genuine deterrent to potential aggressors. The *Flugwaffe*/Swiss Air Force has benefited by selecting aircraft imports that can operate successfully within the country's environment and remain effective over a long time-scale. Therefore, it was known that the victor in the 1957 evaluation would receive a substantial order, plus a spares

proudly emblazoned on the front fuselages.

January 1958 saw the signing of a contract, for Hawker Aircraft to supply 100 Hunter F.6 standard aircraft to the *Flugwaffe*, the Mark 58 designation being given to them, with serial numbers running from J-4001 to J-4100. Modifications to meet *Flugwaffe* requirements included the installation of Swiss UHF, plus STR.9X VHF radios, enlarged link containers in order to collect the shell-cases as well, and the fitting of a brake parachute, deemed necessary for operating from the country's smaller mountain airfields. In order to quicken deliveries, the first twelve aircraft, which were new RAF F.6s held in MUs pending squadron allocation, were returned to Dunsfold for modifications, so that the *Flugwaffe* were able to have the whole dozen by the end of 1958. The rest of the Swiss order were all new-build aircraft, from the Kingston/Langley/Dunsfold complex, the last one arriving in Switzerland on 1 April 1960. Hunter F.58s were

refurbishments, in that the aircraft were delivered, between December 1971 and April 1973, in component form, to the Swiss Federal Aircraft Factory at Emmen, where they were assembled. Two years later, a second follow-up order was placed, for an additional twenty-two F58A aircraft, again to be fulfilled by conversion of ex-RAF aircraft – twenty-one F.4s and an F.6. These later aircraft, delivered, to Emmen between January 1974 and April 1975, were also in component form, and serials J-4131 to J-4152 were allocated.

One final order was received from Switzerland, in 1974. This covered eight Hunter T.7 standard aircraft, to be supplied as Mark 68s to the *Flugwaffe* and fitted with Avon 207 engines. Refurbishment of four ex-RAF F.4s, plus four ex-Swedish F.50s, serviced this order, the work being undertaken by Hawker Siddeley, serial numbers J-4201 to J-4208 given and delivery made between August 1974 and June 1975. F.58As and T.68s operated with Nos. 4, 5, 7, 8, 19 and

As the first twelve Swiss Hunter Mark 58s, with serials J-4001 to J-4012, were ex-RAF ordered aircraft, J-4029, with braking-parachute and gun-blast deflectors, was the sixteenth new-build aircraft. The Mark 58 was a much better-equipped Hunter than its RAF counterpart, the F.6. Besides the brake-chute – dictated by the requirement to operate from small mountain airfields – it had Swiss UHF and VHF radios, a Saab BT-9 bombing computer, plus provision for AIM-9 Sidewinder air-to-air missiles, on the outboard pylons.
M. Fricke

potential for many years. The *Flugwaffe* had been equipped with a mixed force of Vampires and Venoms for several years, but their obsolescence gave them the opportunity to replace them with a front-line aircraft that could undertake defensive, plus attacking, roles when necessary. As has already been said, Hawker were in competition with five other aircraft manufacturers, but their representatives, F.6s XE587 and XE588, proved the Hunter's excellence in performance, weapons delivery and general handling, within the country's geographical confines for which they were awarded the Swiss Alpine Badge,

principally operated from the Dubendorf and Meiringen bases, by Nos. 1, 11 and 18 *Staffen*/Squadrons, within the *Escadre de Surveillance* (Surveillance Wing).

In 1971, Hawker received a follow-up order, for thirty Hunter FGA.9 standard aircraft, but with the added ability to carry Sidewinder missiles. This order would be provided by the refurbishment of a mixture of ex-RAF F.4s, FGA.9s and FR10s, together with two ex-RNethAF T7 airframes, the designation Mark 58A being given to them in the *Flugwaffe*, with serials J-4101 to J-4130 being applied. This order was different from other countries

21 *Staffen* from various bases, including Dubendorf, Meiringen and Mollis.

Starting in 1982, the *Hunter-80* programme got under way, with the Federal Aircraft Factory taking in F.58As for a comprehensive update of armaments and equipment. Provision for operating with the Hughes Maverick air-to-ground guided missile on outboard pylons was made, together with the installation of chaff/flare dispensers in a rearward extension of the link/shell collectors and radar-warning antenna sited either side of the nose-cone. The proof of an air force being satisfied with its aircraft, could not be better

Swiss Hunter Mark 58 J-4025 crossed the threshold at Fairford, in July 1994, declaring to all that it was
the leader of La Patrouille Suisse, who had operated the type, out of Dubendorf, for thirty years. J-4022
was among the remaining five team members, who all carried a vivid red and white undersurface motif.
Author's collection

demonstrated than when F.58 J-4025
joined IAT'95 at Fairford, graphically displaying the fact that *La Patrouille Suisse*
and the Hunter had enjoyed a thirty-year
association.

The aircraft involved in the Swiss orders
(excluding the new-build airfames) are:

Mark 58, first twelve aircraft, ex-RAF F.6s
XE526 to XE529, XE533, XE536, XE541,
XE542, XE545 and XE553 to XE555.

Mark 58A, first order, ex-RAF F.4s
WV374, WV380, WV405, WV411,
XF291, XF303, XF318, XF976, XF981,

XF984 and XF992; ex-FAA GA11s
WT711, WT808, WV257, WW659,
XE674, XE717, XF361, XF365, XF937 and
XF947; ex-RAF FGA.9s XE611, XF462
and XG272; ex-RAF FR.10s XF436,
XF438 and XG127; ex-RNethAF T.7s N-
313 and N-318.

Switzerland's last Hunter order was for eight two-seat T.68 aircraft, the first, J-4201, being a conversion of Kingston-built F.4, WV332, first flown on 7 June 1955, which operated with Nos 67 and 234 Squadrons, before going to Halton as Ground Instruction Airframe 7673M. It was bought by Hawker Aircraft in July 1972 and delivered as J-4201, on 2 August 1974. *Aeroplane Monthly*

Mark 58A, second order, ex-RAF F.4s WT797, WV261, WV266, WV329, WV393, WV404, WW590, XE659, XE678, XF306, XF308, XF312, XF316, XF370, XF933, XF941, XF944, XF973, XF990 and XF998, (F.4 WT716/7790M has been included in some listings, but this has not been confirmed by this author); ex-RAF F.6 XF429.

Mark 68, ex-RAF F.4s WV332, WV398, XE702 and XF951; ex-Swedish AF F50s 34017, 34072, 34080 and 34086

Zimbabwe – see Rhodesia

Hunter Mark 58 J-4079, which had already been upgraded to Mark 58A standard, was further enhanced in the Hunter-80 programme, by having the Hughes AGM-65B Maverick RV-guided missile system installed.
M. J. Hooks

CHAPTER SEVENTEEN

Trials Hunters

While the Supermarine Swift had the distinction of being the first swept-wing aircraft to enter the RAF, the first the Service operated with reheat and the first to operationally deploy air-to-air guided missiles, the fact that it was discontinued after a total production run of 172 airframes does not really qualify it as being mass produced. The Hunter, on the other hand, was the RAF's introduction to handling a swept-wing interceptor in large numbers and many were utilized as trials airframes by experimental establishments, as well as Service units, to further its operational capabilities. It would be impractical to list every aircraft or every trial installation, but the following are some of the Hunters that took part in programmes of signifi-

cance, although the trials were not necessarily converted into Service acceptance.

P.1067 Prototypes

WB188, WB195 and **WB202:** These all participated in the protracted trials, between September 1953 and June 1954, to resolve the optimum airbrake installation. Production F.1s WT566 and WT573 were also involved, while F.6 XF379 had the lateral rear-fuselage airbrake, first tried on WB188 prior to the record flights, fitted for a short time, but it only really proved that such an installation did not work on the Hunter. WB202 also flew with four dummy de Havilland Firestreak

missiles on underwing pylons, to test the aerodynamics of such an installation.

Hunter F.1

WT556: Besides being used at Boscombe Down, to familiarize A&AEE pilots with the flying characteristics of the type, it served on Avon engine trials with Rolls-Royce at Hucknall.

WT558: After participating in the Aden firing trials that showed the Avon RA.7's tendency to surge through gun-gas ingestion, the aircraft was fitted with wing fences of various contours and tested at A&AEE.

XJ615, the first prototype Hawker P.1101, leads a formation of trials aircraft XF310, XG128, XG129 and XG131, on their way to the 1956 SBAC Display. Author's collection

WT560: Following a number of Hawker-conducted equipment trials at Dunsfold, it went to Hucknall to act as a test vehicle in Rolls-Royce testing of the Avon 119, later being joined in the programme by WT573.

WT568: Used for a trial installation of the extended wing leading edge that was adopted as standard on later Marks, the trials being mainly undertaken at Boscombe Down.

WT571: Flown to RAE Farnborough, on 9 April 1954 as a brand new aircraft, where handling assessment throughout the speed and height range was made. Richard T. Whitcombe, of NACA at Langley Field, devised the principal of 'area rule', where a fuselage is 'waisted', so that the cross-section area of a fuselage, plus wing, minimizes transonic drag to a point where it approaches an ideal body. On the Hunter, 'waisting' was not possible, therefore designs were drawn up to attach faired-in bulges on either side of the fuselage, aft of the wings, to produce a more ideal cross-section. RAE Aero Flight made a large number of flights to measure drag at high Mach numbers, both before and after WT571 was fitted with the 'area rule' bulges, so that their aerodynamicists could make an assessment of the principle's practicality. A long nose-mounted instrument boom was fitted during these trials and it is believed that the bulges were later removed, the aircraft reverting to standard.

WT656: Used by RAE and Hawker in a joint trials programme to test the validity of installing flap-blowing on production aircraft, which did not proceed.

WW642: Flown by the AFDS and CFS at West Raynham, following which, it was operated by the Experimental Navigation Division of the A&AEE on TACAN trials. The aircraft's RA.7 Avon was specially overhauled, in order for TACAN sorties to be conducted at 50,000ft (15,240m), during the period October 1956 to January 1957.

Hunter F.2

WN889: Retained at Baginton in January 1954, where it was used in trials with the 8,800lb (3,992kg) thrust Armstrong Siddeley Sapphire ASSa12, which were conducted in conjunction with the AS Flight Test Department at Bitteswell.

Hunter F.4

WT701, WT702 and **WT703:** The first three production F.4s, they were retained by Hawker Aircraft for underwing stores and drop-tank trials, flown from Boscombe Down as well as Dunsfold. A series of radio trials at the A&AEE followed and, in1964, WT703 is believed to have been struck off charge, while the other two are confirmed as being converted to T.8s for the FAA.

WT753: Flown for five years by Hawker and Boscombe Down pilots, on radio trials programmes and the testing of various US electronic apparatus.

WT736: Operated by Rolls-Royce at Hucknall on flight testing of the Avon 121 for over a year, after which it was loaned to the Ferranti Flying Unit at Turnhouse, for PAS trials, in association with the Central Flying Establishment.

WT751: Served with Nos. 118 and 247 Squadrons, before undertaking jettison trials of the 230-gallon (1,046-litre) tanks, conducted at Boscombe Down in 1962.

WT772: Fitted with the trial installation of a retractable Ram Air Turbine, positioned on the starboard side behind the roundel, thought necessary to maintain hydraulic pressure for the proposed 'flying-tail', in the event of engine failure. The system was not put into production.

WT780: Retained by Hawker Aircraft for many trials programmes, including drag parachute and FAA-required tail hook. Used in making *High Flight*, a Warwick Film made at Cranwell, for which the aircraft had five cameras installed in a modified nose.

WV276: Took over Rolls-Royce Avon 121 trials, in conjunction with the A&AEE, when WT736 was loaned to Ferranti.

XE702: Flown by the A&AEE on external stores trials, including various capacity tanks and multi-tier rocket projectile installations. Passed to RAF squadron service and eventually converted to T.66 for the Swiss Air Force.

XF310: Modified by Fairey Aviation in July 1956, for trials of their Blue Sky (Fireflash) beam-riding air-to-air missile carried on underwing pylons and with the nose lengthened to accommodate the missile fire-control radar. Missile test firings were chiefly made on the RAE range, off Llanbedr in North Wales. XF310 was converted to T.7 standard in April 1959.

Hunter F.5

WN954: The first production F.5, it undertook various acceptance testing,

Another product of Kingston's first batch of Hunter F.1s, WT656 was modified to test a flap-blowing system, known as the Attenello scheme. The trials were mainly conducted by RAE Farnborough. Hawker Aircraft

(Left) The ability to operate the Hunter with the Sidewinder air-to-air missile, was a long-standing yearning by the RAF, but it was never sanctioned. One installation proposed by Hawker Aircraft is shown in mock-up form on an unidentified Hunter, the principle being that it left the wing pylons available for additional stores. A similar position was also mooted for the de Havilland Firestreak, but neither got beyond the mock-up stage. Hawker Aircraft

WT780 was a Kingston-built F.4, which first flew on 6 April 1955 and was used for nine years as a test vehicle by Hawker Aircraft. For the filming of High Flight, it was fitted with the five-camera nose installation shown. Hawker Aircraft

associated with the Mark, at Boscombe Down. Later converted for high-speed target-towing trials.

WN955: Operated by Armstrong Siddeley's Flight Test department, for flight trials of the Sapphire ASSa7, at Bitteswell.

WN958: The first F.5 used for external stores trials at Boscombe Down.

WP114: Delivered to Armstrong Siddeley Motors at Bitteswell, on 19 April 1955, for use as a flight test vehicle for their range of Sapphire engines.

Hunter F.6

XF833: The prototype F.6, constructed using the front and centre section of the cancelled P.1083, had its maiden flight on 22 January 1954. Flown from Dunsfold and Boscombe Down on type-evaluation trials

Blackpool-built XF310 flew for nearly three years on Fairey Fireflash missile trials, before being one of six Hunter F.4s converted to T.7 standard. Landing at Farnborough in 1956, the nose profile is much blunter than when it was photographed on its way to the 1957 SBAC Display. There must be a story behind one photograph that was issued at the time, with all national insignia rather crudely retouched out, but it cannot be found.

Author's collection and *Aeroplane Monthly*

until 5 June 1956, when it was passed to Miles Aircraft Limited, under contract to Rolls-Royce, for conversion to test-fly a thrust-reversal installation. The aircraft was flown in this configuration at the 1956 and 1957 SBAC Displays and, while being successful in principle, braking parachutes were considered more cost-effective.

WW594: The third production F.6, it was designated P.1109A and modified with a more pointed nose than F.4 XF310, to act as the aerodynamic test vehicle for the AI.20 fire-control radar associated with the deployment of the de Havilland Blue Jay (Firestreak) air-to-air missile. Missiles were not installed on this aircraft, which was later converted to FR.10 configuration and eventually refurbished to an FGA.70A for the Lebanese Air Force.

WW598: Following company trials at Dunsfold, the aircraft went to the RAE High Speed Flight, flying from both Farnborough and Bedford. Later, it had similar modifications to WW594 and took part in low-level tropical trials. It too was converted to FGA.70A standard for Lebanon.

XE530: Delivered to Rolls-Royce, Hucknall, as a trials aircraft for a range of differ-ent Avon engines. Passed into RAF squadron service and then converted to FGA.9, before finally being refurbished, in May 1969, into a T.67 for Kuwait.

XE531 and **XE532:** These were employed at Hucknall for a variety of tropical trials with Avon engines. Both were later converted to FGA.9 standard, with XE531 ultimately having further conversion, to the one and only Mark 12.

XE587: Going from No.19 MU, the aircraft was one of the pair that won the 1957 evaluation in Switzerland, after which it was used in the tail-parachute development programme and then went to the Empire Test Pilots' School.

XE598: The principal aircraft used for the various gun-gas deflectors evaluated to eliminate pitch-down.

XG131: Originally retained by Hawker Aircraft, to test a wing-tip fuel tank installation that would leave the under wing pylons free for armament stores. The aircraft was statically presented at the 1956 SBAC Display in this configuration, but the project was found to be aerodynamically unsuitable and was not produced. Fol-lowing restoration to F.6 standard in October, XG131 was delivered to No5. MU.

XF378: This, the sixth production F.6 from Baginton, was designated P.1109B and fitted with the full AI.20 radar, in the pointed-nose configuration tested on WW594, two of the Aden cannon being removed to compensate for the AI.20's weight. One Firestreak missile was pylon-mounted under each wing, the aircraft operating out of the de Havilland airfield at Hatfield and RAF Valley. Test firings were made in 1957 on the Llanbedr range and, two years later, the aircraft suffered fire damage and became a 'hangar queen'. The Firestreak was not adopted for the Hunter in the underwing installation, nor in another proposed position of one missile fitted on a pylon, either side of the front fuselage, similar to the English Electric Lightning – a similar fitting for Sidewinders was also abandoned. Neither schemes were test-flown and RAF Hunters were never destined to operate with guided missiles.

XF379: Used as the trials vehicle for another modification of the lateral fuselage airbrakes originally installed on WB188. The aircraft was sold to Jordan in 1958, under the US Offshore Payment scheme.

The first production batch of seven Hunter F.6s built at Kingston, all with pre-Mod 228 Mark 4 wings, were used for trial installations or test programmes, for Hawker Aircraft and the Establishments. WW598, the last of the septet, is seen, liberally stencilled, in P.1109A configuration, at Farnborough. The aircraft had put in nearly 1,300 hours of test flying, prior to being converted, in 1975, into an FGA.70A, for the Lebanese Air Force, where it carried the serial L.280. Author's collection

Seen in the formation at the start of this chapter, Kingston-built F.6 XG131, the test installation aircraft for wing-tip tanks, was displayed in the static park at the 1956 SBAC Display. The pitot tube was moved to the nose of the port-side tip tank and, while the whole conversion blended in with the basic Hunter profile, aesthetics do not hold up in aerodynamics. The concept was far from satisfactory, induced buffeting being such that XG131 was restored to standard configuration and subsequently served with No. 229 OCU.
Aeroplane Monthly and Author's collection

XF452: Retained by Armstrong Whitworth Aircraft in 1957 and used at Bitteswell in connection with Sapphire improvements, before being supplied to the A&AEE the following year for evaluation. On 12 November 1958, this aircraft was also supplied to Jordan under US Offshore Payment.

XF509: Taken out of service with No. 54 Squadron in April 1973 and loaned to the British Aircraft Corporation (BAC) at Filton, to be employed as the chase aircraft for the early test flights of WG774, the first Fairey FD.2. This had been converted at Filton into the BAC221 test vehicle for the ogee wing design on the forthcoming Concorde. Following its BAC uses, XF509 was later delivered to No.4 Flying Training School.

Hunter T.7

XL563: This, the first production T.7, was retained by Hawker Aircraft and delivered to the A&AEE for evaluation in December 1957. On 14 April 1962 it acted as chase aircraft for the maiden flight of the first Bristol Type 188, XF923, from the Bristol Aircraft (later BAC) airfield at Filton, the flight terminating at Boscombe Down. XL563 performed similar duties on subsequent flights of the Type 188, as its test programme was conducted from the A&AEE's airfield. In 1976, XL563 passed to the RAE at Farnborough and later served with the Institute of Aviation Medicine at the same establishment. A Hunter again became associated with the Bristol 188 as, in April 1963, the second prototype XF926 had F.6 XF506 as the chase plane for its maiden flight.

XL574: A Hawker-Siddeley retained aircraft, in April 1958 it was used as a test

(Above) **The beautifully-proportioned P.1101B, XF378, carries a brace of pylon-mounted de Havilland Firestreak missiles, en route to the SBAC Display, on 1 September 1957. This was another Hunter trials application that did not come to fruition.**
Hawker Aircraft

aircraft for windscreen de-icing and rain dispersing, plus some tropical trials, mainly operating from Boscombe Down. In November 1961, the aircraft was finally placed in the fatigue rig at Kingston and tested to destruction.

Hunter T.8

XL580, **XL602** and **XL603** These aircraft, all new-builds and first flown in 1958, served at various FAA stations. In 1980, they were flown to the British Aerospace (BAe) plant at Brough, in Yorkshire, for modification to carry the Blue Fox radar in a recontoured nose. With this equipment, they were designated T.8Ms and flown with No. 899 NAS as airborne instruction aircraft for pilots converting to the Sea Harrier FRS.1.

A quartet of trials aircraft, the farthest, carrying drop-tanks , being the only one fitted with external stores that saw service with the Royal Air Force. The thirty-six rocket projectile load was used by the Indian Air Force, but the Firestreak and Fireflash's association with the Hunter did not go beyond this test application. RAF Museum

Hunter F.50 (J-34)

34085: Delivered to Sweden in 1956, this aircraft was modified to take a Svenska (now Volvo) Flygmotor-designed, afterburner, designated EBK56U and small additional dorsal intakes for the revised cooling system were fitted on the aircraft's centre section The modifications gave 34085 the new type number J-34B and flight trials were made in 1958, these showing a marked improvement in the rate of climb. Problems were encountered however, as the afterburner was found difficult to keep operating above 42,000ft (12,800m). Fuel consumption was also considered unacceptable and the project was abandoned.

CHAPTER EIGHTEEN

Tailpiece

In the case of the Hunter, Hawker Aircraft were in a position with which many a family can empathize. They bore a beautiful infant, that gave cause for concern in adolescence, but matured into a graduate with first-class honours. While it was most likely not considered when Specification F3/48 was written, the P.1067 can be considered as the genesis of one of the world's first multi-role jet-powered combat aircraft. From its conception as an interceptor, it evolved into a good photo-reconnaissance and fast training aeroplane, but it was as a ground-attack aircraft that it really excelled.

The construction of the Hunter followed the Hawker conception – it was built to last. However, they, and their successors, are most likely pleasantly surprised at just how long it *has* lasted. To be in service, forty-three years after the prototype's maiden flight, is stretching a designer's optimism beyond the realms of acceptance. A total of 1,975 production Hunters was built, serving with thirty-eight RAF, plus six FAA, front-line squadrons. Of these, 248 were converted to later marks for UK service and a further 382 refurbished for export to foreign air forces, seventeen of which operated the aircraft. This is a record that has not been matched by any other aircraft and, I think can safely be stated, never will.

One of the main troubles it encountered – lack of range – resulted from the misplaced official conception that a defensive interceptor, as in the days of the Battle of Britain, would not be required to operate far beyond the UK coastline. Consequently, it would not need the encumbrance of carrying a lot of fuel and therefore would be able to intercept sooner. Not a lot of good if, when you reach your target, you have to return to base for a refill!

Hawker's belief that, as the wing/flap airbrake combination worked on their earlier – and slower – jet aircraft, therefore the principle should function on the P.1067, has to be seen as an error (with the resultant delay

in operational squadrons receiving the Hunter) firmly remaining at their door. The finally accepted solution to the problem always looked and operated as a compromise – not to be able to deploy your main decelerator, as you renew acquaintance with *terra firma*, has to be viewed as a disadvantage. Gun-gas ingestion, plus pitch-down, were part of the learning curve, which was shared by Rolls-Royce and Hawker, both companies coming to terms with them. It has to be remembered that the British aircraft industry was treading down new paths, less than a decade after six years of total war, without the vast research facilities enjoyed across the Atlantic Ocean. Nearly every aspect had to be tried *in situ* before it could be proven. I think it can fairly be said that the Hunter most likely suffered from the 'Super Priority' programme, when it was pushed into service at too early a stage of development. Some of the faults would possibly have come to light in a less-urgent atmosphere – and the original order for only three prototypes was downright ridiculous.

The Hunter has been described as a 'pilot's aeroplane' and such a definition may be difficult to quantify, as different aspects appeal to different people. 'Jock' Harvey, former RAE test pilot, told me that 'it was an easy aeroplane to fly, splendid for aerobatics and especially good for inverted flying'. He did add the rider, 'Why any pilot should want to fly inverted has never been clear. Some debris in the bottom of the cockpit is inevitable. When the aeroplane is rolled upside down, the debris goes into the canopy: when rolled right side up, some of it goes down the pilot's neck!'

The sheer joy of flying the Hunter was exemplified to me, one glorious summer day in 1971. I was sitting on the slopes of the Cader Idris mountain range in Mid-Wales, looking down onto the Mawddach Estuary at Barmouth. A pair of FGA.9s came into the estuary at about 50ft (15.2m) above the sea, then banked to starboard and started climbing towards me, hugging the mountain's contours. They passed over my head and continued up towards the summit. I turned to watch and, as they crested Cader Idris, they flipped onto their backs, dived down the other side and disappeared. Those pilots were happy. Happy with their job and happy with their aircraft. Debris down the neck was worth it!

'It's my most beautiful aeroplane.' Sir Sydney Camm

Technical data

Role

(Mark 1, 2, 4, 5, 50, 51 and 52) Single-seat interceptor; (Mark 6, 9, 56, 57, 58, 59, 60, 70, 71, 73, 74, 76 and 80) Single-seat ground-attack interceptor; (Mark 7, 8, 53, 62, 66, 67, 68, 69, 72, 75, 77, 79 and 81) Two-seat operational trainer; (Mark 10) Single-seat photo-reconnaissance and ground-attack aircraft; (Mark 11) Single-seat weapons trainer; (Mark 12) Two-seat special experimental trials aircraft.

Dimensions

Wing Span (all Marks) 33ft 8in (10.25m); Overall Length (all single-seat, except Mark 10) 45ft 10.5in (13.98m); (Mark 10) 46ft 1in (14.02m); (all two-seat) 48ft 10.5in (14.89m); Overall Height (all Marks) 13ft 2in (4.0m); Wing Area (all Marks, without leading-edge extensions) 340sq ft (31.62sq m); (all Marks, with leading-edge extensions) 349sq ft (32.42sq m); Undercarriage Track (all Marks) 14ft 9in (4.48m).

Weights – Empty

(Mark 1) 12,128lb (5,501kg); (Mark 2) 11,973lb (5,431kg); (Mark 4, 5, 50, 51 and 52) 12,534lb (5,685kg); (Mark 6, 56, 58, 59, 66B and 70) 12,760lb (5,788kg); (Mark 7, 8, 53 and 62) 13,360lb (6,060kg); (Mark 9) 13,010lb (5,901kg); (Mark 10) 13,100lb (5,942kg); (Mark 11) 12,510lb (5,674kg).

Power plants

(Mark 1, 4, 7, 8, 50, 52, 53 and 62) One 7,200lb/7,425lb (3,265kg/3,367kg) static thrust Rolls-Royce Avon Mk 104, 107, 113, 115 or 119 (RA.7 rating), Mk 120, 121 and 122 (RA.21 rating); (Mark 6, 9, 10, 12, 56, 58, 59A, 66, 70 and 73) One 10,000lb (4,536kg) static thrust Rolls-Royce Avon Mk 203 or 207 (RA.28 rating); (Mark 2 and 5) One 8,000lb (3,629kg) static thrust Armstrong-Siddeley ASSa6 Sapphire Mk 101.

Performance – Clean

Avon – RA.7 rating (single-seat) – maximum speed: Mach 0.93 at 36,000ft (10,973m); 699 mph at sea level; service ceiling: 48,800ft (14,874m).

Avon – RA.21 rating (single-seat) – maximum speed, Mach 0.94 at 36,000ft (10,973m), 701 mph at sea level; service ceiling: 50,000ft (15,240m).

Avon – RA.21 rating (two-seat) – maximum speed: Mach 0.92 at 36,000ft (10,973m), 693 mph at sea level; service ceiling: 47,000ft (14,326m).

Avon – RA.28 rating (single-seat) – maximum speed: Mach 0.95 at 36,000ft (10,973m), 714 mph at sea level; service ceiling: 51,000ft (15,697m).

Avon – RA.28 rating (two-seat) – maximum speed: Mach 0.93 at 36,000ft (10,973m), 699 mph at sea level; service ceiling: 48,900ft (14,905m).

Sapphire Mk101 (single-seat) – maximum speed: Mach 0.94 at 36,000ft (10,973m), 703 mph at sea level; service ceiling: 50,000ft (15,240m).

Armament – Internal

(all single-seat, except Mark 11) Four 30mm Aden cannon in detachable pack under forward fuselage, with 150 rounds per gun maximum capacity; (Mark 11) No Aden cannon; (all two-seat, except Mark 66) One 30mm Aden cannon under starboard forward fuselage; (Mark 66) Two 30mm Aden cannon under forward fuselage.

Armament – External

(single-seat, Mark 1 and 2) No provision for operational underwing stores; (single-seat, Mark 4, 5, 50 and 51) One inboard pylon under each wing, either capable of carrying a free-fall bomb up to 1,000lb (454kg) in weight or a 100-gallon (455-litre) Napalm tank; (single-seat Mark 6, 10, 11, 56, 58, 60, 71A, 74A and 74B) One additional outboard pylon under each wing, either capable of carrying a 100-gallon (455-litre) Napalm tank, a thirty-seven 2in (52mm) honeycomb rocket projectile pack or being replaced by twelve 3in (78mm) rocket projectiles; (single-seat Mark 9, 57, 59, 70, 71, 73, 74, 76, 78 and 80) Two pylons under each wing, either capable of carrying a free-fall bomb up to 1,000lb (454kg) in weight, a 100-gallon (455-litre) Napalm tank or a thirty-seven 2in (52mm) honeycomb rocket projectile pack, the outboard pylon being replaced by twelve 3in (76mm) rocket projectiles, four 3in (76mm) 60lb (27.2kg) head rocket projectiles or combinations of 5in (130mm) HVAR, Oerlikon, Bofors and Hispano rocket projectiles of various sizes; (single-seat Mark 11 and two-seat Mark 8) Adapted for FAA to carry one Martin AGM-12B Bullpup air-to-air missile on each inboard pylon. Several overseas operators modified their ground-attack aircraft to carry Sidewinder air-to-air missiles, Switzerland adapted outboard pylons to carry ALQ-171 jammer pods and Singapore fitted fuselage centre-line stations to carry two 1,000lb (454kg) free-fall bombs.

Fuel – Internal

(Mark 1) 334 gallons (1,519 litres); (Mark 2) 314 gallons (1,429 litres); (Mark 4, 7, 8, 50, 51, 52, 53, 62, 66, 68, 75, 77, 79 and 81) 414 gallons (1,884 litres); (Mark 5) 388 gallons (1,765 litres); (Mark 6, 9, 10, 11, 12, 56, 57, 58, 59, 60, 67, 69, 70, 71, 72, 73, 74, 76, 78 and 80) 390 gallons (1,774 litres).

Fuel – External, maximum additional to internal

(Mark 4, 5, 7, 8, 50, 51, 52, 53, 62, 66, 68, 75, 77, 79 and 81) 400 gallons (1,820 litres); (Mark 6, 9, 10, 11, 12, 56, 57, 58, 59, 60, 67, 69, 70, 71, 72, 73, 74, 76, 78 and 80) 660 gallons (3,003 litres).

APPENDIX II

Hunter production and serial blocks (new-build aircraft)

The following aircraft were manufactured in the United Kingdom by Hawker Aircraft Limited, Kingston-upon-Thames, Surrey; Hawker Aircraft (Blackpool) Limited, Blackpool, Lancashire, and Sir W. G. Armstrong Whitworth Aircraft Limited, Baginton, Coventry, Warwickshire.

P.1067 prototypes Kingston-built: WB188, WB195 and WB202.

F.1 Kingston-built; Contract No. SP/6/5910/CB.7a; First batch of 113 aircraft: WT555 to WT595, WT611 to WT660 and WT679 to WT700.

F.1 Blackpool-built; Contract No. SP/6/8435/CB.7a;
Second batch of 26 aircraft: WW599 to WW610 and WW632 to WW645.

F.2 Baginton-built; Contract No. SP/6/6315/CB.7a, first part;
One batch of 45 aircraft: WN888 to WN921 and WN943 to WN953.

F.4 Kingston-built; Contract No. SP6/5910/CB.7a; first batch of 85 aircraft: WT701 to WT723, WT734 to WT769, WT771 to WT780 and WT795 to WT811.

F.4 Kingston-built; Contract No. SP/6/6867/CB.7a; Second batch of 100 aircraft: WV253 to WV281, WV314 to WV334 and WV363 to WV412.

F.4 Kingston-built; Contract No. SP/6/7144/CB.7a, first part;
Third batch of three aircraft: WW589 to WW591.

F.4 Blackpool-built; Contract No. SP/6/8435/CB.7a; Fourth batch of 20 aircraft: WW646 to WW665.

F.4 Blackpool-built; Contract No. SP/6/9817/CB.7a; Fifth batch of 100 aircraft: XE657 to XE689, XE702 to XE718, XF289 to XF324 and XF357 to XF370.

F.4 Blackpool-built; Contract No. SP/6/10344/CB.7a;
Sixth batch of 57 aircraft: XF932 to XF953, XF967 to XF991, XG341 and XG342.

F.4 for Sweden (F.50) Kingston- and Blackpool-built; Contract No. HAL/54/S.016;
One batch of 120 aircraft: Kingston-built 34001 (built as WT770 but sold and renumbered) to 34024, Blackpool-built 34025 to 34120.

F.4 for Denmark (F.51) Kingston-built; Contract No. HAL/54/D.017; One batch of 30 aircraft: E401 to E430.

F.5 Baginton-built; Contract No. SP/6/6315/CB.7a, second part; one batch of 105 aircraft: WN954 to WN992, WP101 to WP150 and WP179 to WP194.

P.1099 F.6 prototype Kingston-built; XE833.

F.6 Kingston-built; Contract No. SP/6/7144/CB.7a, second part; First batch of aircraft: WW592 to WW598.

F.6 Kingston-built; second batch of 100 aircraft: XE526 to XE561, XE579 to XE628 and XE643 to XE656.

F.6 Kingston- and Blackpool-built; third batch of 110 aircraft: Kingston-built XG127 to XG137, Blackpool-built XG150 to XG168, Kingston-built XG169 to XG172, XG185 to XG211, XG225 to XG239, XG251 to XG274 and XG289 to XG298.

F.6 Kingston-built; fourth batch of 45 aircraft: XJ632 to XJ646 and XJ673 to XJ718.

F.6 Kingston-built; fifth batch of 53 aircraft: XK136 to XK176 and XK213 to XK224.

F.6 Baginton-built; Contract No. SP/6/9818/CB.7a;
One batch of 100 aircraft: XF373 to XF389, XF414 to XF463 and XF495 to XF527.

F.6 for India Kingston-built; Contract No. HAL/57/I.034; one batch of 160 aircraft (first 32 built as XK157 to XK224, sold unused and renumbered BA201 to BA232, next 16 built as XE537 to XE540, XE547, XE549, XE600, XF463, XF497, XF499 to XF501, XF503, XF505, XG150 and XG163, sold unused and renumbered BA233 to BA248): BA249 to BA360.

F.6 for Switzerland Kingston-built; one batch of 100 aircraft (First 12 built as XE526 to XE529, XE533, XE536, XE541, XE542, XE545 and XE553 to XE555, sold unused and renumbered J-4001 to J-4012): J-4013 to J-4100.

P.1101 T.7 prototypes XJ615 and XJ627.

T.7 Kingston-built; Contract No. SP6/12626/CB.9c; One batch of 55 aircraft (10 transferred for build as T. Mark 8): XL563 to XL579, XL583, XL586 and XL587, XL591 to XL597, XL600 and XL601, XL605, XL609 to XL623.

T.8 Kingston-built; covered by T.7 contract; One batch of 10 aircraft: XL580 to XL582, XL584 and XL585, XL598, XL599 and XL602 to XL604.

T.7 for Holland Kingston-built; Contract No. HAL/55/N/022; One batch of 20 aircraft: N-301 to 310 (balance, 10 aircraft from cancelled RAF contract allocated XM117 to XM126, renumbered N-311 to N-320).

T.7 for Denmark (T.53) Kingston-built; Contract Nos. HAL/56/D.024 and HAL/57/D.026; two aircraft: EP35-271 and EP35-272.

T.7 for India (T.66) Kingston-built; Contract No. HAL/57/I.034; One batch of 22 aircraft: BS361 to BS376 and BS485 and BS490.

T.7 for Jordan (T.66B) Kingston-built; one aircraft: 714.

New-build aircraft, under licence (Holland)

F.4 Fokker/Aviolanda-built; One batch of 96 aircraft: N-101 to N-196.

F.6 Fokker/Aviolanda-built; One batch of 93 aircraft: N-201 to N-293.

New-build aircraft, under licence (Belgium)

F.4 Avions Fairey/SABCA-built; One batch of 112 aircraft: ID-1 to ID-112.

F.6 Avions Fairey/SABCA-built; One batch of 144 aircraft: IF-1 to IF-144.

Index